The Economics of Health Care in Asia-Pacific Countries

ACADEMIA STUDIES IN ASIAN ECONOMIES

General Editor: Sheng-Cheng Hu, *Director, Institute of Economics, Academia Sinica, Taiwan*

Titles in the series include:

Economic Efficiency and Productivity Growth in the Asia-Pacific Region
Edited by Tsu-Tan Fu, Cliff J. Huang and C.A. Knox Lovell

Food Security in Asia
Economics and Policies
Edited by Wen S. Chern, Colin A. Carter and Shun-Yi Shei

The Economic Analysis of Substance Use and Abuse
The Experience of Developed Countries and Lessons for Developing
Countries
Edited by Michael Grossman and Chee-Ruey Hsieh

Productivity and Economic Performance in the Asia-Pacific Region
Edited by Tsu-Tan Fu, Cliff J. Huang and C.A. Knox Lovell

The Economics of Health Care in Asia-Pacific Countries
Edited by Teh-Wei Hu and Chee-Ruey Hsieh

Monetary Policy and Taiwan's Economy
*Edited by Gerald P. Dwyer, Jr., Jin-Lung Lin, Jia-Dong Shea
and Chung-Shu Wu*

The Economics of Health Care in Asia-Pacific Countries

Edited by

Teh-Wei Hu

Professor of Health Economics, Division of Health Policy and Management, School of Public Health, University of California at Berkeley, USA

and

Chee-Ruey Hsieh

Research Fellow, The Institute of Economics, Academia Sinica, Taipei, Taiwan, ROC

ACADEMIA STUDIES IN ASIAN ECONOMIES

Edward Elgar
Cheltenham, UK • Northampton, MA, USA

Published by
Edward Elgar Publishing Limited
Glensanda House
Montpellier Parade
Cheltenham
Glos GL50 1UA
UK

Edward Elgar Publishing, Inc.
136 West Street
Suite 202
Northampton
Massachusetts 01060
USA

A catalogue record for this book
is available from the British Library

Printed and bound in Great Britain by MPG Books Ltd, Bodmin, Cornwall

ISBN 1 84064 929 1

Contents

Figures

Tables

Contributors

Renhua Cai Director, China National Institute for Health Economics, Beijing Medical University, Beijing, P. R. China

Schumarry Chao Associate Vice President for Health Affairs, University of Southern California, Los Angeles, CA, USA

Shou-Hsia Cheng Associate Professor, Institute of Health Policy and Management, and Center for Health Policy Research, College of Public Health, National Taiwan University, Taipei, Taiwan

Martin Gaynor E.J. Barone Professor of Economics and Health Policy, H. John Heinz III School of Public Policy and Management, Carnegie Mellon University, Pittsburgh, PA, USA

Paul Gertler Faculty Director, Graduate Program in Health Services Management, Haas School of Business and Professor, Health Services Finance, School of Public Health, University of California at Berkeley, Berkeley, CA, USA

Chee-Ruey Hsieh Research Fellow, The Institute of Economics, Academia Sinica, Taipei, Taiwan

Teh-Wei Hu Professor of Health Economics, Division of Health Policy and Management, School of Public Health, University of California at Berkeley, Berkeley, CA, USA

Yun-Yi Hung Research Associate, Institute for Health Policy Studies, University of California at San Francisco, San Francisco, CA, USA

Duk Hyoung Lee Director, Disease Control Division, Ministry of Health and Welfare, Republic of Korea

Gordon G. Liu Associate Professor and Director of Graduate Studies Pharmaceutical Policy and Evaluative Sciences, University of North Carolina at Chapel Hill, Chapel Hill, NC, USA

Jui-Fen Rachel Lu Chair and Associate Professor, Department of Health Care Management, Chang Gung University, Tao-Yuan, Taiwan

Ching-to Albert Ma Professor, Department of Economics, Boston University, Boston, MA, USA and Professor, Department of Economics, Hong Kong University of Science and Technology, Hong Kong, P. R. China

Tami Mark Senior Economist/Associate Director, The MEDSTAT Group, Washington, DC, USA

Thomas G. McGuire Professor, Department of Health Care Policy, Harvard Medical School, Boston, MA, USA

Seiritsu Ogura Professor, Department of Economics, Housei University, Tokyo, Japan

John W. Peabody Deputy Director, Institute for Global Health and Associate Professor, Departments of Epidemiology and Biostatistics and Medicine and Health Services, University of California, San Francisco and the University of California, Berkeley, CA, USA

Gabriel A. Picone Associate Professor, Department of Economics, University of South Florida, Tampa, FL, USA

Ya-Chen Tina Shih Research Scientist, MEDTAP International Inc., Bethesda, MD, USA and Research Fellow, Cecil G. Sheps Center for Health Services Research, University of North Carolina at Chapel Hill, Chapel Hill, NC, USA

Frank A. Sloan J. Alexander Professor of Health Policy, Law and Management and Professor of Economics, Duke University, Durham, NC, USA

Reiko Suzuki Senior Economist, Japan Center for Economic Research, Tokyo, Japan

Donald H. Taylor Assistant Research Professor, Center for Health Policy, Law and Management, Terry Sanford Institute of Public Policy, Duke University, Durham, NC, USA

Jung-Der Wang Professor, Institute of Occupational Medicine and Industrial Hygiene, College of Public Health, National Taiwan University, and Department of Internal Medicine, National Taiwan University Hospital, Taipei, Taiwan

Yong Weng Quantitative Strategist, Asset Allocation Group, Bank of America Capital Management, Inc., St. Louis, MO, USA

R. Mark Wilson Associate Professor, Department of Economics, University of South Florida, Tampa, FL, USA

Eric Wu MS in Department of Pharmaceutical Economics and Policy, School of Pharmacy, University of Southern California, Los Angeles, CA, USA

Xianjun Xiong Deputy Director, Department of Medical Insurance, China Ministry of Labor and Social Security, Beijing, P. R. China

Tadashi Yamada Professor of Economics, Institute of Policy and Planning Sciences, University of Tsukuba, Ibaraki, Japan

Tetsuji Yamada Associate Professor, Department of Economics, Rutgers University, The State University of New Jersey, Camden, NJ, USA

Bong-Min Yang Professor, Department of Health Science and Services, School of Public Health, Seoul National University, Seoul, Korea

Jennifer Zeitlin Research Fellow, Department of Health Policy and Management, School of Public Health, University of California at Berkeley, Berkeley, CA, USA

Zhongyun Zhao Senior Health Outcomes Scientist, Health Outcomes Research, Eli Lilly, Inc., Indianapolis, IN, USA

Acknowledgements

Academia Studies in Asian Economies is a publication series that serves to assimilate the findings of research conducted by the faculty of the Institute of Economics, Academia Sinica and studies presented at conferences sponsored by the Institute.

The chapters included in the volume were selected from papers presented at the Taipei International Conference on Health Economics held at the Institute on 25-26 March 1999. Except for the introduction chapter and keynote address (Chapters 1 and 2), all submissions went through a peer review process. We are grateful to anonymous reviewers for their time and effort in providing many constructive comments on early drafts of the chapters. In addition, we thank the conference participants who helped make the conference lively and productive.

Many individuals and institutions contributed to the success of the conference and this volume. We owe a special debt of gratitude to Dr Yuan-Tseh Lee, President of Academia Sinica and Dr Sheng-Cheng Hu, Director of the Institute of Economics, for their encouragement and support. We are grateful to the Health Economics Program of the National Bureau of Economic Research, the National Science Council, the Ministry of Health, and the Bureau of National Health Insurance in Taiwan for generous financial support. We would also like to thank the US National Institute of Aging; China Jiangsu Provincial Bureau of Health and Zhenjiang City Social Security Bureau; the Japan Ministry of Education, Science and Culture, the Institute of Health Economics Policy, the Japan Center for Economics Research and the Research Council of Rutgers University; the Korea Foundation; and the US National Institute of Alcohol Abuse and Alcoholism and National Institute of Mental Health for assisting with the research undertaken by authors of individual chapters presented here. In addition, we thank Min-Hui Hsu and the staff of the Institute of Economics for their efficient logistic support.

Last but not least, we wish to thank the authors for making this volume possible and our wives for making every day worthwhile.

1. Editors' introduction

Teh-Wei Hu and Chee-Ruey Hsieh

1 INTRODUCTION

Although the discipline of economics is over 200 years old, the subdiscipline of health economics is relatively young, nearly 40 years old in terms of the publication of the seminal article by Nobel Laureate Kenneth J. Arrow in 1963 (Phelps 1995; Culyer and Newhouse 2000). During the past four decades, health economics has grown rapidly and become a successful subdiscipline in North America and Europe. As noted in Fuchs (2000), the rapid growth of health economics can be attributed to three principal reasons: (1) intellectual advances; (2) greater availability of data; and (3) ever-increasing health care expenditures. As a result, research into health economics has not only had a great deal to contribute to academic development in economics, but has also provided a valuable input into health policy (Fuchs 2000; Culyer and Newhouse 2000).

In contrast to most developed countries, the development of health economics in Asian countries is even younger, where by almost any standard it is only in the 'infant stage'. For example, researchers from Asian countries account only for 5.5 percent of members in the International Health Economics Association, although Asia accounts for 60 percent of the world's population. From its inauguration to year 2000, the *Journal of Health Economics* (*JHE*) and *Health Economics* (*HE*), which are two leading international journals in their field, have published 471 and 358 articles, respectively. Among them, only 1.5 percent of papers published in *JHE* and 1.7 percent of papers published in *HE* have leading authors who come from Asian countries.

Some researchers have argued that the scarcity of health economics research in Asia is due to the unavailability of micro-level data (Yoshikawa et al. 1996). The other plausible explanation for the underdevelopment of health economics in Asia has been that the average income of Asian countries is lower than their counterparts in North

America and Europe. This is because it has been widely recognized that national spending on research and development is strongly influenced by the income level. However, the most important reason for this research lag, we believe, has been the institutional differences in health care systems between Asian countries and Western nations. Therefore, research advances occurring in Western countries cannot directly apply to Asian countries.

As Fuchs (1996) emphasized, most health economics research is country specific. Therefore, the institutional organization of a health care system plays an important role in health economics research. Compared to Western countries, there are at least four major common features in Asian's health care system. First, most Asian countries adopt a 'closed' hospital system, where physicians who practice in hospitals are employees of hospitals and physicians who practice in clinics are completely independent of hospitals. Under a closed system, clinical physicians do not have admitting privileges at hospitals (Peabody et al. 1995; Yoshikawa et al. 1996). As a result, local clinics and hospitals compete for outpatient services and the referral system of medical services does not play a significant role in the Asian health care market. Patients often self-refer and go directly to a large hospital for care. In other words, there is no referral system in many Asian countries. Second, clinical physicians in many Asian countries can prescribe and dispense drugs. Thus clinical physicians earn most of their revenue from prescribing and dispensing drugs and hence physicians have a financial incentive to overprescribe drugs. As a result, drug expenditures account for nearly one-third of national health care expenditures. Third, most Asian countries are still under the fee-for-services payment system which allows providers to generate a high volume of services, either in outpatient visits, inpatient services, or laboratory tests. These practice patterns have led to cost escalation. To contain the increasing cost of health care, several countries have now initiated a capitation or global budget payment system. Fourth, Asian countries still heavily depend on the family to provide informal care for the elderly as well as other care for patients. As a result, Asian countries on average spend a lower percentage of their gross domestic product (GDP) on health care. For example, Japan only spent 7.3 percent of her GDP on health care in 1997, which is below the average for OECD countries. This percentage is even lower for other Asian countries. For Indonesia, the percentage of GDP spent on health care was only 1.8 percent in 1997 (Table 1.1).

While these common features among Asian health care systems exist, there are also some unique differences within these countries with regard to both the role of government in financing health care services and health

Table 1.1 Health and economic indicators in selected Asia-Pacific
countries, 1997

	China	Indonesia	Japan	South Korea	Taiwan	United States
Economy						
GDP per capita (US$)	500[a]	944[b]	33 269	10 428	11 743	29 297
Average annual economic growth rate (1990–97)	11.6	7.5	1.5	7.2	8.6	3
Population						
Total population (million)	1227.2	200.4	126.1	46	21.7	267.6
Percentage of population aged 65 and above (%)	6.6	4.4	15.5	6.0	8.1	12.3
Health service						
Health expenditure per capita (US$)	19	17	2442	397	607	4093
Percentage of GDP spent on health care	3.8	1.8	7.3	4.0	5.2	14.1
Physicians per 1000 people (1990–97) [c]	1.6	0.2	1.8	1.2	1.2	2.5
Health						
Life expectancy at birth (year)	70	65	80	72	75	76

Notes
[a] Data for 1993.
[b] Data for 1994.
[c] Data of the countries are for the most recent year available.

Sources: The World Bank (1999), *1999 World Development Indicator*, Washington: The World Bank; ROC Department of Health (1997), *Health and Vital Statistics – General Health Statistics*, Taipei: ROC Department of Health; ROC Directorate-General of Budget, Accounting and Statistics (DGBAS), *Statistics Yearbook of the Republic of China 1998*, Taipei: DGBAS.

insurance coverage. For instance, in Taiwan the national health insurance is centrally administered with close to 100 percent population coverage combined with a relatively low co-payment for consumers. On the other hand, even though South Korea has national health insurance, it is more decentralized and has a relatively high co-payment system. For another extreme, Singapore has a Medical Savings Account that places more responsibility on the individual to finance his or her own medical expenses.   Finally, Japan has a national health insurance, but relies on many local insurance societies to finance and monitor physician practices. Each system has its own historical background and political development with its own merits and limitations.

Although the institutional arrangements in their respective health care systems are different in many aspects, both Western and Asian nations face similar challenges on several global issues, such as aging and the spiraling costs of health care. For example, the percentage of the elderly population (age 65 and above) in Japan is even greater than that of the United States. In addition, the population in other Asian countries, such as mainland China, South Korea and Taiwan, is expected to age rapidly over the next two decades, which in turn will increase expenditures on long-term care. Furthermore, the elderly on average have higher health expenditures than people under the age of 65. Thus the rapidly aging population will further escalate rising health care expenditures.

In order to control ever-increasing health care expenditures, both Western and Asian countries are seeking to develop more efficient health care models. This worldwide trend provides a global intellectual community that each country can learn from to reform its health care system. This international interaction in turn will foster a variety of new and exciting environments to help the development of health economics in Asian countries.

To promote health economics research, the Institute of Economics, Academia Sinica (IEAS) organized the Taipei International Conference on Health Economics in Taipei, Taiwan on 25–26 March 1999. The conference attracted many scholars who came together to address the important and timely issue of health care reform and other health policies among Asia-Pacific countries including mainland China, Indonesia, Japan, South Korea, Taiwan, and the United States. As shown in Table 1.1, these countries are fairly diverse in their stage of economic development, social demographic structure, and health care expenditures. Thus the prior agenda on health care reform and health policy is very divergent, as may be expected. This is, of course, one of the reasons why such a conference is worthwhile for providing a forum for comparisons of disparate systems so as to learn from each other.

This volume contains selected reports of studies presented at the above mentioned conference. The 12 chapters that follow extend the frontiers of research on health care economics in a variety of extremely significant ways. As a whole, the book presents quantitative research dealing with various aspects of health care reform and health policy in Asia-Pacific countries. As noted earlier, studies focusing specifically on Asian countries are very rare in the literature of health economics. With the publication of this book, we hope to close the gap between health economics research and the rapid pace of development in Asian health care markets.

2 THE STRUCTURE OF THIS BOOK

The book is organized around five topics: health care reform, production of health, health care utilization, hospital behavior and health care financing. Part I of this volume contains chapters on health care reform, focusing specifically on South Korea, Taiwan, and the United States. Teh-Wei Hu and Yun-Yi Hung (Chapter 2) present an international comparison of health care reform between Taiwan and the United States. Their study focuses on the lessons of change in Taiwan and in the US that may be relevant to each other as both are currently undergoing policy debate of health care cost containment. To draw conclusions and lessons from one health care system reform to the formulation of policy in another country that is socially, politically, economically, and culturally different is far from straightforward. However, they conclude that in principle Taiwan can learn both demand-side and supply-side cost containment instruments from the US.

On the supply side, payment method reforms such as capitation and carve-out will discourage an over-provision of health care services by shifting financial risks to providers. On the demand side, increasing patients' cost-sharing and developing Medisave accounts will decrease over-consumption of medical care. As for the US, even though universal health insurance is not a feasible health policy, the government can extend Medicaid coverage to children of working poor families to protect this vulnerable population. In addition, the authors suggest that both governments can take leading roles in monitoring the quality of care and encouraging the practice of preventive care to improve the health of both countries.

In Chapter 3 Martin Gaynor and Tami Mark shift the focus to the development of managed care in the United States. As noted in their chapter, over the last two decades the US health care market has experienced tremendous growth in managed care and, subsequently, a strong movement toward consolidation. Both trends have led to significant changes in the nature of contracts between physicians and health plans. The authors provide a comprehensive literature review on these developments and the effect of contractual form on physician practice patterns. Their study concludes that incentives matter, emphasizing that there is a trade-off between financial incentives and monitoring (administrative controls). In other words, administrative controls can be used as a partial substitute for financial incentives in the contract between providers and insurers. The empirical evidence from US-managed care plans supports the conclusion that the combination of administrative controls and financial incentive helps reduce the utilization of medical services. The research findings also shed light on the additional policy option for cost containment in Asian countries.

In Chapter 4 Bong-Min Yang presents evidence of health care reform based on South Korea's experience. In recent years South Korea has reformed her health insurance system through consolidation of funds; integrating a multiple fund system into a single payer system. While the reform process is still under way, this study provides a preliminary evaluation by examining the effects of the reform on risk pooling, equity in financing, and economics of scale. Overall, the author confirms that reform can improve the efficiency and equity for the South Korea's health care system. However, two unresolved problems remain: a high co-insurance rate and the crisis of financial insolvency in the system.

Part II of this volume contains two econometric analyses of health production focusing on the inputs of medical care and education investment. In Chapter 5 Frank Sloan and his colleagues empirically investigate the effect of rehabilitation on health outcome among Medicare patients in the United States. The authors construct a sample containing 1493 patients with a stroke or a hip fracture from the National Long-term Care Survey. Based on this data set, two equations are estimated: (1) the receipt of rehabilitation, measured in terms of the probability of receipt of rehabilitation and Medicare program rehabilitation costs for the individual, conditional on receipt, and (2) health outcomes, which include the receipt of rehabilitation as an endogenous explanatory variable. The health outcome was measured by the following six indicators: (1) mortality rate within one year; (2) mortality rate within 2 years; (3) the probability of living in the community; (4) the probability of being cognitively aware; (5) the probability of remaining the same or becoming better in activities of daily living; and (6) the probability of remaining the same or becoming better in instrumental activities of daily living. The major finding is that the effect of rehabilitation is insignificant. Thus the authors conclude that rehabilitation is not productive in terms of improved health, shedding light on future research that investigates the marginal benefits of various medical interventions.

In contrast to the finding that the input of certain medical care is not productive in developed countries, in Chapter 6 Gertler and Zeitlin find that education as an input into health investment is productive in developing countries. Using data from the Indonesian Family Life Survey, which was conducted in 1993 and contained 5584 adult males and 6774 adult females, Gertler and Zeitlin examine the impact of investments in education and nutrition during childhood on adult health by estimating a reduced-form health production function. In their study adult health was measured by five different indicators: (1) self-reported health status; (2) an index of moderate limitations on physical function; (3) an index of severe limitation on physical function; (4) chronic energy deficiency, as defined by a BMI (body mass index) less than 18.5; and (5) obesity, defined as a BMI of 25 or more. Their estimates confirm previous research findings showing that better-educated Indonesians are healthier. However, the relationship between education and health is not always linear. For example, with several health indicators, men seem to benefit only from secondary education, while women benefit more from primary education than from secondary.

Part III of this volume contains three econometric analyses of health care utilization, focusing on mainland China and Taiwan. To reform its public health care system, the PRC government implemented an experimental community-based insurance model in Zhenjiang and Jiujiang cities in December 1994. The experiment was intended to test the feasibility and sustainability of a new model to replace the existing Government Insurance Program (GIP) and Labor Insurance Program (LIP), the two major health programs for urban employees in mainland China. In Chapter 7 Gordon G. Liu and his colleagues present an evaluation of the experiment with a focus on its financing aspect using a series of annual surveys in Zhenjiang City from 1993 (baseline) through 1996 for a total of 44 345 individuals. Major outcomes include health care expenditures, utilization rates of various services in annual visits, and inpatient length of stay per admission. The two-part model is employed as the primary analytical framework for the study.

Their estimates suggest that the reform experiment resulted in an increased likelihood for the general population to seek care, while decreasing total health expenditures resulted among the health care users. With respect to the determinants of cost savings, this study identifies a significant effect of substituting outpatient care for inpatient care for the general population. In addition, they find a substantial reduced utilization of various services, including inpatient admissions, emergency visits, and length of stay per admission, in response to the total cost savings by the experimental model. The study concludes that the community-based health insurance model experimented in Zhenjiang City appeared to be quite effective in containing total health care costs and utilization. The study results at the same time also shed some light on the positive impact of reform on access and equality of health care utilization among the covered populations.

Jui-Fen Rachel Lu (Chapter 8) considers the utilization of health care from the perspective of equity. Theoretical arguments as well as empirical data have shown that demand-side cost sharing, whether in the form of deductibles or copayments, is an effective way to reduce moral hazard to at least some extent (Manning et al. 1987). However, demand-side cost sharing has a disadvantage with respect to socioeconomic equity since the potential financial burden of cost sharing for low-income patients is higher than that for high-income patients. To avoid the side effect of the co-payment policy, the national health insurance (NHI) program in Taiwan adopted a 'catastrophic illness policy' that exempts the insured with a defined catastrophic illness from the co-payment requirement.

Lu's research aims to investigate the equity issue of the catastrophic illness policy based on the principle of horizontal equity where persons in equal need of medical care should receive the same treatment. In her study patients with similar needs for health care were grouped to construct two comparable groups. Diagnosis-related Group (DRG) was adopted as the grouping criteria based on its theoretical design. Data on 827 patients with principal discharge diagnoses of DRG 561 (255 ICD-9-CM codes) in a medical center were collected in 1996. Among them, 506 people (Group A) are classified as NHI-defined catastrophic illness patients (the fifth category, systemic autoimmune syndrome) while the other 321 patients are not (Group B). To examine whether patients in equal need receive the same treatment, Group B patients are compared with those in Group A, in terms of medical expenses incurred. The results indicate that Group B patients incurred higher average NHI expenses in inpatient care and physician visits than Group A patients. Further examination of the out-of-pocket expenses between these two groups has shown persistent differences. Therefore, Lu concludes that a catastrophic illness policy does not serve its distributive justice, but creates inequity among the NHI-insured population.

In Chapter 9, in contrast, Shou-Hsia Cheng and Jung-Der Wang consider the utilization of health care from the effect of supplemental health insurance, using survey data obtained from Taiwan. In addition, they examine the demand for supplemental health insurance under a universal health insurance program. Several interesting findings emerge from their analysis. Cheng and Wang find that 43 percent of the study sample own some kind of supplemental health insurance. Their estimates also confirm the findings of previous research showing that the important determinants of supplemental health insurance purchases are education, employment status, and income level. However, they find that health status has no effect on the purchase of supplemental health insurance, which may imply the absence of adverse selection. Furthermore, they provide estimates on the effect of supplemental health insurance, concluding that under the universal health insurance program, supplemental health insurance does not have a significant effect on the probability or the amount of health care utilization.

Part IV of this volume focuses on the effect of reimbursement policy on hospital behavior. Ya-Chen Tina Shih (Chapter 10) considers whether hospitals in the United States have a cost-shifting behavior under the multiple-payer system. Based on a 1995 nationwide sample, her study compares charges of surgical admissions for patients with a diagnosis of back pain, by taking into account the possibility of selection bias associated with treatment selections. Her main finding is that patients under workers' compensation have higher charges than those covered by other payers. More importantly, she finds that after adjusting for biases in the selection between medical and surgical treatment, differences between surgical charges for back pain patients covered by worker compensation versus other payment sources were augmented. This result provides supporting evidence of hospital cost shifting.

In 1990 the Japanese government introduced a partial capitation fee, which is a prospective reimbursement with the point system, on elderly care services in geriatric and general hospitals. In Chapter 11 Tetsuji Yamada and his colleagues empirically investigate the effect of this capitation system on hospital services for elderly patients, using a data set merged from three different surveys. In particular, they address three questions relevant to hospital decisions: (1) whether the hospital decides to participate in the capitation program; (2) the effect of the capitation program on the total quantity of services (measured by total points) provided by the hospital; and (3) the effect of the capitation program on the intensity of hospital service, which in turn includes four different measures: service intensity per day, unit of service, length of stay, and service intensity per treatment.

Their answer to the first question is that hospitals with a higher number of inpatient admissions per month are less likely to choose the capitation program. In response to the second question, they present consistent evidence from their regression model demonstrating that the capitation program has a significantly positive effect on the quantity of hospital services. With regard to the third question, they find that an introduction of the capitation program to general hospitals reduces the resource intensity of hospital services. Based on these findings, they conclude that transferring elderly care from acute-care oriented general hospitals to less resource intensive managed geriatric hospitals with the capitation program will be a viable option in a government's cost containment policy.

The chapters in part V consider the issue of health care financing. In Chapter 12 John W. Peabody and his colleagues examine the financial crisis of national health insurance following the rapidly aging population in South Korea. They argue that the demographic transition to an elderly population decreases the relative number of individuals participating in the workforce. This transition, in turn, decreases revenues paid into the national health insurance (NHI) and increases demand for care by an aging population. As a result, South Korea's NHI, a pay-as-you go system funded through a combination of earmarked payroll taxes and government subsidies, will fall into a crisis of financial insolvency.

Using data from government and public records, Peabody and his colleagues model the trends in costs and utilization. Their principal finding is that expenditures rise exponentially while revenues rise linearly. As a result, expenditures of South Korea's NHI will exceed revenues by 2005, and NHI reserves will be exhausted by 2010. The unmet needs for the elderly such as improved access, high co-payments for chronic conditions, and lack of coverage for selected geriatric services, are likely to accelerate this timetable. Thus they conclude that under the current financial structure the future viability of that NHI will jeopardize the remarkable accomplishments of the past and the health care for the elderly in the future. In particular, they point out that these problems are similar to the challenges faced in the Philippines, Singapore and the United States. In all these countries, policy options such as decreasing benefits or raising taxes may not be politically viable. Therefore, they conclude that an alternative approach is to distribute risk over time rather than individuals using medical savings accounts.

In the final contribution, Ching-to Albert Ma and his colleagues (Chapter 13) provide a special example of health care financing from the experience of the United States. Beginning in 1982, the US federal government used a 'block grants' policy to fund state mental health and substance abuse services. Based on state-level pooling data for the period between 1984 and 1994, Ma and his colleagues assess an element of the success in using block grants to fund substance abuse spending in the US. They find that block grants are effective as a source of funding for state substance abuse expenditures: an increase in block grant funds is associated with an increase in state spending. In addition, they find that an increase in general enforcement (announcement by the federal government of an intention to monitor the situation more closely) appears to have a positive effect on state spending, but specific enforcements, such as technical reviews, waiver application, and general audits, appear to have no discernible effect.

REFERENCES

Arrow, K.J. (1963), 'Uncertainty and the welfare economics of medical care', *American Economic Review*, **53**(5): 941–73.

Culyer, A. and J.P. Newhouse (2000), 'Introduction: the state and scope of health economics', in A. Culyer and J.P. Newhouse (eds), *Handbook of Health Economics*, Amsterdam: Elsevier Science, **1A**: 1–8.

Fuchs, V.R. (1996), 'Economics, values, and health care reform', *American Economic Review*, **86**(1): 1–24.

Fuchs, V.R. (2000), 'The future of health economics', *Journal of Health Economics*, **19**(2): 141–57.

Manning, W.G., J.P. Newhouse, N. Duan, E.B. Keeler, A. Leibowitz and M.S. Marquis (1987), 'Health insurance and the demand for medical care: evidence from a randomized experiment', *American Economic Review*, **77**(3): 251–77.

Peabody, J.W., J.C.I. Yu, Y.R. Wang and S.R. Bickel (1995), 'Health system reform in the Republic of China: formulating policy in a market-based health system', *Journal of the American Medical Association*, **273**(10): 777–81.

Phelps, C.E. (1995), 'Perspectives in health economics', *Health Economics*, **4**: 335–53.

Yoshikawa, A., J. Bhattacharya and W.B. Vogt (1996), *Health Economics of Japan*, Tokyo: University of Tokyo.

PART I

Health Care Reform

2. Health care reforms in Taiwan and the US: what we can learn from each other

Teh-Wei Hu and Yun-Yi Hung

1 INTRODUCTION

A usual framework for assessing the performance of a health care system is to consider three key parameters: access, costs, and quality. It would be ideal to have a system that can provide a population with full and easy access to care, efficient and affordable costs, and delivery of satisfactory and desirable health outcomes. In reality, this ideal goal is almost impossible to reach, since these three parameters are not always complementary. Achieving full access to care would require more resources and thus an increased cost burden to society. To contain cost increase, providers or payers may have to compromise the service quality or outcome. Health care systems around the world are all facing this dilemma to find an optimum balance among these three prongs (these are, access, costs, and quality). Each health care system, depending on its economic, political, social, and cultural background, places its relative emphases on goals of access, costs, or quality. For instance, the UK health care system has employed universal coverage with reasonable success in cost containment, but access and quality have been major concerns. Taiwan has achieved universal coverage through the establishment of the National Health Insurance (NHI) program in 1995, but costs of health care have increased rapidly. Because of the difficulty in achieving an optimum balance among these key parameters, each health care system is constantly finding policy alternatives to modify its system. It has been said that health care reform is now a world epidemic.

A World Health Organization (WHO) study defined 'reform' of health care as an intentional, sustained, systematic process of structural changes to one or more major health care sector subsystems (Saltman and Figueras 1998). By this definition, Taiwan indeed had a health care reform in 1995,

15

by transforming three separate health insurance programs and 45 percent of the uninsured population into one single national health insurance plan. Does US health care have a reform? According to this WHO definition, the United States had an intentional health care reform during 1993–94 under the Clinton administration, but the reform collapsed in 1994. Yet, while the goal of universal health insurance coverage failed, its intent to use managed care for cost containment has been widely adopted in the past five years. Therefore, if one uses a less rigid definition of reform, as simply meaning changes in a health care system, then US health care in fact has been reformed or transformed, especially in financing and delivery of health care services. This chapter will examine the lessons of changes in Taiwan and in the US health care financing and delivery systems that may be relevant to each other, as both currently undergo policy debate on health care cost containment.

Lessons of health policy learned from a foreign country are not easily transferable, because of the economic, social, political and cultural differences between countries. Therefore, it would be much easier to learn from a conceptual point of view rather than the practice of a policy. With this in mind, this chapter will address possible lessons that countries can learn from each other.

First to be considered will be health care reform and current issues in Taiwan. Next, some important US health care reform strategies of the past 30 years and the economics of managed care will be reviewed. Finally, lessons from both countries will be analyzed, with attention to the limitations and implications for future health care reform in Taiwan.

2   HEALTH CARE REFORM IN TAIWAN

2.1   A Brief History of Taiwan Health Care Reform

Until March 1995, Taiwan had three separate health insurance programs: Labor Insurance, Government Employers' Insurance, and Farmers' Health Insurance. Labor Insurance covers private sector employees; Government Employees' Insurance covers all government employees, retirees, and their family members; and Farmers' Health Insurance covers all farmers. Each of these programs provides a similar range of benefits, including outpatient visits, hospital inpatient services, and prescription drugs. These three programs were all administered by different government agencies and together they covered about 55 percent of the population. The remaining 45 percent uninsured were children, the elderly (those that were not farmers), dependents of Labor Insurance employees, and unemployed.

Because of rapid economic growth in Taiwan during the mid-1980s and concerns about social welfare for the voluminous uninsured population, the government started the planning of the national health insurance by integrating these three health insurance programs and expanding the program to cover the remaining 45 percent of uninsured population. Originally it was proposed to take a phased-in approach to be completed by the year 2000. However, due to the political pressure from the opposition party, concern over the financial crisis of three separate health insurance programs, and the pending major election of the legislative representatives in December 1995, an official legislation on National Health Insurance Law was passed in July 1994. The Bureau of National Health Insurance (BNHI) was established in January 1995 and the government ordered the BNHI to fully implement the NHI on 1 March 1995. Needless to say, it was a major system change that presented many administrative challenges in terms of population registration, premium setting, and provider contracting. The NHI is a government run and single payer insurance program which consolidated the three insurance programs and extended coverage to the previously uninsured population (Chiang 1997). By 1997, 96 percent of the population of Taiwan were fully insured under the National Health Insurance Program (Yeh 1997). This is indeed a major achievement in the social legislation of Taiwan: another miracle for Taiwan's pride, in addition to her economic miracle achieved during the 1980s.

The objective of Taiwan's health care reform was to establish national health insurance to provide equal access to medical services for all of the population. To achieve this objective, the NHI program was designed with the following three features: (1) compulsory universal coverage, (2) uniform comprehensive benefits, and (3) financing by payroll tax with large government subsidies from general revenue.

To control health care cost inflation, the NHI program implemented a cost sharing scheme which includes a minimum registration fee of NT$50 (current exchange rate between US and NT is 1:33) for a private clinic visit or visit to the district hospital physician, NT$100 for a visit to the regional hospital, and NT $150 for a visit to the Academic Medical Center (Yeh 1997). The actual percentage of copayment for a hospital ambulatory visit is about 6–7 percent (Yeh 1997). There is also a 10 percent copayment for inpatient services lasting 30 days, 20 percent between 31 and 60 days, and 30 percent for more than 61 days stay (Yeh 1997). Low-income families, families residing in mountain areas or on offshore islands and patients with catastrophic diseases are exempted from cost-sharing.

The major payment method under the NHI program is fee-for-service (FFS). The NHI program has many thousands of fee schedules for procedures and medications on the reference list. The current FFS system has been criticized for its relatively low fee for hospital physician visits, inpatient per diem rate, and surgical procedures. The initial design of the NHI program proposed to implement a global budget system with supplemental diagnosis-related-group (DRG) models for paying inpatient services. The DRG payment schedule has been under study for several years, but has not yet been implemented.

By March 1997, at the end of a two-year period, the NHI program received 75 percent consumer satisfaction, increasing from a 33 percent satisfaction rate at the beginning of the implementation period, March 1995. The more than two-fold increase in the satisfaction rate was largely due to the removal of financial barriers to health care for those newly insured and full coverage extended to chronically ill patients. Of course, with this generous coverage, NHI has faced rapid increases in total health care costs: about 19.6 percent annual growth rate in 1996–97, as compared to a 15.3 percent annual increase between 1990 and 1994 (Chiang 1997). Between the 1995 and 1997 fiscal years, the total health insurance premium collected has exceeded the total health care expenditures under the BNHI program. In fact, there have been savings accumulated throughout these three years. However, according to statistics from the Bureau of NHI, in 1998 the NHI program received NT$23.9 billion, while the expenditure was NT$25.0, leaving a shortage of NT$1.1 billion (Lai 1998). The outlook for future financial status indicates that expenditures will continue to exceed total premium collections, if there is no additional premium increase or implementation of cost containment policies.

The rapid increases in health expenditure are attributable to two factors: increase in unit cost of services and increase in amount of services. At the beginning of the NHI program, physicians and hospitals requested an increase in their reimbursement rate. Due to the threat by physicians and hospital providers to sabotage the NHI program, NHI paid 17–34 percent more per physician visit and 19–33 percent more per patient day than before the NHI period (Chiang 1997). Furthermore, the universal coverage increases the use of health care services. For example, per capita physician visits among the previously insured groups increased by 23 percent. Among those previously uninsured, per capita physician visits increased by 129 percent (Cheng and Chiang 1997). The annual number of physician visits increased from 12.8 in 1995 to 13.8 in 1996 and is projected to be 14.3 in 1998 (Lai 1998). In essence, NHI has provided equal access and removed financial barriers for almost the entire population of Taiwan. However, under the fee-for-service system, the total payments by NHI are increasing rapidly and have exceeded the revenue. A financial crisis is foreseen for the coming years.

2.2 Proposed Options for Further Reform

Since raising premiums in the near term could face very strong opposition from employers and employees, one viable alternative to resolving the financial crisis is to contain the cost increase. Currently, there are a number of proposals under discussion. One is to privatize the national health insurance, so that even though it is financed by public funds, the management could be organized by private entities that insure financial self-sufficiency. Perhaps this will shift the financial risk from the government to the private entity. The other alternative is to let the private sector organize not-for-profit insurance organizations and compete against the Bureau of National Health Insurance. It is hoped that through competition among multiple carriers, either the premiums will be reduced or the efficiency will be improved, so that costs can be contained.

Another alternative under consideration in payment reform is to move from fee-for-service to case payment, DRG, capitation, health maintenance organizations, or the global budget system. Thus far, 28 procedures such as vaginal delivery, Caesarean section, hernia repair, appendectomy, and others have been implemented as pilot experiments. The global budget system has been implemented in dental care since July 1998, starting with a small figure (5 percent) as a first step toward the global budget experiment.

Finally, there is a consideration of demand side cost control, by either increased copayments for outpatient visits to Chinese Medicine doctors and prescription drugs or the adoption of a Medical Savings Account (MSA) approach, similar to programs that have been implemented in Singapore, some parts of urban China, or current experiments in the US Medicare program (Medisave). These options are under discussion and require further legislation and the public are largely opposed to increasing patients' cost sharing.

The Taiwan National Health Insurance program is still relatively new compared to many other national insurance programs found internationally. In fact, one may consider this as an experiment which is early enough in development to allow for modification and revision to take advantage of experiences learned from other countries to improve Taiwan's future national health insurance program.

3   US HEALTH CARE REFORM AND ECONOMICS OF MANAGED CARE

3.1   A Brief History of US Health Care Reform

From 1964 to 1994, US health care costs experienced double-digit growth rates in the percentage of national health care expenditure and rose faster than growth rates in the overall economy (Levit et al. 2000). Therefore, a major issue facing health care policymakers in the United States has been containing health care costs. Although the problem of the uninsured population was also a major concern, it had not been on the political agenda until the 1992 Clinton campaign.

The failure to control health costs would affect the cost of health care for the consumer, escalating employers' costs of benefit packages, and the cost of private and public health insurance programs. In the end, the economy would be left with fewer resources for other national priorities such as education and housing. With these negative consequences in mind, the United States, largely on the part of government, introduced numerous policy alternatives to control and contain the health care cost increases of the past 30 years.

In the 1960s and 1970s, the US health insurance plan and government Medicare program introduced the patient copayment and deductible schemes as a means to discourage consumer over-use, the moral hazard problem in the health insurance market. In fact, the Rand Health Insurance experiment (Newhouse 1993) was designed to find the effects of copayment variation on health expenditures, with hopes that the government would be able to benefit from these findings in their health insurance reform.

With debate and research on the possibility of provider-induced or created patient demand for usage of health care services, and with the continuous increase in health care cost in spite of the existence of copayment and deductible schemes, the US government policies have focused on regulating the provider side of health care. The government strategies included regulation of hospital capital investment, certification of need (CON), hospital rate setting, peer utilization review, payment to hospitals according to diagnostic-related-groups (DRGs), and payment to physicians according to relative value of services (RBRVS). However, studies have shown that none of these control instruments have shown significant cost containment during the 1980s and into the 1990s (Rice 1992).

The failure to control costs on either the consumer or provider side has led policymakers and health economists to realize the obvious concept that health care expenditure consists of two components: (1) unit price of the services (P), and (2) quantity of services (Q). The total health expenditure is the product of P and Q. If one only controls the health care services price (P), such as by rate setting or physical fee schedules, providers can increase quantity (Q) of services and thus total revenue can continue to increase under the fee-for-services system. If one intends to control quantity of services (Q), such as by peer utilization review, providers could increase their price (P) of services. DRGs were an initial attempt to control both P and Q, through a fixed payment according to a diagnostic disease group. However, the incentives of DRGs are limited to only inpatient care and public insurance (Medicare) programs. Hospitals can still shift costs to private insurance carriers or shift them from inpatient to outpatient services. Therefore, DRGs had limited success in controlling the total health expenditure. The failure of past payment system reform provides a lesson on the importance of developing a prepaid fixed payment scheme which covers both inpatient and outpatient care for a population-based payment program. In thinking of this, one may wonder why it took the US 30 years to learn that either control of P or Q would not achieve the goal of cost containment. Perhaps the reason lies in the relative administrative costs of implementing cost containment policies. Generally speaking, it is easier to set up a fee schedule or copayment rate than to set up a prepaid payment scheme.

The 1993–94 Clinton health care reform mainly proposed to create a universal insurance coverage system by using health maintenance organizations (HMOs) as a means to control costs and generate savings. An HMO is a prepaid health care delivery system with a capitation basis which provides comprehensive outpatient, inpatient, and preventive services to its members. Because of the capitation payment system, there is an economic incentive for providers to keep members healthy and to control the use of medical services. HMOs usually use primary care physicians as gatekeepers for referral to specialty physicians and inpatient services. Also, HMOs use many methods such as hospital pre-admission, concurrent utilization review, and case and disease management to control the use of health services. The methods are also called the 'managed care' approach. Thus it is quite often that the public considers the HMO as the managed care organization. The Clinton health care reform failed due to a variety of oppositions through interest groups, the complexity of the proposal, and the lack of financial resources to pay for the proposed system. However, the concept of managed care was adopted either with the anticipation of the pending health care reform, or due to the failures of previous alternative cost containment methods.

One of the largest changes in the US health care system since 1992 has been the exploding growth in managed care enrollment in both private employer sponsored and public insurance programs. According to the American Association of Health Plans, managed care enrollment increased to 60 percent of the population in 1996, up from 30 percent in 1992 (American Association of Health Plans 1998). The record of success of implementing managed care, at least until 1998, is quite impressive. Ever since 1992, the rate of growth of annual national health care expenditures fell drastically from the double-digit increases of the 1970s, 1980s, and even the early 1990s, to 5.5 percent in 1994, 4.8 percent in 1995, 4.6 percent in 1996, 4.7 percent in 1997 and 5.6 percent in 1998 (Levit et al. 2000). This marks the slowest growth since 1960. After adjustment for inflation, the real rate of growth during 1994–97 registered 3.0 percent in 1994, 2.4 percent in 1995, 2.7 percent in 1996, 2.8 percent in 1997 and 4.5 percent in 1998. The health care profession has largely attributed the success of cost containment during this period to the implementation of managed care. However, the 1998 health care financing statistics indicate that the nominal rate of health care expenditure has increased by 6.5 percent and the real rate of growth was 5.0 percent (US Department of Commerce 2000). It now has been debated within the US health care profession whether the managed care approach can continue to contain health care costs, or whether the cost-reducing effect by managed care is just a short-term (that is, five-year) phenomenon.

3.2   Economics of Managed Care

It should be noted that, in reality, an HMO is a health care delivery organization as well as a payment system, while managed care is a process or method to deliver health care services. By the nature of HMO structure, managed care methods have been implemented within the system. However, without being an HMO, one can still implement managed care practice within an insurance carrier, such as a preferred provider organization (PPO). Therefore, managed care is a much broader practical concept than an HMO system. In our opinion, it is the underlying economic concepts of managed care that contribute to the success of the managed care plan in cost containment, rather than the HMO structure per se. The success of cost containment in the US relies on the working of some basic economic concepts such as changes in economic incentives for providers and shifting financial risk to providers.

Economic incentive
Under fee-for-service systems, providers have incentives to maximize revenue by ordering more services and this may lead to overconsumption

of medical care resources, largely due to supplier-induced demand. Under the prepaid capitation system, such as HMO, the incentive for providers is to minimize costs of services by eliminating unnecessary services, which may, in contrast, lead to underconsumption.

The US health care reform experience of the past 30 years has shown that the most effective cost containment strategies are those aimed at providers of care, since providers respond easily to changes in price or quantity. Also, through the managed care mechanism such as capitation payment, providers have economic incentives to closely monitor their service referral. Therefore, if the economic incentive is to be emphasized on the provider side, then a capitation payment to the provider would be a logical payment financing method to implement. This economic incentive leads to a shift of the demand curve downward.

Financial risk
Under FFS, financial risk of illness rests entirely on the payer (that is, the patient or insurance carrier). Given the pivotal role of the physician provider, the prepaid capitation system has shifted the financial risk to the provider. The more services they provide to the consumer, the more resources required by the provider, thus the higher financial risk for the provider. In this case, it would be advantageous for providers to emphasize preventive care, health promotion, and to manage the delivery of health care. In addition, the provider also tends to be more cost efficient by reducing capital investment, such as hospital facilities, expansion, equipment acquisition, and even by mergers with other facilities to take advantage of economy of scope and economy of scale. Literature (Miller and Luft 1994) has shown that unit costs of patient services are reduced by substituting less costly services (for example, outpatient care) for more expensive services (for example, inpatient care). More efficient production of health care services leads to the reduction of the average cost curve.

Market responses to managed care
In practice, managed care has made a large impact on the interaction among patients, payers, and providers. To survive successfully in the new era of managed care, the health care system in the US has experienced significant changes in recent years. These changes include vertical and horizontal integration of providers, managed competition, and risk-contracting.

1. Integrative health care delivery systems. Until 1993, under the FFS system, the US operated with a generally unintegrated system of health care treatment, except for those under HMOs. Through the capitation

payment system and managed care practices, it is necessary for health care providers to coordinate primary care, specialty care, outpatient and inpatient service, surgery, and drug prescriptions. The economic incentives for cost efficiency have led to the development of vertical integration among physicians, clinics, and hospitals so that redundancy and over-capacity can be eliminated.

2. Information development. To implement managed care and to accept a reasonable capitation rate from employer-based payer or public insurance programs, providers need more comprehensive clinical and cost information. Computerized clinical information would enhance the coordination of services and the monitoring of quality of services. Cost information systems are critical to monitoring the impact of physician clinical practice patterns on costs, to developing an incentive or bonus scheme for clinicians and cost centers, to planning for managed care program development, and to negotiating with payers for risk-adjusted capitation rates. This information development would enable providers to be more efficient and lower the cost of overall services.

3. Risk shifting. Risk shifting has been a key element in the health care financing scheme during recent years. Health insurance payers can contract services to providers at a fixed cost for a special service (for example, mental health services) or a special population (for example, Medicaid or Medicare). If it is a special service, because of the uncertainty of incurring high costs and high use, another form of contracting, carve-out, has also been implemented in the US. It has been found that risk shifting through contracting or carve-out has reduced the cost of services (by substituting outpatient care for inpatient care) or reduced the utilization and sometimes access of health care services (Dickey 1997; Bloom et al. 1998).

4. Competition among providers and carriers. With the increase in managed care practice, which leads to fewer specialty and inpatient services, specialist and hospitals have to compete for fewer available clients. One of the reasons for vertical integration is to enable better competition for the market share of patient services. Competition among providers would also lead to horizontal integration, through mergers among hospitals and clinics. So, as a result, they can negotiate a better capitation rate with carriers. Furthermore, providers could also establish a managed care organization (that is, HMO or PPO) to serve as a financial entity as well as a provider organization to compete with insurance carriers. The increasing competition among financial carriers has led to the reduction of insurance premiums during the past four years, while the increasing competition among providers has led to the reduction in price and costs of services (Melnick and Zwanziger 1995). These reductions, to

some extent, are due to the managed care and capitation systems.

The discussion so far shows that the US care reform has succeeded, at least until 1998, in containing the health care cost increase. However, the issues of access and universal health insurance coverage for the entire US population have not been resolved. In fact, the uninsured population has increased from 15.2 percent in 1994 to 16.3 percent in 1998 (US Census Bureau 1995, 1999).

4   WHAT WE CAN LEARN FROM EACH OTHER

4.1   Lessons to Learn from Taiwan

Taiwan's provision of full access to health care services without financial barriers for the entire population within a short time period is a major success. This success can be attributed to a number of reasons which provide lessons in health care reform for other countries.

First, one of the challenges in developing a national health insurance is the integration of various health insurance programs with a uniform health budget. Taiwan was fortunate that she had only three major health insurance programs, all administered by the government, with no private health industry to resist such integration. Even though there were still conflicts and confusion among these public insurance programs, it turned out that a single payer insurance program has its advantage in financing as well as administration of health insurance programs. The administrative cost of the national insurance program was only 2.32 percent of the total health insurance program expenditure in 1997 (Lai 1998). In addition, when a health care system becomes a single payer, it has its monopsony power in setting fees, monitoring, and contracting with providers.

Second, it is quite obvious that a successful health care reform requires not only financial resources, but also the political environment and opportunity. It is important for government policymakers to have a vision and to take advantage of opportunities with a decisive policy implementation. For instance, in the late 1980s and early 1990s, Taiwan had excellent economic growth and the ruling party sensed the political timing was right to shorten the planning period. On the other hand, histories of health care reform in the US have shown that the Truman administration in the early 1950s, the Nixon administration in the early 1970s, and the Clinton administration in the early 1990s all failed in their agenda for a national health insurance program and one of the key factors for these failures was timing. The beginning of the Korean War in the early 1950s, the Watergate event in the early 1970s, and the indecisiveness of the 1990s Clinton health care reform all took the momentum away from the legislation of national health insurance.

Third, during the implementation of the NHI, Taiwan has devoted a large amount of resources to setting up a health care expenditure reimbursement claim information system, which includes outpatient, inpatient, medication, laboratory, and other service utilization and payment information. This information can be linked to each individual or each provider by unique identifications. In other words, this is a population-based health care services utilization and costs data system. This population-based information system is a golden opportunity for NHI program management, health service policymakers, and health service researchers to monitor the health status of the population and health care costs and utilization patterns. Although this unique information system is still in its early stages, through this information the BNHI can construct physician and hospital provider files, plan treatment outcome evaluations, and design alternative health care payment systems. Obviously, this population-based information is envied by many health service policymakers and health service researchers from other countries. In the US, only small sectors of the population, such as HMO, Medicaid, and Medicare, have this population-based data.

4.2   Lessons to Learn from the US

As Reinhardt (1996) has mentioned, the US is a 'laboratory' of innovative health care systems. Through all 30 years of experimentation, it seems clear now that cost control has been more effective on the provider side than on the consumer side. The managed care system developed in recent years is a cost control mechanism directed at the supply side. Managed care practice has been defined as applying one or more of several practice options, such as limited choice of providers, selective contracting, financial incentives for providers, gatekeeping, physician profiling, and utilization review. However, these are operational practices. The main reason for managed care's success so far is the transfer of financial risk from the insurance carrier to the provider, therefore changing the economic incentive of providers. In other words, it is the change in payment system from fee-for-service to capitation that has led to the changes in provider practice. This, in turn, has affected the amount of intensive services use (these are hospital inpatient, high cost procedures, medication, and so on.) provided, and finally has been reflected in the reduced rate of health care cost increase.

In our opinion, Taiwan can learn, as far as cost containment is concerned, to use the capitation payment system which will induce providers to preserve resource use, as the US experience suggests. Thus it is the principles of risk shifting and economic incentive that can help Taiwan reform its payment system. Managed care is a tool to achieve or to respond to the change in payment system. Different health care systems, different health care provider organizations, and different health care information systems may have different managed care practices. In fact, there is no uniform managed care practice system. Cost may be contained with the implementation of the capitation payment system alone. Capitation is a necessary condition, while managed care is merely a sufficient condition for cost containment.

There are a number of capitation systems, such as pure capitation, risk contracting (risk sharing), and carve-out. In a pure capitation system, a provider accepts payments per person per year, and the provider earns a profit if the patient costs are less than the capitation revenue, and vice versa. Another system is a risk sharing capitation. In many US capitation systems, such as mental health services, both the provider and the payer can share the risk of profit or loss. A risk sharing capitation system could help providers to avoid experiencing extreme losses and this may reduce incentives for providers to limit patient treatment on the one hand or, on the other, may limit the provider from reaping the entire profit so that part of the profits can go back to the payer. Furthermore, payers can impose performance indicators, consumer satisfaction reports, and quality measurements as additional incentives in risk sharing capitation, which can create incentives to economize while limiting profit through undertreatment.

Under the concept of risk shifting and risk contracting, a particular feature of the payment system is to subcontract one special type of service (for example, mental health services) to providers who manage to be responsible in paying for these services. This type of arrangement is called 'carve-out'. The carve-out system requires the provider to bear financial risks (or profits) but also makes the provider responsible for providing services. Cases have been shown where managed care vendors achieved most savings by diverting inpatient services to outpatient services and by negotiating substantial price reductions from both hospitals and physicians. The argument in support of the carve-out concept is that a special organization is established or contracted to manage the cost and the quality or appropriateness of care for a particular type of illness. Furthermore, carve-out guarantees the fixed amount of funding for services which can mandate a set of benefits covered for a particular population, including chronic illness, so that carve-out would reduce adverse selective problem (Frank et al. 1995).

Implementing capitation, risk contracting, or carve-out, requires considerable information on both costs and services utilization distribution of a service population being served. If the capitation rate is higher than costs of treatment, the goal of cost containment may not be realized. The contractor may end up with huge profits without being efficient. If the capitation rate is much lower than treatment costs, the provider may be pushed to unacceptable reductions in quantity and quality of care. Therefore, a reliable record of past service utilization, cost of services, and case mix will be important in carrying out the risk adjusted capitation rate. The US health care system has made significant advances in the development of the capitation system.

Implementing capitation also requires a mechanism to negotiate between payers and providers which leads to contracting. Contracting has been a popular method of risk shifting which guarantees a legal and stable financial and service provision relationship between payer and provider. In Taiwan, there are numerous contracts between the Bureau of National Health Insurance and providers (those are hospitals, clinics, and physicians). However, contracts in Taiwan are not focused on price, efficiency, or quality. Rather, the contracting in Taiwan serves as a network for consumers to access providers' services and the providers do not bear any financial risk.

One of the successful factors in both capitation contracts and carve-out contracts in the US is the selective mechanism which uses a competitive procurement process. In other words, there is competition among potential contractors. During such a process, potential, qualified contractors are identified and invited to bid. Introduction of market mechanisms is often considered a means of encouraging efficiency. Competition may be used to promote efficiency and quality of services and to control costs for a contract or for enrollees. Under the single payer system in Taiwan, it would be best to use competition for a contract. Competition for a contract could result in cost efficiency, but not in quality of care. Competition for enrollees gives providers the incentive to achieve or maintain quality of care. However, currently there are no network providers which are organized to compete for enrollees, since the entire population in Taiwan is enrolled under the Bureau of National Health Insurance.

The major drawback of capitation or carve-out systems is that they have an incentive to limit use of all services. They have an especially strong incentive to avoid persons who are expensive to treat or to reduce their access to health care services. Therefore, in recent years, there have been serious concerns about the issues of quality and access of care, patient satisfaction, and treatment outcomes for the vulnerable population. Thus there has been the development of the Health Plan Employer Data and Information Set (HEDIS) and other consumer satisfaction indicators as report cards to evaluate quality of provider services. These quality indicators include the health promotion and disease prevention services provided for the covered populations, waiting time for appointments, waiting time in clinics, services to patients with chronic illnesses such as diabetes, asthma, mental illness, and so on. These quality and outcome indicators have become an integral factor when employers contract with a provider or when consumers choose a health plan.

In the quality assurance area, Taiwan has a great deal to learn from the US. In fact, Taiwan has a unique advantage in implementing quality assurance programs, since the Bureau of National Health Insurance has collected service utilization information through computerized records from each insured member's ID card. This information includes type of services, number of services, and type of provider, together with the disease diagnosis and procedure codes. These data can be linked to treatment outcomes and provide longitudinal patient/provider-based outcome and quality indicators which can be used by the government to monitor services outcqme and quality of services.

5   CONCLUDING REMARKS

Given the current economic and health care system in the US, it would be difficult for the US to implement a single payer health care system with wage payroll as a major financing scheme. Also, with the current political environment in the US, national health insurance is not an attainable goal in the short run. What the US can learn from Taiwan is that, perhaps at the state level, integration of various private and public health insurance programs can be used as an experiment toward future national health insurance. Furthermore, a uniform health care claims information system would also be a useful goal for future population-based health care data. As we have learned from Taiwan, the political environment is another important factor in health care reform success. Future political leaders perhaps can seize the opportunity to make another effort to achieve national health insurance in the US. Finally, the US government can extend Medicaid coverage to children of working poor families to protect the vulnerable population.

There are several lessons that Taiwan might learn from the US health care reform.

1. Reform payment system. While Taiwan has been debating for some time about the possibility of privatization of health insurance or

promotion of multiple insurance carriers to compete against each other to replace the current single payer system, not much progress has been made in the health care financing reform. Given the rigidity of the legislative process and the political environment of Taiwan, it may not be possible to move from the current government run, single payer system to a privatized multiple carrier system. Therefore, the immediate direction of reform should be focused on payment system reform, namely, cost containment through payment reform.

Most effective cost containment strategies are those aimed at providers of care. With asymmetric medical information, providers are a major source of generating medical services utilization. Therefore, it is important to shift financial risk and develop financial incentives for providers to conserve medical service resources. Given that Taiwan is a single provider, Taiwan can start with capitation, risk contracting, and carve-out at the regional level or at the specialty services level (those are renal dialysis and mental health services), before a global budget system is implemented. With the current health care provider system in Taiwan, it is difficult to start a global budget system. Perhaps a mixed system of capitation with fee-for-service would be an initial payment reform method.

2. Increase competition. The US experience shows that competition among contractors is an efficiency mechanism to contain cost and perhaps maintain quality of care. Taiwan has a contracting system, but without competitive bidding and without risk sharing. Taking advantage of being a single payer, the government can promote competition among providers or promote service integration so that competition for contracting can be implemented easily.

3. Assure Service Quality. Data collection of the information on utilization of service and treatment outcomes is important when formulating capitation and risk-adjustment strategies, and for monitoring perverse outcomes of capitation, such as adverse selection, undertreatment, denial of access, and others. It is the government's role to take full advantage of the population-based computerized information system. Linking payment systems with quality of care or treatment outcomes would be a favorable initiation. The performance-based payment system would encourage providers to take initiatives such as practical guidelines and a total quality management program to improve quality of care. Low cost and high quality could be contradicting goals because resource is restricted. However, if preventive services such as immunization, cancer screening, and behavioral changes through health

promotion are encouraged, then cost-effective strategies to achieve cost containment can also improve quality of care.

4. Limit the supply of physician and hospitals. In 1995, in Taiwan, the number of physicians per 1000 population was about 1.2 and the number of acute hospital beds per 1000 population was about 4.7 (BNHI 1998). Even though the number of physicians per 1000 population in Taiwan is lower than in the US (2.3), Japan (1.6) and the UK (1.4), we think health policies should focus on encouraging doctors to practice in remote areas, rather than continuously increasing the supply of physicians. Also, the number of acute hospital beds per 1000 population in Taiwan is higher than in the US (3.8) and the UK (3.2) and the overall hospital occupancy rate has been maintained at the level of 85 percent at the medical centers and 75 percent at the regional hospitals. Since the US experience shows that the oversupply of hospital beds and physicians induces more health services use, Taiwan should make careful plans for future expansions of hospitals and medical schools.

To draw conclusions and lessons from one health care system reform to the formulation of policy in another country that is socially, politically, economically, and culturally different is far from straightforward. It is quite possible that lessons from the US may not be directly transferable to Taiwan and vice versa, because of the major differences in their health care systems. However, we believe, at least in principle, that developing financial risks for providers, while considering additional demand-side management (that is, cost sharing or Medisave accounts, and so on.), would be useful cost containment policy instruments for both countries. Finally, both governments should take more proactive roles in monitoring the quality of care, providing consumer medical information, and encouraging the practice of health behaviors to improve the health of both countries.

REFERENCES

American Association of Health Plan (1998), 'Annual report of the American Association of Health Plan', Washington, DC.

Bloom, Joan, Teh-Wei Hu, Neal Wallace, Brian Cuffel, Jackie Hausman and Richard Scheffler (1998), 'Mental health costs and outcomes under alternative capitation systems in Colorado: early results', *The Journal of Mental Health Policy and Economics*, 1: 3–13.

Bureau of National Health Insurance (1998), 'Comparisons of national health insurance program with other health care systems (in Chinese)'.

Cheng, Shou-Hsia and Tung-Liang Chiang (1997), 'The effect of universal health insurance of health care utilization in Taiwan', *Journal of the American Medical Association*, **278**: 89–93.

Chiang, Tung-Liang (1997), 'Taiwan's 1995 health care reform', *Health Policy*, **39**: 225–39.

Dickey, B. (1997), 'Assessing cost and utilization in managed mental health care in the United States', *Health Policy*, **41** (Suppl): S163–74.

Frank, Richard, Thomas McGuire and Joseph Newhouse (1995), 'Risk contracts in managed mental health care', *Health Affairs*, Fall, pp. 50–64.

Lai, M. (1998), 'The current status and the future of national health insurance program in Taiwan (in Chinese)', Bureau of National Health Insurance.

Levit, K., H. Lazerby and B. Braden (2000), 'National health spending trends in 1998', *Health Affairs*, Jan/Feb, pp. 124–32.

Melnick, Glen and J. Zwanziger (1995), 'State health care expenditures under competition and regulation, 1980 through 1991', *American Journal of Public Health*, **85**(10): 1391–6.

Miller, Robert and Harold Luft (1994), 'Managed care plan performance since 1980: a literature analysis', *Journal of the American Medical Association*, **271**(19): 1512–9.

Newhouse, Joseph (1993), *Free for All: Lessons from the Rand Health Insurance Experiment*, Cambridge, MA: Harvard University Press.

Reinhardt, Uwe (1996), 'A social contract for 21st century health care: three-tier health care without bounty hunting', *Health Economics*, **5**: 479–99.

Rice, Thomas (1992), 'Containing health care costs in the United States', *Mental Health Review*, **49**(1): 19–65.

Saltman, Richard and Joseph Figueras (1998), 'Analyzing the evidence on European health care reforms', *Health Affairs*, March/April, pp. 85–108.

US Census Bureau (1999), 'Current population reports: health insurance coverage', Series P60–190, 1995 and Series P60–208.

US Department of Commerce (2000), 'Statistical abstracts of the United States', Washington, DC, p. 109.

Yeh, Ching-Chuan (1997), 'Overview of national health insurance in Taiwan', presented at International Symposium on Health Care and Payment System Reform, Taipei, Taiwan, 23 June.

3. Physician contracting with health plans: a survey of the literature

Martin Gaynor and Tami Mark

1 INTRODUCTION

During the 1980s and 1990s, health care markets in the United States have been dominated by two major trends: tremendous growth in managed care and, most recently, a strong movement toward consolidation, both horizontally and vertically (Gaynor and Haas-Wilson 1999). Both of these developments are characterized by changes in the nature of contracts between physicians and health plans. In this chapter we review trends in physician contracting with health plans and other financial intermediaries, describe the characteristics of physician contracts, and review the theoretical and empirical literature on the effect of contractual form on physician practice patterns.

Physician contracting with health plans and other financial intermediaries raises a number of questions. How has physician contracting affected physicians' practices, such as their work load and income? How has physician contracting affected patient care, such as the amount of time physicians spend with patients and medical outcomes? Does physician/health plan contracting affect the price of health care? Because health care resource utilization is controlled in large measure by physicians, and because physicians are the cornerstone of managed care organizations, understanding contracting between health plans and physicians, and how contracts influence physicians' behavior is also essential for understanding the potential effects of managed care and for predicting its long-run viability. Further, information about the relationship between physicians and intermediaries can inform the debate over policies aimed at regulating these relationships.

In the next section, we provide some information on trends in the health care market affecting physician practices, such as the growth of managed care, recent trends toward consolidation in health care markets, and new legislature affecting physician contracts. The third section

33

characterizes different types of health plans, managed care arrangements, and physician contracting. The fourth section discusses theoretical issues in physician contracting, the fifth section reviews the empirical evidence on the decision to contract, the sixth section reviews the empirical evidence on the effect of contractual form on physician behavior, and the final section contains the summary and conclusions.

2   RECENT TRENDS IN US HEALTH CARE MARKETS

2.1   Insurance

Until the 1980s, most insurance was reimbursement insurance, first predominantly provided by Blue Cross and Blue Shield, and later also by commercial carriers. Under these traditional insurance contracts, a consumer (or more accurately, an employer) pays a premium[1] and after paying a deductible, is reimbursed a predetermined percentage of covered expenses, usually 80 percent.[2,3] This traditional insurance contract is characterized by fee-for-service (FFS henceforth) reimbursement for physicians. In some cases consumers pay the physician's bill and are reimbursed directly by the insurer for the covered amount of the total. A more typical case is for the physician to submit a bill directly to the insurer. In this case, the contract between the physician and the insurer specifies that the insurer will reimburse the physician a predetermined usual, customary, and reasonable (UCR) rate as a fee, and that the insurer has the right to disallow a claim, either because of coverage restrictions or limits, or inappropriateness of treatment. No other restrictions on the physician apply. Under 'pure' reimbursement insurance physicians are reimbursed on a fee-for-service basis, with little oversight or involvement on the part of the plan, and consumers are free to receive care from any provider. The growth of myriad forms of managed care organizations during the 1980s and 1990s, stemming largely from employers' concerns about medical costs, dramatically altered this arrangement (Miller and Luft 1994).

In 1980, 9.1 million persons (about 5 percent of all Americans) were enrolled in health maintenance organizations (HMOs), most of which were so-called closed staff or group-model HMOs – where the physicians practiced in large organizations or multispecialty group settings (Weiner and de Lissovoy 1993). By 1998, HMOs had over 78.8 million enrollees, or over 30 percent of the total US population (Interstudy 1999). Most growth occurred not in staff and group-model HMOs, but through the creation of newer forms of managed care organizations, such as

Independent Practice Associations (IPAs). An IPA is an HMO that primarily contracts directly with physicians in independent practices; and/or contracts with one or more associations of physicians in independent practice. Approximately 40 percent of total HMO enrollment in 1998 was in IPA-model HMOs (Interstudy 1999). Other forms of managed care, such as PPOs, have been growing as well and by 1998 less than 15 percent of active employees covered in employer-sponsored health plans were enrolled in traditional indemnity insurance (Mercer/Foster Higgins National Survey of Employer-Sponsored Health Plans 1998).

The term 'managed care' has been applied to a wide range of associations among physicians, hospitals, and other health care providers. While this term is used in a variety of ways, it essentially denotes explicit efforts by insurers to influence utilization through their relationships with providers. This clearly includes alternative health plans such as HMOs, IPAs, PPOs, and their variants. It also includes traditional reimbursement insurers' amendments to the traditional physician FFS payment contract.

2.2 Physicians

Managed care organizations have grown by employing or contracting with physicians. At present, most physicians are involved in managed care. Eighty-three percent of physicians had a contract with at least one managed care organization in 1995 (that is, IPA, HMO, or PPO), up from 61 percent in 1990 (Emmons and Simon 1996). Thirty-nine percent reported a contract with an IPA, 64 percent with an HMO, and 69 percent reported a contract with a PPO (Emmons and Simon 1996). For most patient care physicians who have contracts, revenue from HMOs or PPOs alone represented, on average, 33 percent of total revenue in 1995, up from 28 percent in 1990 (Emmons and Simon 1996). Another study reports approximately one-third of physicians participating in alternative health plans (HMOs, PPOs, IPAs) in 1984 (Rosenbach et al. 1988). Those who participated received on average 28.6 percent of their net income from alternative health plans.

The extent of physician/health plan contracting varies by physician specialty and region of the country. Emmons and Simon (1996) report that physicians specializing in emergency medicine and psychiatry have the lowest rates of contracting with HMOs, IPAs, or PPOs, while medical and surgical subspecialties have the highest rates (physicians employed by staff-model HMOs are excluded). They also indicate that the prevalence of contracting between physicians and insurance plans varies by region. In 1995, IPA contracting in the New England and Pacific states was estimated to be nearly double that in the West North Central and East South Central states. In addition, rural physicians are much less likely than urban physicians to have contracts with health plans. Rosenbach et al. (1988) report that primary care physicians and the medical and surgical specialties are most likely to participate, while radiologists, anesthesiologists, pathologists, and psychiatrists are the least likely. They also find a participation rate for urban physicians which is 2.6 times higher than that for rural physicians, and the highest regional participation rates in the West and North Central regions, with the lowest in the Northeast and South regions.

Physician practices have been changing in other ways as well. Today, very few physicians in solo practice remain. Only one-fourth of physicians were in solo practice in 1995, down from over a third in 1991 (Emmons and Kletke 1996). Further, the size of medical practices has been increasing. Physicians in medical groups are more likely to have contracts with HMOs than are solo physicians and the likelihood of contracting with a managed care organization increases with group size (Emmons and Simon 1996).

2.3 Health Care Restructuring

A third important, and relatively recent, trend in health care markets is the dizzying pace of alliance and network formation, mergers, and acquisitions (Gaynor and Haas-Wilson 1999). While there is no systematic information as of yet about these changes, there does seem to be a clear trend toward consolidation. One such trend is in physician practices. New physician practice management companies have sprung into being and are achieving rapid growth by purchasing private physician practices (Jaklevic 1995). Phy-Cor, Inc. and Pacific Physician Services are two such corporations, expanding at a rate of 30 percent per year (Anders 1993). MedPartners, the largest physician practice management company in the United States in 1998, grew from 190 physicians to 7914 physicians between 1994 and 1996 (Robinson 1998). These firms provide capital, managed care expertise, economies of scale, and marketing services. Typically, physician practice management firms own the physical facilities of a physician practice, employ the nonphysician staff, and manage the business operations of the clinics or IPAs (Robinson 1998). An important role filled by these firms is to market the physician practices to managed care organizations. In some cases, these networks are themselves being bought by insurers or managed care organizations (Lipin 1995). As a result of this consolidation, physicians with established practices are relinquishing their managerial role due to increased administrative requirements (Anders 1993; Freudenheim 1993).

Consolidation is also occurring in hospital markets and insurance markets. In Worcester, Massachusetts, for example, the number of hospitals dropped from seven independent hospitals in 1979 to four in 1992, three of which were affiliated with health systems (Shactman 1994). The number of hospitals in Minneapolis/St Paul dropped from 24 independent hospitals in 1981 to 19 hospitals belonging to three health networks by 1992 (Shactman 1994). Overall, in 1998, there were 198 hospital merger deals involving 687 hospital facilities (Bellandi 1999).

Further, mergers and acquisitions between managed care organizations themselves are leading to consolidation and increasing size of managed care organizations (Anders and Winslow 1995). California's HMOs have declined from 25 less than a decade ago, to about 15 HMOs in 1995 (Anders and Winslow 1995). Between 1987 and 1997, enrollment in large HMOs (those with more than 200 000 members) increased from 32.6 percent to 57.6 percent of the industry (Interstudy 1998).

2.4   Legislation Regarding Physician Contracts

Contracts between financial intermediaries and physicians must be crafted within the confines of Federal and state laws. As managed care proliferates, Federal and state governments are passing legislation to regulate managed care contracts with physicians (Cooper and Green 1991). Perhaps the most important (and contentious) types of legislation for the health plan/physician contracting environment are the '*any willing provider*' or '*any willing physician*' laws. These laws dictate that any provider or physician willing to accept a plan's terms and who practices within the plan's geographic service area may apply and must be accepted into a health plan's network. Typically, these laws only apply to plans that contract with physicians and not to HMOs that hire physicians as employees. As of October, 1994, three states had enacted any willing physician laws (Texas, Utah and Virginia), but none applied to HMOs (GHAA October, 1994). Ten states had enacted broader any willing provider laws (Florida, Georgia, Idaho, Illinois, Indiana, Kentucky, Utah, Virginia, Washington and Wyoming). Any willing provider laws offer physicians some protection against being cut off from their patient base. Physicians and others also make the case for any willing provider laws on the grounds that patients should be free to choose their own physician. In contrast, health plans perceive any willing provider laws as curbing their ability to manage costs by selecting the most efficient physicians, and by de-selecting physicians that are not managing care in a manner consistent with their goals (Hudson 1994).

3   PHYSICIAN/HEALTH PLAN CONTRACTING: A DESCRIPTION

In this section we describe the basic types of financial and administrative relationships that health plans establish with physicians. Because the market for health care in the United States is so diverse and dynamic, it is important to begin this background section with a definition of terms. We use the term *health plan*, or *health benefit intermediary*, to mean an organization that contracts with employers or government sponsors to offer its health plans to potential enrollees and acts as a conduit between the employer or government entity and providers (Weiner and de Lissovoy 1993; Miller and Luft 1994). A health benefit intermediary can be an HMO, insurance carrier, third-party administrator, or independent provider organization.[4]

In general, health plans may influence physician's practices through both financial incentives and administrative controls. In this section we describe common forms of financial arrangements and administrative structures that are established between health plans and physicians.

Typically, three forms of payment arrangements between health plans and physicians are distinguished: (1) fee-for-service, (2) capitation, and (3) salary. Under, *fee-for-service* payment, physicians may bill the insurance carrier for the service provided and are retrospectively reimbursed for the charges billed on a per service basis. Alternatively, patients may pay physicians directly and then submit the claim to their insurance plan. Under discounted *fee-for-service*, the health plan negotiates a discount from a given base, such as usual and customary fees or charges, or establishes a predetermined list of prices per service with the physician, such as Medicare's Relative Value Scale (RVS). The plan then reimburses the physician retrospectively according to the agreed upon price.

In contrast, under *capitation*, a physician or a physician group receives a fixed predetermined payment in exchange for a commitment to provide a particular set of services to a defined population of plan members, based upon their medical need. The capitated amount may apply to only primary care services, to all physician services, or to all health care services. Under capitation, physicians are at risk for expenses that are higher than the capitated amount, and will benefit if expenses are lower than expected. *Salaried* physicians are employees of the health plan. Barring any other financial incentives, salaried physicians' incomes remain constant regardless of the amount of care provided.

Health plans often establish other financial incentives in addition to a 'basic' or predominant form of compensation. These include various types of revenue-sharing plans, bonus incentives, and financial penalties

(Hillman et al. 1989). Some managed care organizations base primary care physicians' compensation on the plans' expenditures on specialists or expenditures on specialists and inpatient treatment. If the plans' expenditures on specialty and inpatient care are less than expected, primary care physicians who act as gatekeepers may receive a bonus payment (surplus sharing). Alternatively, part of a physician's compensation may be withheld against a deficit in the pool allocated for specialty and hospital care (a 'withhold'). In addition, plans may pay physicians bonuses based on certain performance standards such profitability or expenditures. These financial incentives may apply to individual physicians or to a group of physicians.

To protect physicians from excessive financial risk arising from capitation, health plans may also establish a stop-loss plan, which sets a dollar ceiling on a physician's financial liability for services provided to the plan's enrollees. Similarly, health plans may exempt physicians from the costs incurred for enrollees with certain diagnoses that are likely to require services outside the norms for the physicians' specialties (General Accounting Office 1988).

Arrangements between managed care plans and physicians are also typically characterized by administrative controls. When physicians are employees of a health plan, a variety of factors – such as the plan's corporate culture, promotions, perks, and performance reviews by peers and superiors – may be brought to bear to influence physician behavior. When physicians are independent contractors for health plans, administrative controls may be more limited, and may include post-payment review of practice patterns (such as through physician profiles), prepayment review (such as utilization review), and selective contracting.

Another way to characterize the relationship between a physician and a health plan is by the contract's relative importance to the physician's practice. Physicians may receive most or all of their income from a health plan, for example, in the case of salaried physicians employed by staff-model HMOs. Alternatively, physicians may contract with various types of health insurance plans each of which have different types of payment structures ranging from fee-for-service, to discounted fee-for-service, to capitation. One might anticipate that the degree to which a particular managed care plan can influence a physician's practice depends on the extent to which the physician's patient base comes from that plan. Physicians with a small percentage of their income derived from managed care organizations may be less willing to cooperate with administrative controls and less responsive to financial incentives than those who derive a large portion of their income from patients in managed care organizations.

Health plans can sometimes increase their leverage over physicians by developing contracting relationships that prevent physicians from participating in any other managed care organization (called 'exclusivity clauses'). In a similar vein, some contracts include 'Most Favored Nation' pricing that requires a physician to reduce the level of his or her billings to the managed care plan, if contracting for a lower level of fees with another plan (Jensen 1991). For a review of some of the antitrust issues that arise with respect to such clauses see Gaynor and Haas-Wilson (1999).

Managed care organizations may contract with various forms of physician organizations. Contracts may exist between a single physician in a solo practice or between a physician group. Groups may be single-specialty or multispecialty groups. Groups may also differ in their degree of physical integration. Groups may consist of physicians who operate separate practices but are organized as a legal entity for contracting purposes (for example, an independent practice association); they may comprise physicians who practice in separate offices but share administrative services and contract collectively (sometimes called a group practice without walls), or groups may be physically and administratively integrated. The organization of a physician group, such as its size, internal administrative controls, and financial structure, has the potential to mediate the effect of a health plan's contract. For example, a health plan may contract with a physician group on a capitated basis, but some physicians within the group may be paid on a salaried basis by the group. Similarly, the importance of a 'withhold' may be substantially diminished if it is spread across a large group.

4   THEORETICAL ISSUES IN THE ECONOMICS OF PHYSICIAN CONTRACTS

The previous two sections have documented the extent and growth of managed care, physician contracting, and the relevant legal environment and have defined the types of physician contracting currently in existence. In this subsection we discuss the theoretical impacts of the different forms of physician contracting. In the next subsection we discuss the empirical evidence on the impacts of forms of physician contracting.

Many studies have considered physician response to the form of the compensation contract, generally focusing on fee-for-service versus capitation reimbursement (see Newhouse 1991 and Ellis and McGuire 1993 for reviews).[5] Some studies that have considered this problem with a single insurer are Ellis and McGuire (1990), Selden (1990), Blomqvist

(1991), and Ma and McGuire (1997). These authors have focused on deriving the optimal contract. Nonetheless, these models contain frameworks for predicting physician response to variation in incentives, since this response must be modeled in order to derive the optimal contract.

Ellis and McGuire (1990) consider a model of bargaining between patient and physician. There is no asymmetric information between the patient and physician, although physicians are modeled as patients' agents by placing a weight on the patient's preferences as part of their own utility. Patient–physician pairs are assumed fixed, so market equilibrium is not considered. The forms of physician payment considered are fixed prepayment and cost-based reimbursement. The major finding is that an optimal payment for health care will lead to conflict between patient and physician. Insurance for the patient carries with it moral hazard. The optimal payment for the physician will lead him or her to provide less than the patient's insured demand, hence the conflict. They also find that supply-side policies are optimal for controlling costs and that pure cost-based reimbursement to providers is never optimal. The optimal payment will often be a blend of prepayment and cost-based reimbursement.

Selden (1990) derives the third party payer's optimal provider reimbursement where treatment may be influenced by the provider. Selden explicitly considers capitation versus cost-based reimbursement. Quantity is determined by a function that has the patient's and physician's objective functions as arguments. The optimal payment system is a mix of capitation and cost-based reimbursement, similar to Ellis and McGuire (1990). Here also there is no explicit modeling of the patient–physician agency relationship nor of the insurer–physician agency relationship.

Blomqvist (1991) considers a problem in which the patient knows whether they are ill or not, but they do not know the exact nature of the illness. Physicians can observe the exact nature of the illness, and insurers cannot observe if the patient is actually ill. Under a fee-for-service payment contract from the insurer, the physician will always have an incentive to supply too much. If patients pay only a small fraction of the cost, they do not necessarily act as a sufficient check on this behavior. There is a welfare loss due to this opportunistic behavior, which is essentially a welfare loss due to moral hazard. If physicians were to reveal the true nature of the patient's illness to the insurer, then it would be possible to write contingent contracts against the state of health (for example, these could take the form of indemnity insurance in which the insured is paid a prespecified dollar amount for each state of nature). However, these contracts are not possible, since patients and physicians always have an incentive to misrepresent the patient's state of health as worse than it truly is. Blomqvist assumes that HMO type contracts in which doctors are employees of the insurer solve the physician–insurer agency problem, but the patient–physician problem remains. However, physician behavior is not explicitly modeled nor is it shown that the strategies analyzed are a best response.

Ma and McGuire (1997) consider the optimal insurance and payment system in a game between a single physician and a patient. Doctors choose the effort they put into producing health for the patient, and patients choose the quantity of treatment. The doctor's effort is observable to the patient, but not *verifiable*, thus it is *non-contractible*.[6] Physicians can only be paid on the basis of verifiable activities; for example, the quantity of treatments. When the insurer has perfect information, and when the physician's and patient's choices are complements in the production of health, the form of physician payment can solve the non-contractibility problem completely. In this case this involves paying the physician some fee over their marginal cost. If the physician's and patient's choices are substitutes, the second best may not be achieved, but physician ethics in the form of a minimal patient health level can improve matters. They also consider the impact of competition, which is found to provide an incentive for physicians for greater effort.

These studies all focus on optimal payment methods for health providers. They do not, however, explicitly model asymmetric information problems between the insurer and physician. Neither do they consider market equilibrium.

Other theoretical approaches to this problem could yield important insights. It is important to emphasize the problem of asymmetric information in contracting. The optimal contracting literature (Hart and Holmström 1987) suggests it should be possible for insurers to write better contracts with physicians than pure reimbursement insurance.

Gal-Or (1993) uses contracting theory to analyze the agency relationship between an insurer and provider. She shows that the optimal contract will be a combination of a fixed rate and a share of costs. Further, the levels of the fixed rate and cost share will vary with the reported severity of a case. In order to induce truthful reporting of severity by providers it is necessary that the fixed rate be a non-increasing function of reported severity and that the cost share be a non-decreasing function of severity. Insurers' objective functions are a weighted sum of consumers' and providers' surpluses. When consumers' welfare is more important the provider will optimally be reimbursed a larger share of costs, and vice versa. If cost sharing is not employed (for example, capitation reimbursement), the threat of losses from malpractice can improve outcomes, but will in general be inferior to a combination of cost sharing and a fixed rate. Competition in the insurance and provider markets is not modeled explicitly.

More recently Gal-Or (1999) considers optimal payments to physicians by insurers when the insurer may have information obtained through monitoring such as utilization review. As indicated previously, when the insurer has full information they simply force physicians to use the desired treatment. If the insurer has only partial information from monitoring, then minimal acceptable standards will be established, and incentive payments will be used in combination with them. The resulting outcomes will be better than those which would occur if no monitoring information were available.

Considering the agency problem between physicians and insurers in a market equilibrium model may lead to important results. Consider contracting between physicians and insurers in markets with multiple insurers. Suppose there exists an optimal contract between an insurer and a physician. Will this optimal contract be offered by insurers? If there are many insurers, competition for physicians may force insurers to offer more generous contracts that are non-optimal. This will be tempered by competition in the insurance market itself, as well as by competition in the market for physician services. There should be important differences across medical specialties. Presumably markets for general practitioners are more competitive than the markets for the services of pediatric oncologists.

However, there is an additional issue associated with optimal contracting with multiple insurers. Many insurers report that physician response to incentives is weak or nonexistent because they do not command a large enough proportion of the physician's caseload. What this may suggest is that as the diversity of insurance plans in a physician's patient population increases, the cost to the physician of determining each patient's insurer and the incentives in that contract prior to diagnosis or treatment may be too high. Given the tremendous advances in information technology, it seems hard to believe that these information costs are particularly large for any computerized physician's office. Further, it should be the practices with the largest, most diverse (in terms of insurance contracts) patient populations for which computerization is most useful, if the incentives in insurers' contracts are strong enough to be important. We are not aware of any research on this topic. Since the evidence is anecdotal, some careful systematic empirical research is necessary to first establish whether there is convincing evidence of the existence of this phenomenon. If this phenomenon exists, theoretical explorations into the form of optimal contracts in this situation would be useful.

Considering dynamic aspects of the relationship between physicians and insurers may also be important. Insurers presumably learn about physician behavior over time. They also observe the behavior of other physicians. Trigger strategies may be available which would punish a physician when some aspect(s) of his or her claims deviate by too much from some standard. The 'double agency' problem proposed by Blomqvist could be considered as a problem of common agency (Bernheim and Whinston 1986).

Monitoring as a choice for the insurer, and its impact on the form of physician–insurer contract, is an important factor to be incorporated into theoretical models. We are aware of only one study (Gal-Or 1999) which considers monitoring at all, albeit as exogenous information. The accounting literature on agency relationships often focuses on monitoring and would undoubtedly yield useful insights (Baiman and Demski 1980; Baiman 1982).

Certainly there are strategic aspects to the problem as well. Groups of physicians may contract with insurers collectively as a way to increase market power. The case of provider organized PPOs (preferred provider organizations) has been extensively discussed (see Leffler 1983; Dranove et al. 1986; Frech 1986). Leffler (1983) discusses a case in which such a contract can be anticompetitive in the context of the *Maricopa* case in which physicians agreed to a price ceiling. Greaney and Sindelar (1987) discuss how such contracts may provide opportunities for anticompetitive behavior. Vistnes (1992) formally models such contracts using the concept of network goods. He finds that these associations can increase the market power of the firms in them. Pauly (1988) considers the effects of insurer market power on the medical care market. He shows that insurers with market power can enforce prices to providers that are welfare reducing. Gaynor and Ma (1996) consider exclusive deals between insurers and providers. They show that exclusive deals are not anticompetitive, in the sense of raising price above marginal cost, but they do reduce consumer welfare by restricting choice of providers.

A great deal of progress has been made in the theoretical literature on physician contracting. However, there is still room for substantial contributions. For example, contracting in market equilibrium, has not been extensively modeled, in particular the impacts of market power on either side of the market. As both health care provider markets and health insurance markets become more concentrated, this assumes greater importance. In addition, the role of monitoring and information has not been modeled explicitly for the most part. The increasing efforts devoted to measuring outcomes, and profiling providers, combined with advances in information technology, make this an area where effort may have a significant payoff.

5 EMPIRICAL EVIDENCE ON THE DECISION TO CONTRACT

A few studies have empirically investigated factors which influence a physician's decision to have a contractual relationship with a health plan. Rosenbach et al. (1988) report on results using data from the Physicians' Practice Costs and Income Survey (PPCIS), conducted in 1984. In the survey physicians were asked about their reasons for participating in managed care plans (those are prepaid group practices, independent practice associations, and preferred provider associations). Three-quarters of all participants in managed care plans said they joined a managed care plan to maintain or increase their patient load. This was the most common response to the question. Slightly fewer than one-half of managed care participants said they joined to have a more regular source of income and caseload and 39 percent said they joined because of a philosophical commitment. Eighteen percent said they joined because of increased competition. Other reasons were cited as well, but by less than 10 percent of participants.

These results are consistent with subsequent findings from the 1992 Socioeconomic Monitoring System (SMS) survey, conducted by the AMA. The SMS survey asked physicians to rate the competitiveness of their practice environment as either 'very competitive,' 'somewhat competitive' or 'not at all competitive'. Physicians who rated their environment competitive were more likely to have contracts with HMOs, IPAs or PPOs than physicians who rated their environment not competitive (Gillis and Emmons 1993).

Rosenbach et al. (1988) also report on physicians' reasons for not participating in managed care. The PPCIS asked physicians who were not participating in managed care plans why they were not participating and whether there was a managed care plan in their area. Nearly one-half of nonparticipants said there was no managed care plan in the area. Of the remaining non-participants, three-quarters chose not to participate because they did not want to give up their independence. In addition, concerns over quality were cited by 71 percent of the physicians. Sixty-two percent also said they did not join because they were busy enough in their current practice, and 52 percent had other reasons for not joining.

Freund and Allen (1985) report on factors that influenced physicians in the Research Triangle area (Chapel Hill, Durham, and Raleigh) of North Carolina to join a primary care network type of IPA. Those physicians who had less experience, lower incomes, fewer visits, or were new in the community were more likely to join. Concerns with paperwork, low fees, and negative impacts of cost control efforts on quality of care were very important factors for those physicians who did not join.

These studies collectively are consistent in finding economic factors as being crucial determinants of a physician's decision to contract with a managed care plan. Quality concerns, paperwork, and independence appear to mitigate against affiliation.

6   EMPIRICAL EVIDENCE ON CONTRACTUAL FORM AND PHYSICIAN BEHAVIOR

Up until recently, relatively few studies have examined the effect of managed care contracts on physician behavior. In what follows, we survey the empirical literature on contractual form within physician groups, within HMOs and fee-for-service plans, and generally for a given group of physicians. By and large, the evidence reviewed here indicates that the form of the contract established between a physician and a financial intermediary can have a significant impact on medical care utilization. More specifically, studies suggest that capitation will decrease utilization, while fee-for-service payment, and bonuses based on utilization, will increase utilization.

6.1   Contracting Within Medical Groups

Over 50 percent of American physicians actively engaged in patient care are members of medical group practices. Further, that proportion has been growing over time, with most of the recent growth occurring in small and large groups, rather than medium sized ones (Marder and Zuckerman 1985). One explanation for the growth in small and large groups is the technology of monitoring. In small groups, monitoring is informal and inexpensive. If there are fixed costs to monitoring (for example, cost of a manager, information system), then there may be a critical group size necessary to cover these fixed costs. Thus small groups and groups of at least the critical size would be the most viable.

In a typical medical group practice there is some sharing of revenues and costs. Decisions about pricing and the hiring of inputs are made collectively (Held and Reinhardt 1979; Kralewski et al. 1985). In addition, there may be some internal administrative controls. Nonetheless, there is a great deal of variation in the internal organization of these firms. Some share income equally, some allocate it on a purely productivity basis; some are small and some are large; some have extensive internal controls and monitoring, some have none; some have a hierarchical structure while others are completely horizontal. A few studies have examined contracting among physicians within these organizations.

Gaynor (1989) specifies and tests a theory of competition within the firm. He shows that pure productivity compensation may lead to excessive competition within the firm if physicians compete with each other over patients. Thus the optimal contract is not pure fee-for-service, but some combination of fee-for-service and revenue sharing. Gaynor and Pauly (1990) show that physicians are strongly responsive to financial incentives. They find that physicians with compensation contracts based on their individual productivity take on over 31 percent more office visits than those who have no such incentive. Further, groups that have more than 50 percent of their revenues from prepayment (that is, from HMOs) have compensation contracts that are based significantly less on individual physician performance. They find no independent effect of HMO participation on physician productivity. This resonates empirically with the suggestion made previously that managed care may involve less use of financial incentives and more use of direct controls, although this study contains evidence on only the first point.

Evidence also indicates that physicians are significantly risk averse with regard to their compensation. Gaynor and Gertler (1995) show that compensation contracts within physician groups trade off moral hazard for risk spreading. Physicians in more risk averse groups adopt compensation contracts with more revenue sharing, such that the most risk averse sacrifice approximately 10 percent in income relative to the least risk averse.

Lee (1990) considers groups' use of payment schemes and internal administrative controls, in particular, the impact of HMO and PPO contracting on internal organization. He shows that internal controls are adopted to reduce opportunism. Further, participation in managed care plans affects the internal structure of these groups. HMO share (the percentage of revenues from HMO contracts) has a negative and significant impact on whether the group uses compensation based on individual physician productivity, consistent with the results of Gaynor and Pauly (1990). HMO and PPO share collectively have positive impacts on the use of various types of administrative controls (productivity standard, monitoring preventive services, use of a colorectal cancer screening protocol, the distribution of clinical algorithms, that is, guidelines, the presence of a quality assurance procedure, monitoring of physician costs, monitoring of hospital use). This evidence is consistent with the more extensive use of administrative controls being associated with managed care organizations, and there being a tradeoff between financial incentives and monitoring.

6.2   Contracting with Health Plans

In this section we review the research on the effect of physician contracts with health plans, and more broadly the effect of different types of physician financial arrangements, on the rate of various types of medical care utilization and on physician behavior. Table 3.1 summarizes the research. Column two of Table 3.1 describes the incentive structures that were compared. For example, some studies compare HMOs to FFS plans. In these studies the incentive structure is all the aspects of the contract between the HMO and the physician, such as risk sharing and profiling, that affect physicians' incentives. In HMO/FFS comparisons contracts may vary between HMOs as well as between HMOs and FFS plans. In other studies the incentive structure examined was more specific and uniform. For example, some studies compare the behavior of physicians paid a fee for each patient seen to that of physicians who are salaried.

The third column of Table 3.1 indicates whether the study used a cross-sectional design, a pre/post design, was a randomized trial, or was a literature review. Individual studies comparing HMOs to FFS plans were not reviewed since an excellent review by Miller and Luft (1994) already exists. The fourth column indicates the unit of analysis of the study, the fifth column indicates whether the study focused on a particular disease, service, or physician specialty, and the last column describes the findings of the study.

This section is organized by the aspect of care that was studied as being influenced by physician financial incentives. Specifically, we look at: hospitalizations, office visits, tests and procedures, physician labor supply, and physician earnings.

Hospitalizations

The review by Miller and Luft (1994) of studies comparing HMOs to FFS plans, in which the health plan was the unit of analysis, found consistent evidence that HMO enrollees have fewer hospitalizations than their counterparts in FFS plans. Reduced hospitalizations have been long been hypothesized to be an important source of cost saving from HMOs. The cause of the reduction, however, is not clear from these studies. Lower hospitalization rates might be the result of physician contracts; for example, primary care physicians' compensation may be adjusted based on patients' hospitalization expenditures thus providing an incentive not to hospitalize. Alternatively or additionally, reduced hospitalizations may result from utilization reviews whereby hospitalizations must be approved by the plan in order to be reimbursed, or by other aspects of managed care. Two studies that look more specifically at the nature of physician–health

Table 3.1 Studies of impacts of contracting

Author(s), date	Incentives compared	Study design	Unit of analysis	Disease/ service/ physician specialty	Findings
Miller and Luft 1994	HMO vs. FFS	Review	Health plan	Various	HMOs have few hospitals rates and more visits
Hillman et al. 1989	Various physician compensation arrangements within HMOs	Cross-section	Health plan	Various	Fewer hospitalizations when HMOs pay physicians using capitation or salary than when use FFS
Stearns et al. 1992	FFS with per head capitation vs. fixed capitated payment with profit sharing.	Pre/post	Patient	Primary care physicians	Reduction in hospitalizations but increases in LOS and number of ambulatory visits, particularly to specialists
Epstein et al. 1986	FFS physician groups vs. salaried groups	Cross-section	Patient	Internists treating uncomplicated hypertension	Greater use of electrocardiography in FFS practices. No difference use of chest radiography, blood counts, or urinalysis, average charges
Murray and colleagues 1992	Patients with prepaid or FFS insurance treated by same physicians	Variation across patients with different types of insurance	Physician	Hypertensive patients	Physicians ordered one-third fewer tests for patients who had prepaid insurance and total charges for prepaid patients were half those of FFS patients
Clancy and Hillner 1989	Patients with prepaid or FFS insurance treated by same physicians	Variation across patients with different types of insurance	Patient	Various	HMO patients underwent fewer tests but received the same amount of preventive services.
Hickson et al. 1987	Physicians paid FFS or salary	Randomized physicians into FFS or salary	Patient	Pediatric residents treating children	FFS physician's patients had 22% more visits per capita, especially more well-child visits

49

Table 3.1 Studies of impacts of contracting (cont.)

Author(s), date	Incentives compared	Study design	Unit of analysis	Disease/ service/ physician specialty	Findings
Hemenway et al. 1990	Physicians paid flat per hour rate vs. profit sharing based on percentage of gross monthly charges generated	Pre/post	Patient	15 physicians employed by chain of ambulatory care centers	After incentive was instituted laboratory tests, x-ray films, patient visits, and total charges all increased significantly
Hughes and Yule 1992	Per-time fee system vs. bonus based on percentage of women given pap smears	Pre/post	Patient	UK general practitioners and cervical cytology services	System of bonus payments was associated with a rise of almost 50% of pap smear tests
Ferrall et al. 1998	FFS payment vs. salary	Cross-section	Physician	Canadian physicians	FFS payment led to more hours worked seeing patients and overall
Hadley and Mitchell 1997	HMO penetration	Cross-section	Physician	Physicians under age 45	HMO penetration reduces physician hours worked, reduces the number of patients seen, and decreases physician satisfaction with their practice
Simon et al. 1997a	HMO contract	Cross-section	Physician	All physicians	Primary care physicians with a managed care contract provide more primary care than those who do not. The effect is the opposite for specialists.

Table 3.1 Studies of impacts of contracting (cont.)

Author(s), date	Incentives compared	Study design	Unit of analysis	Disease/ service/ physician specialty	Findings
Baker et al. 1996	Percentage of revenues from PPO, IPA, HMO or FFS	Cross-section	Physician	All physicians except hospital-based physicians and physicians working part time	General practitioners, internists, pediatricians, and other specialists who derive a larger proportion of their practice revenues from HMOs spend less time in patient care, and vice versa for ob/gyns and emergency medicine physicians. HMO contracting associated with an increase in office visits by internists, pediatricians, ob/gyns, and other specialties. No statistically significant effect for general practitioners, general surgeons, or emergency medicine.
Hadley and Mitchell 1997	HMO penetration	Cross-section	Physician	Physicians under age 45	HMO reduce physician earnings
Simon et al. 1997b, 1998	Managed care penetration	Time-series	Physician	All physicians	Incomes of primary care physicians rose more rapidly in states with higher managed care growth, while the relative incomes of hospital based physicians and physicians practicing in medical or surgical subspecialties experienced lower growth

51

plan contracts and physician financial arrangements indicate that physician incentives in and of themselves can indeed influence hospitalization rates.

Using data from a survey of HMOs, Hillman et al. (1989) studied the effect of different compensation arrangements on utilization within HMOs. They found that HMOs that paid primary care physicians on a capitated or salary basis had lower hospitalization rates than HMOs that used fee-for-service payment.

Stearns et al. (1992) examined the response to a change in the reimbursement mechanism by a group of physicians who participated in a fee-for-service plan and then formed an IPA. Under the fee-for-service plan the primary care physician group received a capitation payment for each enrollee and fee-for-service payments for each visit. Under the IPA, for each signee, the primary provider's group received a fixed capitation payment. If a surplus for the HMO was left at the end of the year, it would first go to primary care physicians by increasing the capitation per patient, and second to the specialists, who would be paid at an increased percentage of their usual fees. The hospital had a third claim on any surplus. Analyses of data for a group of continuous enrollees showed that the change in physician payment mechanism was associated with a reduction in hospitalizations.

Physician visits
The findings of studies of the effect of physician financial arrangements on patient visit rates differ depending on the research design. The majority of comparisons of visit rates in HMOs and FFS plans show that HMOs have more visit rates, although some studies show the opposite (Miller and Luft 1994). The difficulty with drawing conclusions about the effect of physician financial arrangements from these HMO/FFS comparisons is that there are differences between HMO and FFS plans besides the nature of the physician contracts. In particular, the lower patient cost-sharing characteristics of HMOs could result in greater visits by patients independent of physician incentives.

Hillman et al.'s study (1989), which focused on physician incentives within HMOs, found that HMOs that placed primary care physicians at financial risk as individuals, or imposed penalties for deficits in the HMO's hospital fund beyond the loss of withheld funds, had fewer outpatient visits per enrollee. Neither general withholds nor bonuses had any impact on utilization. In contrast, Stearns and colleagues (1992) found that ambulatory visits increased after the FFS physicians formed an IPA and surmise that the increase in ambulatory visits may be a result of primary care physicians only being capitated for primary care services and specialists still being paid fee-for-service.

A small randomized control trial by Hickson et al. (1987) found that physicians randomized to a fee-for-service payment system provided more visits per patient than physicians paid a salary. The study was performed in the Vanderbilt pediatric residents' community clinic. Study subjects were pediatric residents who worked in the clinic between September 1983 and June 1984: ten second-year and eight third-year residents were placed into nine pairs, each matched for year of training and the day of the week that their clinics were held. Each pair was randomized into one individual who received $2 per patient visit (fee-for-service group) and another who received $20 per month (salary group). Payments were designed, using data collected before the study, such that total reimbursement between groups would be approximately equal.

The study showed that patients assigned to the fee-for-service physicians had 22 percent more visits than patients assigned to salaried physicians, the difference being due, almost entirely to a greater number of well-child visits. Children assigned to fee-for-service physicians had more visits in excess of American Academy of Pediatrics' guidelines, and missed fewer recommended visits. This suggests that the fee-for-service doctors may have been engaging in overprescribing, while the salaried doctors may have been undertreating.

Hemenway and colleagues (1990) studied the effect of a payment change on services provided by 15 physicians employed by a chain of walk-in ambulatory care centers. Until 1985, physicians working for the ambulatory care centers were paid a flat rate of $28 per hour. In the middle of 1985, a payment system involving bonus incentives was instituted, according to which physicians would receive either a flat fee or a percentage of the gross monthly charges they generated, whichever was higher. After the bonus system was instituted the average number of patient visits per month rose by 12 percent. The increase was significantly greater than increases experienced nationally (for example, nationally, visits increased by 3.7 percent).

Thus all of the studies reviewed indicate that physician financial incentives can influence visit rates, although the direction of effect depends on the type of the incentive structure.

Tests and procedures
Several studies have examined how physician financial incentives influence the rate at which physicians prescribe tests and conduct procedures.

The study by Hemenway and colleagues (1990) of the effect of changing payment in ambulatory care centers from a flat rate to one based on a percentage of the gross monthly charges generated found that laboratory tests per patient visit increased by 23 percent and x-ray films per visit increased by 16 percent under the bonus system.

Hughes and Yule (1992) conducted a study in the United Kingdom and found a significant increase in utilization following the implementation of a bonus system. In 1990 the United Kingdom's per-time fee system for cervical cytology services was replaced with 'target payments' whereby general practitioners were paid a lump sum if they achieved 50 percent coverage for cervical smears among the eligible women on their practice list, with a higher sum if they reached 80 percent coverage. The new system of target payments was associated with a rise of almost 50 percent in smear tests performed by general practitioners in the year following the implementation of the payment change.

Epstein et al. (1986) found that internists in five large fee-for-service groups were more likely to perform some common diagnostic tests on patients with uncomplicated hypertension than their counterparts in prepaid groups. Specifically, Epstein and colleagues found that use of the two high-profit tests – electrocardiography and chest radiography – was 30 percent higher in the fee-for-service practices; however, only the difference for electrocardiography approached statistical significance. Neither use of blood counts nor urinalysis were significantly different across settings. Comparisons were adjusted for the physicians' year of medical school graduation, and patients' mean age, gender, number of medications received, diastolic blood pressure, and duration of hypertension. Because visit rates were higher in the HMOs than in the fee-for-service practices, it was unlikely that visit rates explained the higher testing in the fee-for-service practices.

Murray and colleagues (1992) examined the number of tests received over a 12-month period by 165 patients who were diagnosed as hypertensive and were treated at two primary care outpatient clinics staffed by 23 full-time faculty. Physicians were either paid on a fee-for-service basis or on a prepaid basis. Physicians were found to have ordered one third fewer tests for patients whose insurer paid the clinic on a prepaid basis.

Clancy and Hillner (1989) studied 17 physicians enrolled in an IPA who treated FFS and HMO patients concurrently. They found that patients in the HMO underwent fewer tests than did patients in the FFS system, but received the same proportion of preventive services. This was true even after controlling for the age and sex of the patient.

Physician Labor Supply (hours worked and patients treated)
Three studies have examined the effect of physician contracts with

managed care plans on physician labor supply as measured by hours worked. Each found that FFS payment is associated with a greater supply of hours. One of the studies also examined the effect of HMO penetration on the number of patients treated, and one examined the effect of HMO contracting on the number of patient visits provided. A fourth study examined the effect of HMO contracting on the amount of primary care provided.

Using data from a survey of Canadian physicians, Ferrall et al. (1998) simultaneously estimated equations for group size, payment method (fee-for-service vs. salaried), hours per week of patient care, and total weekly work hours. They found that fee-for-service payment led to 11 more hours per week seeing patients, and 1 to 2 more total hours per week, controlling for the simultaneous determination of whether a physician is primarily reimbursed by fee-for-service.

Baker et al. (1996) examined the relationship between patient care hours worked and the percentage of physician income from HMOs, PPOs, IPAs and FFS plans. Data came from a 1991 American Medical Association sponsored national survey of physicians throughout the United States. They found that general practitioners who derive a larger proportion of their practice revenues from HMOs spend less time in patient care. Similarly, HMO contracting had a negative (albeit smaller) effect on patient care hours provided by internists, pediatricians, and other specialists. In contrast, HMO contracting actually increased the amount of patient care hours provided by obstetrician/ gynecologists and emergency medicine physicians. HMO contracting was associated with an increase in office visits produced by internal medicine physicians, pediatricians, and obstetrician/gynecologists, and other specialties. In contrast, there was no statistically significant effect for general practitioners, general surgeons, or those in emergency medicine.

Using data from a nationally representative sample of 4373 physicians under age 45 conducted in 1991, Hadley and Mitchell (1997) found that a doubling of the average level of HMO penetration is associated with a statistically significant difference of 4 percent fewer hours worked per week and 13.7 percent fewer patients seen per week.

Simon et al. (1997a) examined whether managed care affects the provision of primary care. Using data from the AMA's annual random sample of physicians for 1995, they found that primary care physicians with a managed care contract provide more primary care than those who do not. Interestingly, the effect is the opposite for specialists: those without managed care contracts spend more time delivering primary care than those who do have managed care contracts.

Physician earnings

Simon et al. (1997b, 1998) used state-level data to examine the impact of managed care growth on changes in physician incomes over the period 1985 to 1993. They found that incomes of primary care physicians rose more rapidly in states with higher managed care growth, while the relative incomes of hospital based physicians (radiologists, anesthesiologists, and pathologists) and physicians practicing in medical or surgical subspecialties experienced lower growth.

Using data from a nationally representative sample of 4577 physicians under age 45 conducted in 1991, Hadley and Mitchell (1997) found HMO penetration had a negative and statistically significant impact on physicians' earnings in 1990. A doubling of the average level of HMO penetration in the market was estimated to reduce annual earnings by 7–10.7 percent, and hourly earnings by approximately 6–9 percent.

7   SUMMARY AND CONCLUSIONS

The growth in managed care may be the most important phenomenon characterizing the changing structure of markets for health care in the 1980s and 1990s. Managed care is in part identified by contracting with physicians. Consequently, understanding the potential impacts of these contracts is crucial to understanding the likely impacts of managed care on health care delivery in the United States.

Research has lagged behind the rapid pace of developments in these markets. Nonetheless, there are small, but significant theoretical and empirical literatures which are generally informative. Theory indicates that incentives should matter, that risk aversion should cause less than full use of incentives, and that financial incentives and monitoring (administrative controls) will be used as (partial) substitutes. The empirical evidence (from various studies using different data sets) is consistent with these points. What is necessary at present is more detailed empirical study of the specific impacts of managed care on physician behavior and the determinants of physician contracting with managed care plans.

NOTES

[1]   Note that even if the employer pays the premium, a worker will indirectly share part of the expense through reduced wages. Recent evidence suggests that insurance expenses are shifted almost entirely onto workers through reduced

wages.

2   Although this kind of traditional insurance is often called indemnity insurance, it is more accurately labeled reimbursement insurance. Under indemnity insurance a consumer is indemnified against a loss. If the loss occurs, payment is made, regardless of whether repairs are undertaken. For example, automobile insurance will make a dollar payment for damage caused by an accident. The consumer can then undertake repairs or not. Medical insurance, by contrast, does not indemnify consumers against a loss due to illness, it reimburses them for treatment (repair) expenses associated with the illness.

3   Insurance contracts are usually more complex than this. The copayment rate may vary by type of service (it is often higher for mental health or substance abuse treatment), there may be a stop-loss limiting the consumer's total out-of-pocket expenses, insurance companies may limit the percentage reimbursement to a particular fee (usual, customary, and reasonable) with the consumer being fully responsible for any excess above that, there is usually a lifetime limit on total reimbursements, and there may be extensive restrictions or exclusions in coverage.

4   Although the focus of this report is on physician/health plan contracting, it is useful to note that some large employers are contracting directly with organizations of physicians and hospitals (known as Physician Hospital Organizations or PHOs) and by-passing the services of intermediaries (Johnsson 1992).

5   There are many studies that have considered optimal fee schedules for physicians (that is, price regulation), taking fee-for-service compensation contracts as given. See Glazer and McGuire (1993), Frech (1991), and Wedig et al. (1989) for theoretical treatments. Most of the empirical work has examined the effects of changes in public programs' physician fees; see also Mitchell and Cromwell (1982). Sloan (1982) and Lee (1991) examine physician response to private insurance companies' reimbursement policies.

6   *Non-verifiable* refers to something which cannot be verified to a third party. Consequently, even if something is observable to both parties, if it is non-verifiable, any contract based on it cannot be enforced, hence it is *non-contractible*.

REFERENCES

Anders, George (1993), 'McDonald's methods come to medicine as chains acquire physicians' practices', *The Wall Street Journal*, 24 August.

Anders, George and Ron Winslow (1995), 'The HMO trend: big, bigger, biggest', *The Wall Street Journal*, 30 March.

Baiman, Stanley (1982), 'Agency research in managerial accounting: a survey', *Journal of Accounting Literature*, 1: 154–213.

Baiman, Stanley and Joel Demski (1980), 'Economically optimal performance evaluation and control systems', *Journal of Accounting Research*, 18 (Supplement): 184–220.

Baker, Loren, Christopher Ferrall, Martin Gaynor and Tami Mark (1996), 'Managed care contracts and physician behavior', unpublished manuscript, Carnegie Mellon University.

Bellandi, D. (1999), 'A year of more and less. Number of hospital deals drop, but more facilities change hands', *Modern Health Care*, 29(2): 48–62.

Bernheim, B. Douglas and Michael D. Whinston (1986), 'Common agency', *Econometrica*, 54(4): 923–42.

Blomqvist, Åke (1991), 'The doctor as double agent: information asymmetry, health insurance, and medical care', *Journal of Health Economics*, 10(4): 411–32.

Clancy, C.M. and B.E. Hillner (1989), 'Physicians as gatekeepers: the impact of financial incentives', *Archives of Internal Medicine*, 149 (April): 917–20.

Cooper, Paul P. and Kylanne Green (1991), 'The impact of state laws on managed care', *Health Affairs*, Winter, pp. 161–9.

Dranove, William, Mark Satterthwaite and Jody Sindelar (1986), 'The effect of injecting price competition into the hospital market: the case of preferred provider organizations', *Inquiry*, 23: 419–31.

Ellis, Randall P. and Thomas G. McGuire (1990), 'Optimal payment systems for health services', *Journal of Health Economics*, December, 9(4): 375–96.

Ellis, Randall P. and Thomas G. McGuire (1993), 'Supply-side and demand-side cost sharing in health care', *Journal of Economic Perspectives*, 7(4): 135–51.

Emmons, David W. and Phillip R. Kletke (1996), 'Physician practice size, 1991–1995', unpublished manuscript, American Medical Association, forthcoming in Ronald Conners (ed.), *Organization and Management of Physician Services*, American Hospital Publishing, Inc.

Emmons, David W. and Carol J. Simon (1996), 'Managed care: evolving contractual arrangements', in Martin L. Gonzalez (ed.), *Socioeconomic Characteristics of Medical Practice 1996*, Chicago: American Medical Association.

Epstein, Arnold M., Colin B. Begg and Barbara J. McNeil (1986), 'The use of ambulatory testing in prepaid and fee-for-service group practices', *New England Journal of Medicine*, 314(17): 1089–94.

Ferrall, Christopher, Allan W. Gregory and William G. Tholl (1998),

'Endogenous work hours and practice patterns of Canadian physicians', *Canadian Journal of Economics*, **31**(1): 1–27.

Frech, H.E. III (1986), 'Preferred provider organizations and health care competition', in H.E. Frech III (ed.), *Private and Public Health Insurance: Research and Policy*, Cambridge, MA: Ballinger Publishing Co.

Frech, H.E. III (1991), *Regulating Doctors' Fees: Competition, Benefits, and Controls under Medicare*, Washington, DC: AEI Press.

Freudenheim, Milt (1993), 'Physicians are selling practices to companies as changes loom', *The New York Times*, 1 September.

Freund, Deborah A. and Kathryn S. Allen (1985), 'Factors affecting physicians' choice to practice in a fee-for-service setting versus an individual practice association', *Medical Care*, **23**(6): 799–808.

Gal-Or, Esther (1993), 'Asymmetry of information and optimal reimbursement rules in health care markets', unpublished manuscript, Pittsburgh: University of Pittsburgh.

Gal-Or, Esther (1999), 'Optimal reimbursement and malpractice sharing rules in health care markets', *Journal of Regulatory Economics*, **16**(3): 237–66.

Gaynor, Martin (1989), 'Competition within the firm: theory plus some evidence from medical group practice', *Rand Journal of Economics*, **29**(1): 59–76.

Gaynor, Martin and Paul J. Gertler (1995), 'Moral hazard and risk spreading in medical partnerships', *Rand Journal of Economics*, **26**(4): 591–613.

Gaynor, Martin and Deborah Haas-Wilson (1999), *Journal of Economic Perspectives*, **13**(1): 141–64.

Gaynor, Martin and Albert Ching-To Ma (1996), 'Insurance, vertical restraints and competition', unpublished manuscript, Pittsburgh: Carnegie Mellon University.

Gaynor, Martin and Mark V. Pauly (1990), 'Compensation and productivity in partnerships: evidence from medical group practice', *Journal of Political Economy*, **98**: 544–73.

General Accounting Office (1988), *Medicare. Physician Incentive Payments by Prepaid Health Plans Could Lower Quality of Care*, GAO\HRD-89-29, December.

Gillis, Kurt D. and David W. Emmons (1993), 'Physician involvement with alternative delivery systems', in Martin L. Gonzalez (ed.), *Socioeconomic Characteristics of Medical Practice, 1993*, Chicago: American Medical Association.

Glazer, Jacob and Thomas G. McGuire (1993), 'Should physicians be permitted to "balance bill" patients?', *Journal of Human Resources*,

12(3): 239–58.

Greaney, Thomas L. and Jody L. Sindelar (1987), 'The anticompetitive effects of preferred provider organizations', *Inquiry*, 24(4): 384–91.

Group Health Association of America (1994), 'Any willing provider laws by type', unpublished document, 4 October.

Hadley, Jack and Jean M. Mitchell (1997), 'Effects of HMO market penetration on physicians' work effort and satisfaction', *Health Affairs*, November/December, 16(6): 99–111.

Hart, Oliver and Bengt Holmström (1987), 'The theory of contracts', in Truman Bewley (ed.), *Advances in Economic Theory, Fifth World Congress*, Cambridge: Cambridge University Press, pp. 71–155.

Held, Philip J. and Uwe E. Reinhardt (1979), *Analysis of Economic Performance in Medical Group Practices*, Project Report 79-05, Princeton, NJ: Mathematica Policy Research, Inc.

Hemenway, David, Alice Killen, Suzanne B. Cashman, Cindy Lou Parks and William J. Bicknell (1990), 'Physicians' responses to financial incentives: evidence from a for-profit ambulatory care center', *New England Journal of Medicine*, 322(15): 1059–63.

Hickson, G.B., W.A. Altemeier and J.M. Perrin (1987), 'Physician reimbursement by salary of fee-for-service: effect on physician practice behavior in a randomized prospective study', *Pediatrics*, 80(3): 334–50.

Hillman A.L., M.V. Pauly and J.J. Kerstein (1989), 'How do financial incentives affect physicians' clinical decisions and the financial performance of health maintenance organizations', *New England Journal of Medicine*, 321(2): 86–92.

Hudson, T. (1994), 'State laws: a stumbling block for systems integration?', *Hospitals & Health Networks*, April, pp. 40–5.

Hughes, David and Brian Yule (1992), 'The effect of per-item fees on the behaviour of general practitioners', *Journal of Health Economics*, 11: 413–37.

InterStudy (1998), *The InterStudy Competitive Edge, Part II: The HMO Industry Report 8.2*, St Paul, MN: Interstudy Publications.

InterStudy (1999), *The InterStudy Competitive Edge, Part II: The HMO Industry Report 9.1*, St Paul, MN: Interstudy Publications.

Jaklevic, Mary Chris (1995), 'Doc practice management set to explode', *Hospitals*, August, pp. 26–31.

Jensen, Harold L. (1991), 'The impact of managed care on physicians', *Quality Assurance and Utilization Review*, 6(4): 109–14.

Johnsson, Julie (1992), 'Direct contracting: employers look to hospital–physician partnerships to control costs', *Hospitals*, February, pp. 56–60.

Lee, Robert H. (1990), 'Monitoring physicians: a bargaining model of medical group practice', *Journal of Health Economics*, 9(4): 463–81.

Lee, Robert H. (1991), 'Insurance and medical list prices', *Journal of Human Resources*, 24(4): 689–708.

Leffler, Keith B. (1983), '*Arizona v. Maricopa County Medical Society*: maximum-price agreements in markets with insured buyers', *Supreme Court Economic Review*, 2: 187–211.

Lipin, Steven (1995), 'California blue shield bids $4.5 billion for WellPoint,' *The Wall Street Journal*, 27 March.

Ma, Ching-to Albert and Thomas G. McGuire (1997), 'Optimal health insurance and provider payment', *American Economic Review*, 87: 685–704.

Marder, William D. and Stephen Zuckerman (1985), 'Competition and medical groups: a survivor analysis', *Journal of Health Economics*, 10 (4): 385–410.

Mercer/Foster Higgins National Survey of Employer-sponsored Health Plans (1998).

Miller, Robert H. and Harold S. Luft (1994), 'Managed care plans: characteristics, growth, and premium performance', *Annual Review of Public Health*, 15: 437–59.

Mitchell, Janet B. and Jerry Cromwell (1982), 'Physician behavior under the Medicare assignment option', *Journal of Health Economics*, 1: 245–64.

Murray, J.P., S. Greenfield, S.H. Kaplan and E.M. Yano (1992), 'Ambulatory testing for capitation and fee-for-service patients in the same practice setting: relationships to outcomes', *Medical Care*, 30 (March): 252–61.

Newhouse, Joseph P. (1991), 'Pricing and imperfections in the medical care marketplace', in H.E. Frech III and Peter Zweifel (eds), *Health Economics Worldwide*, Dordrecht: Kluwer Academic Publishers, pp. 3–22.

Pauly, Mark V. (1988), 'Market and power monopsony, and health insurance markets', *Journal of Health Economics*, 7(2): 111–28.

Robinson, James C. (1998), 'Consolidation of medical group practices into physician practice organizations', *JAMA*, 279(2): 144–9.

Rosenbach Margo L., Brooke S. Harrow and Sylvia Hurdle (1988), 'Physician participation in alternative health plans', *Health Care Financing Review*, 9(4): 63–79.

Selden, Thomas P. (1990), 'A model of capitation', *Journal of Health Economics*, 9(4): 397–410.

Shactman, David (1994), 'Market concentration, antitrust, and public policy in the health care industry', manuscript, Council on the

Economic Impact of Health Care Reform, Washington, DC.

Simon, Carol J., William D. White, Sandy Gamliel and Phillip R. Kletke (1997a), 'The provision of primary care: does managed care make a difference?', *Health Affairs*, **16**(6): 89–98.

Simon, Carol J., David D. Dranove and William D. White (1997b), 'The impact of managed care on the physician marketplace', *Public Health Reports*, **112**: 222–30.

Simon Carol J., David D. Dranove and William D. White (1998), 'The effect of managed care on the incomes of primary care and specialty physicians', *Health Services Research*, **33**(3, Part 1): 549–69.

Sloan, Frank A. (1982), 'Effects of health insurance on physicians' fees', *Journal of Human Resources*, **17**(14): 533–57.

Stearns, Sally C., Barbara L. Wolfe and David A. Kindig (1992), 'Physician responses to fee-for-service and capitation payment', *Inquiry*, Winter, **29**: 416–25.

Vistnes, Gregory (1992), 'Strategic alliances, cliques, and competition in markets with network goods', unpublished paper, Washington, DC: Antitrust Division, US Department of Justice.

Wedig, Gerard, Janet B. Mitchell and Jerry Cromwell (1989), 'Can optimal physician behavior be obtained using price controls?', *Journal of Health Politics, Policy and Law*, **14**(3): 601–20.

Weiner, Jonathan P and Gregory de Lissovoy (1993), 'Razing the tower of babel: a taxonomy for managed care and health insurance plans', *Journal of Health Politics, Policy, and Law*, **19**(1): 75–103.

4. Health insurance reform in Korea: consolidation of funds

Bong-Min Yang

1 INTRODUCTION

Health care reform is a popular trend in many parts of the world. Both developed and developing countries are trying to create different models of their health care systems through health system reform. Some are moving into a more regulated system, while others are introducing competition strategies. Whatever means the different countries are using, they have a common goal; achieving an increase in efficiency and an improvement in equity in health care delivery. Korea is no exception in this respect.

Twenty-two years after the initial implementation of the National Health Insurance (NHI) program in 1977, Korea is adopting a major change in the structure of health insurance. The health insurance system is in transition from the German type multiple fund system to the Canadian type single payer system. The change is dramatic in that its impact on various sectors of the economy could be diverse and significant. It may be too early to assess the impact of this reform because the reform process is still under way. However, to both developing and developed countries that consider similar changes for their systems, the Korean experience could be of interest.

After starting with a brief description of Korea's health care system and health insurance system, this chapter introduces the reform of the health insurance structure, and discusses the implications of this dramatic change. Remaining issues in the health insurance system will then be briefly mentioned. Among various health care issues, this chapter's scope is limited to health insurance only. Other issues in the delivery of health care, such as the payment reimbursement system, primary health care, referral channels, government regulations, and the role of the private sector, will be handled in a separate study.

2   HEALTH SERVICE DELIVERY

The Korean health service delivery system has been basically a market-oriented, private sector-dominated, fee-for-service payment system. The role of the government has been limited primarily to the public health area. There has been very little regulation or monitoring of the ever-growing number of private providers to discourage excessive technology acquisition, excessive provision of services, unethical behavior (selective abortions, for example), fraudulent insurance claims, and income tax evasion.

It is a market-oriented system in the sense that health care is viewed, in general, as an economic good, but not as a social good. Access to health care is selective, guided by the willingness and the ability to pay. How much and what level of care one receives depends largely on one's income level. For example, there are the so-called special treatment charges (STCs). When patients prefer to be treated by regular staff physicians (board specialists) in a general hospital, they have to pay STCs in addition to the scheduled fees. If they cannot afford the STCs, interns or residents are automatically assigned to them.

The private sector, which was dominant in Korea before the insurance plans, has been growing further with the increase in per capita income and with the expansion of health insurance coverage. As shown in Table 4.1, in 1977, the year when a health insurance program was first introduced, 53.2 percent of all beds were either public or non-profit (Ministry of Health and Social Affairs, *Yearbook of Health and Social Statistics*, various years; Korean Hospital Association, *Membership Reports*, various years). Seventeen years later, the share dropped to 23 percent, with 77 percent of total hospital beds in private hospitals. In 1975, two years before the health insurance programs started, 34.5 per cent of all hospitals were public. In 1994, the share dropped to 4.9 per cent and the remainder (95.1 percent) are now owned and operated by private or non-profit organizations. Hospitals specializing in traditional medicine are not included in the figures. The shares of the private sector would be even greater if their numbers were taken into account, because most of the facilities and human resources in traditional medicine are in the private sector. The change has been dramatic, and the trend is expected to continue at least in the near future.

Patients pay a fee for service (FFS) for all services at all referral levels. FFS has been the dominant method of payment for physicians (both Western and traditional), clinical services, and pharmacists. A trial of case payment structure[1] (called DRG) began in early 1997. It is the first time that a payment structure other than FFS has been tried in the Korean

Table 4.1 Number and percentage of public and private hospital beds

	1962	1977	1987	1994
Public:				
National[a]	2564 (24.5%)	8504 (33.3%)	10 580 (12.4%)	10 642 (8.6%)
Local government/ Non-profit	3535 (33.7%)	5078 (19.9%)	14 759 (17.3%)	18 228 (14.6%)
Total public	6099 (58.2%)	13 582 (53.2%)	25 339 (29.7%)	28 870 (23.2%)
Private [b]	4378 (41.8%)	11 941 (46.8%)	59 841 (70.3%)	95 727 (76.8%)
Total	10 477	25 523	85 180	124 597

Notes
[a] National encompasses national leprosy, mental, and tuberculosis hospitals.
[b] Private includes for-profit corporate, for-profit proprietary, non-profit welfare organizations, and private university hospitals.

Source: Ministry of Health and Social Affairs, *1963 Yearbook of Health and Social Statistics*; *Membership Reports* of the Korean Hospital Association; from Lee (1995).

market. Physicians at hospitals are paid salaries, and occasionally they are paid bonuses based on their performance.

In most cases, patients are given a choice from various providers at multiple referral levels. Because there is no patient referral channel, they can go directly to the outpatient departments of general hospitals. In 1989 some regulatory provisions were introduced governing the choice of providers under the NHI. However, most patients did not abide by the rules, and hospitals, for fear of losing revenue, did not enforce these rules. As a result, the provisions have become ineffective.

Within the system, a 'gatekeeper' – someone who could guide the patient to a proper provider or proper level of care – is virtually unknown. Since most patients prefer to be treated in general hospitals, both the outpatient and inpatient departments in these hospitals are overcrowded. Consequently, the concepts of patient referral channels and primary health care hardly exist.[2] For many Koreans – and even for some health bureaucrats – primary health care is considered a synonym for public health or low-quality care for the poor.

In the absence of 'gatekeepers' in the system, there is inefficiency and a lack of cost effectiveness. Simple illnesses are treated expensively; for example, a good proportion of common cold patients are treated by internists in general hospitals, and simple headaches are treated by neurosurgeons in outpatient departments of university hospitals.

Moreover, patients often seek care from both Western and traditional physicians, and sometimes also from pharmacists, for the same episode of illness, increasing the revenues of the providers but not necessarily giving the patients the proper care.

3   HEALTH INSURANCE

3.1   Evolution of NHI

A blueprint for the Korean health insurance system was initiated by the Health Insurance Act of December 1963, when Korea's per capita GNP was still under US$100. This scheme was primarily aimed at voluntary coverage. However, little was accomplished due to limited financial resources and lack of participation. The government then implemented the first stage of its compulsory social security program for health care in July 1977, by enforcing observance of the scheme for corporations hiring 500 or more workers. In 1983 the corporate health insurance program was extended to firms hiring 16 or more employees.

A special program for civil servants and private school teachers began in January 1979. In January 1980 the scheme was extended to cover families of military personnel and pensioners. An occupational health insurance program was introduced as a voluntary scheme in December 1981 to cover groups of self-employed workers with similar occupations. In January 1988, the rural regional health insurance program was initiated for people in rural farming and fishery areas. Finally, a program to cover self-employed and unemployed populations in urban areas – the urban regional health insurance program – began in July 1989. Until then, they were the only population group excluded from insurance benefits.

In addition to the health insurance schemes, there are government financed public assistance programs for medical care: (1) Medical Aid for the destitute, and (2) Medical Assistance for the medically indigent. The first category of beneficiaries consists of individuals who are extremely poor, or those living in public facilities, such as the elderly and homeless and elderly people without supportive family members. The second category includes individuals whose income and other means falls below a specified standard. As of 1997, 95.7 percent are under health insurance plans and the remaining 4.3 percent are under the Public Assistance Medicaid program (*Yearbook of Health and Social Statistics*, Ministry of Health and Social Affairs 1997).

The development of Korea from an agrarian to an industrial society served as the vehicle for all these changes. After all, consumers approved the idea of universal health insurance, politicians pushed forward in recognition of public demand, the growing economy helped form NHI financially, and no influential opposing forces existed in the market economy. As far as achieving NHI is concerned, fortunately all sectors of the economy worked in a harmonized way.

However, not much analytical work was conducted prior to the introduction of health insurance. Government did not have much information on the various impacts of insurance programs. For example, in setting up fee schedules, Korea borrowed Japanese fee schedules with only slight deductions and additions. Disputes on the appropriateness of relative value scale, consequently, continue between government and provider groups.

The introduction of compulsory universal health insurance transmitted different signals to different economic agents. Many Koreans now regard health (or basic health care services) as one of their rights. Unlike other goods or services, everyone in the population is presumed to be entitled to minimum health services for survival, regardless of their wealth or social standing.

Providers can no longer enjoy unchecked autonomy as they are subject to the many constraints inherent in the system. Physician and hospital charges are contingent on government fixed-fee schedules, and the acquisition of certain equipment and expansion or establishment of hospitals in certain areas needs the approval of the Ministry of Health and Welfare.

For the government, the transition implies enhanced financial and social obligations. Even with an economy in recession, it would be very difficult for the government to cut budgets or reduce benefits in the future, because people are accustomed to the welfare state and would not accept such a change. On the contrary, it is more likely that the government will face an even greater burden as certain groups, such as the elderly and the handicapped, demand their fair share of the pie.

3.2   Payment and Reimbursement of Insurance Services

In most cases, as mentioned above, patients are given a choice of hospitals and clinics. Providers are paid by FFS in return for providing services that are covered by insurance. Total expense is reimbursed, in part, by the insurance funds, and the rest by patients' out-of-pocket payments. Two types of cost-sharing features are incorporated into each service utilization. The first feature is a deductible applied to each unit of service. For example, a flat fee of about US$4 has to be paid by a patient for each physician visit. On top of the deductible, a patient pays coinsurance rates of 30 per cent for clinic outpatient services, 50 percent for hospital outpatient services, and 55 per cent for general hospital outpatient services. The coinsurance rate for inpatient services is 20 percent across all types of providers .

Under the NHI, for insurance-covered services, providers (hospitals and clinics) are reimbursed according to a set of fee schedules. The government plays a major role in setting the fee schedules, although the level of fees is negotiated at the national level by parties concerned.

3.3   Insurance Administration

As of December 1997, there were 373 insurance funds. Each fund was financially autonomous. The size of each insurance fund was small, covering 30 000 to 200 000 people. With the structure of a large number of small insurers in which each fund covered only a small fraction of the population, two problems arose. First, the system could hardly realize economies of scale and, second, there was inequitable and insufficient risk pooling among beneficiaries. The proportion of administrative costs to total expenditure was 8.5 percent on average. Some regional funds had as high as 15.6 percent (KMIC 1996). This high figure, when compared with 1.5 percent in Canada and 2.6 percent in the UK, indicates a high degree of administrative inefficiency, which could have been reduced by increasing funds.

3.4   Coverage

Not all health services are covered by the NHI in Korea, which remains the most controversial part of the Korean health insurance system. The extent and the level of insurance coverage are determined by the government. Figure 4.1 shows the division of health services into insurance covered and non-covered services, and their respective payments. New or expensive high-technology medical services account for most of these non-covered services. Examples include Gamma Camera, Magnetic Resonance Imaging (MRI), most nuclear scanning, some chemotherapy, PET, and ultrasonography. CT scans only became an insurance-covered service in January 1996. For insurance-covered services, patients are required to pay 20 percent of inpatient charges, 30 percent of clinic outpatient charges, and 55 percent of general hospital outpatient charges out of pocket. On top of these user fees, patients at general hospitals pay special treatment charges (STC) when they see staff physicians. STC are totally out of pocket.

While government-controlled prices are applied for insurance covered

Special *Treatment* *Charges*	*Special* *Treatment* *Charges*	
Market fee Stated price of service	Deductibles and Copayment	Payment by Insurance

| ←Services Not Covered by Insurance→ | | ← Services Covered by Insurance → |

Note: Special treatment charges = Out-of-pocket payments to providers beyond stated price of service.

Figure 4.1 Components of total payments for services

services, for services not covered by insurance, providers charge unregulated market prices. When prevailing market prices of the services are compared with production costs of such services, one finds enormous differences between the two. The difference is purely the monopoly rent created by factors such as consumer ignorance and imperfect hospital market conditions. This high monopoly rent from non-insurance services acts as a strong incentive for providers to invest more in expensive medical technologies not covered by insurance. This has resulted in active acquisition of expensive high-technology products and equipment by hospitals in recent years.

The diffusion of selected technologies over time is shown in Table 4.2. A significant jump in the rate of technology adoption is observed in 1989 and 1990, when NHI was fully implemented. The marked difference in the rate of diffusion between 1987 (before NHI) and 1990 (after NHI) can be noted in the table. This rapid adoption of medical technology has resulted in Korea having more MRI machines per million population than European countries and more lithotripsy machines per capita than the USA (Yang 1997). Adoption of such technology results in cost increases for the system.

In sum, insurance coverage under NHI is limited in several respects: the rate of out-of-pocket payment is still high, even with covered services; some of the expensive services are outside the domain of health insurance; STCs come along with both covered and uninsured services in general hospitals. In addition, there is an upper insurance coverage in terms of the number of days of hospitalization and care covered (300 days, as of 1998). The result is that, as Table 4.3 and Figure 4.1 show, only a fraction of total medical expenditures are covered by health insurance schemes in

Table 4.2 Number of selected medical technology units per million population (1977–96)

Year	Whole-body CT	MRI	Lithotripsy (ESWL)
1977	2	–	–
1980	8	–	–
1983	23	–	–
1986	73	–	1
1987	81	–	25
1988	104	–	30
1989	159	10	37
1990	227	33	42
1993	507	71	53
1996	733	194	52**
Number/million population in 1988	2.42	0.00	0.70
Number/million population in 1990	5.28	0.77	0.98
Number/million population in 1993	11.79	1.65	1.23
Number/million population in 1996	16.66	4.41	1.18**

Note: ** Data from 1995.

Source: Internal report, Ministry of Health and Social Affairs, various years.

Table 4.3 Out-of-pocket payments as percentage of total treatment costs

	University hospital		Private hospital		Public hospital	
	OP	IP	OP	IP	OP	IP
Internal medicine	63.9	51.8	63.1	50.6	49.9	23.6
Surgery[a]	63.5	58.0	75.5	54.55	61.0	38.3
Pediatrics	70.7	49.6	83.1	54.55	55.7	23.0
Obstetrics and gynecology	90.6	59.95	93.5	67.4	87.4	47.0

Notes
OP = outpatient service; IP = inpatient service.
[a] Cosmetic surgery is not included.

Korea. User charge rates higher than 30 percent are seldom found in other insurance schemes. Based on available information, the Korean out-of-pocket cost rates appear to be the highest in the world (OECD, 1995, p. 50).

4   REFORM IN HEALTH INSURANCE: CONSOLIDATION OF INSURANCE FUNDS

4.1   Background

In February 1999, 22 years after the introduction of the first public health insurance scheme, and 12 years after the inauguration of the NHI, the Korean parliament passed the 'National Health Insurance Act', which mandates the consolidation of all health insurance funds into a single fund. With this law, Korea embarked on a transition from a multiple sickness fund system to a single fund system. This transition is part of the health care reform package that the country has been pursuing during the last five years. It is a rather big change, a change that has been supported by various social groups, including civil non-governmental organizations (NGOs).

The impact of this change would hardly be insignificant, although it is difficult to assess its impact before the new system is completely incorporated into Korea's existing health care system. The change could be the starting point for several other health system reform agendas to follow. It will be interesting to observe how the Korean health care system and its subsectors adjust to this new environment, because not many countries have undergone these types of changes so far. Korean experience may provide an important lesson to other countries that consider similar changes in their health insurance structure.

4.2   New Structure

The basic philosophy underlying the consolidation of insurance funds is the solidarity principle. The proponents of the consolidation of funds argued that social cohesion among different social groups could be strengthened through having the solidarity principle in the delivery of health services. They further argued that applying the solidarity principle to the health insurance scheme was an important and necessary first step toward strengthening 'social safety net' in Korea.[3]

Consolidation of insurance funds was made possible with the support from various social groups, including the unified labor union belonging to regional insurance funds, some academicians, civil NGOs, bureaucrats, and politicians. Despite the resistance from interest groups such as Association of Corporate Insurance Funds and business corporations, it is interesting to see that in response to the growing support for a single payer system, both the leading and the opposition parties unanimously agreed to pass the new Act. The Association of Corporate Insurance

Before Oct. 1998   Oct. 1998–June 2000   July 2000
                                          (Stage I)   (Stage II)

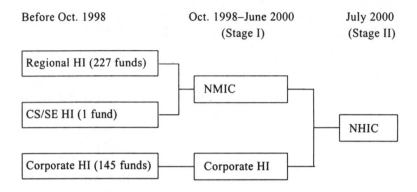

Figure 4.2 Two stages in the process of consolidation

Funds and business corporations think that (1) their premiums go up under a unified system, and (2) the solidarity concept is hardly acceptable within the market economy framework. Nevertheless, the process of consolidation of insurance funds has been generally smooth.

As shown in Figure 4.2, the transition from 373 insurance funds to a single fund involves two stages. In the first stage (Stage I), 227 regional insurance funds are being merged with the Civil Servant insurance fund, thus creating a single fund which is named the 'National Medical Insurance Corporation' (NMIC). This process had been complete as of September 1998, and the NMIC was launched on 1 October 1998. In the second stage (Stage II), all corporate HI (health insurance) funds are planned to be merged into the NMIC, thus creating a nationwide single fund which covers the whole population under one umbrella. The single fund, National Health Insurance Corporation (NHIC), will be established in July 2000. The NHIC will function as the central cortex of health insurance administration and delivery of insurance services.

The consolidation process is seperated into two phases in order to reduce the potential shocks that might result from an abrupt one-phase change. The problems encountered in the first stage of partial consolidation will be carefully examined, and solutions will be sought in time, before the system moves to a unified system.

By July 2000 when Stage II is complete, the structure of the national health insurance system will be as shown in Figure 4.3. The business of public health insurance will be separated into two parts: administration and delivery of health insurance services by the NHIC, and review of claims and technology assessment by HIRA (Health Insurance Review Agency). Both will be under the supervision of the Ministry of Health and

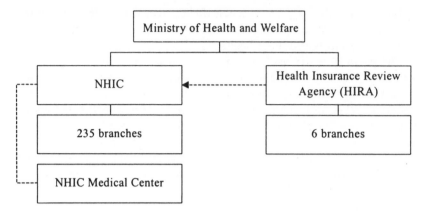

Figure 4.3 Administration structure of the national health insurance system

Welfare in terms of operational budgets, but they will be independent in their functions.

Major operations, such as determining level of contributions, level of service fees, reimbursement to providers, fund management, will be the role of NHIC. Meanwhile HIRA will take the role of (i) reviewing the appropriateness of claims made by providers and (ii) assessing new medical technologies, including development of drugs.

The role of NHIC will be assisted by 161 branches that are geographically spread over the nation. The NHIC will also run a medical center, a general hospital with 650 beds, to have on-site experience in both clinical and health promotion services.

4.3 Expected Performance

Risk pooling
Since the whole population (farmers, business employees, and the self-employed) will be under one insurance scheme, risks by different population groups can now be pooled and spread over the entire population. The highly skewed nature of health expenditure makes risk pooling essential. The pooling of resources sets up a natural tradeoff between protecting individual patients from financial ruin and the moral hazard problem (Nichols et al. 1997). Further investigations are necessary to find out empirically the pattern and the level of risk pooling among groups in the society. However, it is evident that the level of risk pooling

under a single fund system is much higher than that under the previous multiple fund system in which the population was segmented into smaller groups of people with similar health risks.

The result of wider risk pooling is an enhancement in both equity and efficiency. People with higher risk will be better protected under the new system, by contributions from lower-risk population groups. The new system will be more equitable and efficient, especially when the higher-risk groups are the elderly and the less affluent. By helping the poor to get necessary health services for survival, the marginal benefit of insurance expenditure will certainly be increased. Improved risk pooling will also enable the system to have better predictions on insurance expenditures and levels of contributions.

Equity in financing
Under the unified system, the same contribution scheme will be applied to all Koreans in the employment sector. In other words, those with a monthly income of one million Won, for example, will pay the same amount of insurance premium regardless of their type of occupation or of the size of their employment. Under the previous multiple fund system, where each fund was financially autonomous, the financial status of each fund often dictated the contribution scheme. In some cases, for example, an employee in firm A whose monthly income was 1.0 million Won paid a higher insurance premium than one in firm B whose income was 1.5 million Won. In general, government employees paid higher premiums than those in the business sector mainly because they used more health services. The level of premuim had been closely tied with the level of utilization, rather than with the level of income. The financing was inequitable in the sense that contributions were not fully connected to the ability to pay. Under the unified system, that aspect of inequitable financing will disappear at least in the employment-based insurance sector.

Economies of scale
A substantial reduction in administration costs is expected under the single fund system. Table 4.4 shows the change in the number of funds and the number of beneficiaries in each fund (branch) before and after the consolidation of funds. In the case of NHIC, although it is a single fund, since its operation is based on 235 branches, as far as insurance administration is concerned the system is similar to the case of 235 funds. The result is a decrease in the number of funds from 372 to 235, and an increase in the number of beneficiaries per fund from 106 694 to 190 305. This means the size of each fund is nearly doubled after the consolidation.

Table 4.4 Change in the number of funds and beneficiaries with
  consolidation

	Number of funds/ branches	Number of beneficiaries per fund/per branch
Before consolidation	372 funds	106 694/fund
After consolidation (NHIC)	1 fund and 235 branches	190 305/branch

With this increase in fund size, the annual reduction in administrative costs is estimated to be about 11 billion Korean Won.[4]

The new structure can witness good sized economies of scale. The saved administration costs could be used, for example, to lower user changes for low income class or to expand insurance coverage for the currently uncovered services.

5 REMAINING ISSUES

Even with the consolidation of funds, and with the resulting positive aspects, experts argue that several basic problems remain unsolved in the Korean NHI. Two major problems are limited insurance coverage especially in cases of major risks, and cost increase that may precipitate financial insolvency in the system.

5.1 Limited Coverage/ High User Charges

The combination of the FFS payment-reimbursement system, the dominance of for-profit providers and the current structure of health insurance resulted in high level of reliance on direct payments in Korea. A high coinsurance rate is useful in that moral hazard can be reduced. However, it has a few shortcomings as well. First, a high coinsurance rate is hardly consistent with the principle of social insurance that Korea has adopted (Korea Health Insurance Act). Health care needs may not be adequately met when you pay a substantial proportion of service charges. Second, a high coinsurance rate raises an equity issue. When a coinsurance rate is applied irrespective of family income, as in Korea, it becomes a greater burden to low-income families than to high-income families. Seeking needed care by high-risk, low-income families is often deterred by financial barriers, whereas use by high-income families is rarely affected.

If equity is considered to be one important goal of the Korean health care system, the priority of reform should be to lower user charges through expansion of coverage. To lower user charges it is necessary to, first, bring most health services under the NHI umbrella; second, remove STCs in hospital service provision; third, install income-related cost-sharing features; and finally, make upward adjustments in fee schedules and premiums so that the system can be sustained.

A major impact of this reform is cost shifting between insurers and consumers, which will make the whole system considerably more equitable than before. For example, through utilization of health services, there will be cross-subsidization among income groups, from the rich to the poor. The combination of higher (income proportional or progressive) premiums and lower (income regressive) user charges will certainly bring about monetary transfers from the rich to the poor, compared with the reverse case (current situation) of low premiums and extensive user charges. The more direct user charges are replaced by premium payments, the greater cross-subsidization will be.

After the health insurance reform, changes can occur in the conduct, behavior, and performance of the system as a result of a reformed incentive structure. The most important of all is the gain in efficiency through change in provider behavior. As insurance coverage becomes comprehensive, the misleading incentive to provide non-insured services will be reduced. Excessive adoption of some new technologies will be eased, as profit opportunities from non-insured high-technology services are largely reduced.[5]

An alternative to the expansion of coverage is shifting insurance coverage from the current minor risks to major risks. This alternative can be considered when raising the level of contributions is politically unacceptable. As is known, expansion of insurance coverage and reducing user charges will require a large increase in contribution levels of the insured. If people are unwilling to accept the increase in the contribution (that is, quasi tax) levels, an alternative to the expansion of coverage needs to be considered. This is the shift of insurance coverage from outpatient services to major risks. As shown earlier, insurance coverage for major risks is very weak in the current system. Many expensive services and drugs are outside the domain of insurance system. Coverage needs to be shifted from low-cost, high-probability outpatient care to high-cost, low-probability inpatient care. Minor risks, for which insurance does not produce much welfare gain, are generally affordable as part of routine consumption expenditures, and a significant amount of resources can be freed and redirected to high-cost cases. By concentrating coverage on major risks, the system can shield individual patients from financial ruin, and at the same time, can solve the moral hazard problem. There will also be a gain in efficiency.

5.2   Cost Increase/ Insolvency of Health Insurance

The gradual expansion of health insurance plans during 1977–89, in conjunction with the growth of the private health care sector, has resulted in increased demand for services and higher quality care. The nationwide coverage of health insurance has contributed to increases in health service utilization and to upgrading the level of health of the people. The growing private sector imported new medical technologies aggressively and competitively, resulting in an apparent increase in the technological quality of health care.

However, these changes involve substantial cost increases. Rising health costs are now viewed as a growing problem in Korea. The health care system of Korea is inflationary by design. It is inflationary not simply because people demand more health care services, but also because of the way the system is structured. It can be characterized by dominance of the private sector, FFS, and inadequate government regulation. They induce an expanding amount of service provision and consumption, and services that are more expensive.

As shown in Figure 4.4, from 1975 through 1995, the health care share of the total economy has grown from a mere 2.8 percent to 5.4 percent, with an annual rate of increase of around 28 percent. (Between 1975 and 1995, the Korean economy recorded unprecedented high growth rates. The increasing share of health costs as a proportion of GDP, therefore, signifies how fast the health sector expanded during this period.) It is expected that the rate would be much higher in recent years as Korea's economic growth rate has slowed significantly since 1996.

Many factors contributed to the rapid increase in the national health expenditure. A substantial part of the total cost escalation is attributable to the increase in treatment costs. Data from health insurance expenditure shows that total insurance expenditure has been increased by 26.6 percent in 1995, and 29 percent in 1996 (NFMI, Statistical Yearbook, various years). A similar increase is observed in KMIC data files.

The continuing increase in treatment costs in health insurance has profound implications for the financial insolvency of the NHI. As shown in Table 4.5, in all three types of health insurance, expenditures exceed revenues in recent year, thus reducing accumulated surpluses. It is required by law that the insurance system as a whole has to hold at least 20 percent and up to 50 percent of annual outlay (about 8000 billion Won) as a reserve. According to the current trend, it is likely that not only will

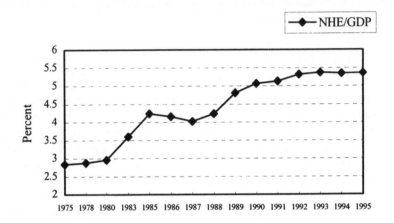

*Figure 4.4 National health expenditure as percentage of gross domestic
product (1974–95)*

Table 4.5 Trend of financial status of the health insurance system

(Unit: 1 billion won)

		1993	1994	1995	1996	1997	1998*	1999*
Corporate health insurance	Annual surplus	408	445	345	149	−227	−245	−234
	Accumulated surplus	2024	2259	2450	2608	2503	2258	2023
Regional health insurance	Annual surplus	259	226	133	−34	129	39	−136
	Accumulated surplus	551	769	952	962	885	857	721
Civil Servant health insurance	Annual surplus	84	81	32	−95	−167	−144	−65
	Accumulated surplus	316	368	427	454	397	141	77
Total	Annual surplus	751	752	510	20	−265	−350	−435
	Accumulated surplus	2891	3396	3829	4024	3785	3256	2821

Note: * predicted values based on past trends.

Source: National Federation of Medical Insurance, *Medical Insurance Statistical Yearbook*,
various years.

the minimum reserve (about 1800 billion Won) hardly be maintained, but
also the overall fund will go into deficit very soon.

This is the case even when the financial pressure generated by the aging population is not fully taken into account. Korea's NHI, like insurance systems in many other countries, is a pay-as-you-go system. The fact that the population is aging very rapidly (Bureau of Statistics, Government of Korea 1997) puts added strain on both revenue and expenditure sides of insurance financing. The work force making contributions to insurance is shrinking while the number of elderly who use large amounts of resources is expanding in size, making the support ratio of the number of workers to each older Korean smaller and smaller. The financial status of NHI will be jeopardized further with the population aging.

Although there could be cost savings from consolidation of insurance funds, that would still by far not be enough to cover the trend of cost increase, nor would it solve the problem of financial insolvency in health insurance. How to resolve the problem of financial insolvency of NHI is an issue in hand now. OECD (1995) introduces both macro and micro reforms; budgetary caps and other macro measures to control expenditures and increasing efficiency (by strengthened role of payers, increased accountability of purchasers, better purchasing agents, etc.) to lower cost pressures. Macro and micro reforms in the Korean context are becoming essential.

6 CONCLUSION

The government of Korea introduced various reforms in the health insurance system recently. Some minor proposals were made to lower the rate of user charges and to expand health insurance coverage. One major proposal was to consolidate the multiple insurance funds into a single payer.

Consolidation of many sickness funds into a single payer could mean a dramatic change in the delivery of health care in Korea. One expects substantial savings in the system's administration costs, improved equity among social classes in financing health insurance, and enhanced efficiency through better risk-pooling among different population groups. On top of this, tackling the remaining issues in health insurance, such as the expansion of insurance coverage and the containment of escalating costs, is becoming a possibility under the consolidated fund system. Before the consolidation, where each financially autonomous individual fund took its own position with the problematic issues, it was not easy to have a consensus among the funds on how to resolve the issues in hand. However, all the above expectations can only be sustained by evaluation and evidence.

One is not saying that the consolidation of funds itself will automatically lead the system to perfect solutions. However, it is evident that a powerful single payer, as a representative body of all premium contributors, will have the monopsony bargaining power to lead the insurance system toward a more reasonable paradigm.

NOTES

[1]   It is a form of fixed compensation per episode which was originally developed by the US. In the US, the method is called DRG (diagnostic related groupings).

[2]   Primary health care refers to service category provided by general practitioners and family physicians, including preventive and health promoting services.

[3]   The need for a 'social safety net' was particularly emphasized with the rising unemployment rate at that time. As one of the conditions of World Bank Loan (after the economic crisis), the Korean government agreed with the Bank to have a reasonable social safety net for the destitute, including the unemployed.

[4]   The estimate is based on the average cost equation that appeared in a recent journal article (Yang and Kim 1998). The equation was derived from pooled cross-sectional data of 373 funds during 1990–96.

[5]   As explained in Figure 4.1 and in Table 4.2, exclusion of high-technology services from insurance coverage produced perverse incentives to providers. Under the current system, high mark-ups from uncontrolled fees for non-insured services (mostly high-tech services) triggered extensive adoption and use of high-cost medical technologies.

REFERENCES

Bureau of Statistics, Government of Korea, *Statistical Yearbook of Population Dynamics*, various years.

Korea Medical Insurance Corporation (KMIC), *Statistical Yearbook*, various years.

Korean Hospital Association, *Membership Reports*, various years.

Korean Ministry of Health and Social Affairs, *Yearbook of Health and Social Statistics*, various years.

Lee, K.S. (1995), 'Expansion of the hospital sector', *Korean Health Economic Review*, 1(1): 92–120.

National Federation of Medical Insurance (NFMI), *Statistical Yearbook*, various years.

Nichols, L.M., N. Prescott and K.H. Phua (1997), 'Medical savings account for developing countries', *Innovations in Health Care Financing*, World Bank Discussion Paper, No. 365, World Bank.

OECD (1995), *New Directions in Health Policy*, Health Policy Studies No. 7.

Yang, B.M. (1997), 'The role of health insurance in the growth of the private health sector in Korea', in W. Newbrander (ed.), *Private Health Sector Growth in Asia*, West Sussex, England: John Wiley & Sons Ltd., pp. 61–82.

Yang, B.M. and Y.M. Kim (1998), 'Empirical estimate of optimum insurance fund size: pooled data of 1990–96', *Korean Health Economic Review*, 4(1): 116–34.

PART II

Production of Health

5. Is rehabilitation following an acute hospital stay productive? Evidence from elderly patients in the United States

Frank A. Sloan, Donald H. Taylor, Gabriel A. Picone and R. Mark Wilson

1   INTRODUCTION

In fiscal year 1984, Medicare – a government program insuring almost all persons over age 65, seriously disabled persons under age 65, and persons with end stage kidney disease in the United States – introduced prospective payment for hospitals. Under this new system, which replaced retrospective cost-based reimbursement, hospitals were paid a fixed price per case that varied by diagnosis. Care delivered prior to or after the hospital stay was not included in the fixed price. By paying a fixed amount to hospitals per covered patient, irrespective of hospital input use, the new payment system offered hospitals a greater incentive to be efficient. Under the cost-based system it replaced, hospitals generated higher revenue by increasing cost. Under the new system, hospitals can keep the residual amount between revenue and cost as profit.

However, the new system also has had the effect, among others, of encouraging provision of care before or after the hospital stay. If provided in other settings, care is reimbursed separately by Medicare. In this way, the hospital can collect the same per case payment, and possibly other payments for care delivered before and after the stay as well, from Medicare while reducing the cost of the stay. Since 1984, the share of Medicare-covered services provided in acute hospital settings has decreased markedly (*Health Care Financing Review* 1998, pp. 96–7; US Medicare Payment Advisory Commission 1998) with corresponding increases in the share of program cost attributable to care in other settings, such as in physicians' offices, nursing homes, and in the patients' homes (for example, home health).

Provision of care in less costly settings than hospitals may be efficient to the extent that equivalent or even better outcomes are achieved at lower cost. However, especially when payment for the non-hospital services is on a piece rate basis and/or based on retrospective cost, it seems unlikely that potential efficiencies are being realized, especially when there is little patient cost-sharing. Because of the rise in Medicare expenditures for such care, prospective payment methodologies have recently been extended to several types of non-hospital services, but this change did not occur during the observational period covered by this study.

Rehabilitation occurs after the immediate effects of an acute event leading to the hospitalization have been alleviated, for example after the repair of a fractured hip. The goals of rehabilitation are to prevent secondary complications, to reduce deficits attributable to the acute episode, to help patients compensate for or adapt to residual disabilities, and to maintain function over the long term (see, for example, US Department of Health and Human Services 1995, p. 10). Rehabilitation includes therapies administered by several types of health professionals, including physical, occupational, and recreational therapists, speech–language pathologists, vocational rehabilitation specialists, physiatrists (physicians specializing in rehabilitation), neurologists and others. Rehabilitation is provided in acute care and rehabilitation hospitals, nursing homes, ambulatory care settings (such as hospital outpatient facilities), and in patients' homes. Rehabilitation in hospital-based facilities tends to be more expensive than in skilled nursing facilities (Schlenker et al. 1997).

When provided by Medicare in hospitals, rehabilitation is excluded from the prospective price and reimbursed up to a limit that reflects Medicare payments to the hospital in a base year (Chan et al. 1997). Thus a patient may receive coverage for an acute event and then be transferred within the same facility to receive rehabilitative care. Like other Medicare-covered, post-acute care services, the quantity of Medicare-paid rehabilitative services has grown rapidly since 1984, without, as explained more fully below, clear evidence that such care is effective. Nor for that matter are there evidence-based criteria on the types of patients that would most be likely to benefit from such interventions.

In this study, we analyzed care patterns following hospital admission of Medicare beneficiaries who were admitted with a primary diagnosis of a disease or disorder of the nervous system or musculoskeletal system. Within these two categories, major reasons for admissions to hospitals are for stroke and hip fracture, respectively.

Diseases and disorders of the nervous system and of the

musculoskeletal system and connective tissue are common diagnoses leading to hospital admissions and are frequent causes of long-term disability. Both are 'major diagnostic categories' (MDCs) in the Medicare prospective payment classification system. MDCs are an aggregation of diagnosis related groups (DRGs). Payment to hospitals under Medicare is now based on the patient's DRG. The nervous system diagnostic category (MDC 1) includes strokes, injuries to the nervous system, neoplasms of the nervous system, and concussions. The musculoskeletal category (MDC 8) includes hip fractures and other procedures involving repair of joints.

Stroke and hip fracture are two very common disabling adverse health events among the elderly. For strokes, 40 percent of stroke survivors have some disability at six months following the acute event (Dombovy et al. 1987). Forty to 60 percent of the elderly who suffer a hip fracture have reduced ability to walk and elevated health care use (Brainsky et al. 1997; Cooney 1997; Koval and Zuckerman 1994). Both hip fracture and stroke are determinants of institutionalization and death. Death rates from stroke have been declining in the United States and most Western European countries (Wolf et al. 1992; Broderick et al. 1989; Cooper et al. 1990; Sloan et al. 1999). The decline has been attributed to better control of modifiable risk factors such as hypertension, earlier diagnosis, and better therapy (see, for example, Wolf et al. 1992). Although having a hip fracture raises the probability of death, mortality is generally attributed to another cause. In analysis of mortality of stroke and hip fracture among elderly patients in the United States, mortality among stroke patients declined by about 5 percent per year between 1984 and 1994. For hip fracture, mortality rates improved by 2 percent a year, with determinants of death held constant, but the trend was not statistically significant at conventional levels ($p = 0.16$) (Sloan et al. 1999). Another study in the US found statistically significant increases in survival rates for males over age 85 and for females over age 75 (Bacon 1996). The greatest increase was for older males. In spite of decreases in mortality, for other outcomes, there were improvements over the same period in instrumental activities of daily living (preparing meals, doing laundry, shopping for groceries, managing money/paying bills, taking medicine, and making telephone calls) for both hip fracture and stroke (Sloan et al. 1999). Cognitive status improved for patients with hip fracture. Some higher level functioning improved for hip fracture (combing/brushing hair, using fingers to grasp/handle small objects) and for stroke (washing hair).

Because these two conditions lead to high rates of residual disability (Flick 1999), the probability that persons admitted for the major diagnostic categories of nervous and musculosketal diseases is highest among the 25 MDCs. Using Medicare claims data for 1991, Lee et al.

(1996) found that 73 percent of stroke survivors receive some rehabilitation within the first six months following their strokes. Preliminary analysis of our data showed MDC 1 and MDC 8 to have the highest probability of receipt of rehabilitation among all MDCs.

2   CONCEPTUAL FRAMEWORK

The objective of this analysis was to assess the effect of rehabilitation on various health outcomes using a two-equation model in which rehabilitation and outcomes are jointly determined. Decisions of whether or not to obtain rehabilitation and the amount of rehabilitation to obtain, conditional on receiving any rehabilitation, is the result of an optimization decision. Conditional on the patient surviving the health shock, families with their physician agents weigh marginal benefit against marginal cost. Marginal benefit logically reflects the patient's survival probability and, given survival, the marginal product of investments in rehabilitation, where output is measured by functional and cognitive status and residential location. Marginal product depends in part on the patient's health before the shock occurred and the severity of the shock.

However, physicians observe much more about the patient's condition than does the researcher. Therefore, because part of the information about the severity of the patient's condition is not known to the researcher but may determine the patient's receipt or nonreceipt of rehabilitation, receipt of rehabilitation is endogenous. Not accounting for the omitted heterogeneity would probably lead the researcher to overstate the marginal benefit of rehabilitation.

Although explicitly not a purpose of Medicare-subsidized rehabilitation, some families may also benefit from having publicly sponsored care following the hospitalization, even if rehabilitation per se is not productive. Especially when care is provided in a hospital or nursing home, there is also a benefit from provision of formal care which is supplied in addition to rehabilitative services.   This is true to a greater extent when there are no potential family caregivers, spouses or children. In principle, Medicare only pays for rehabilitation that is likely to be productive in terms of improved health.   The fact that prior health is not fully captured, and more importantly, severity of the shock is hardly recorded at all in the data gives rise to simultaneous equation bias discussed below.

The marginal cost to the patient depends on the extent of the Medicare subsidy and availability of rehabilitation facilities near the patient's home. Since Medicare benefits are uniform geographically, there is no exogenous variation in the extent of subsidy, except perhaps to the extent Medicare coverage is not supposed to be available when rehabilitation is not productive. Unfortunately, there is no empirical evidence on the extent to which Medicare actually enforces this rule.

This type of variation is similar to what is termed 'practice patterns,' and represents the unwritten rules of how physicians determine who gets rehabilitation. There is considerable geographic variation, however, in availability of rehabilitation services.

3 DATA

The study sample was drawn from the National Long-term Care Survey (NLTCS) which is a panel study fielded in 1982, 1984, 1989, and 1994. Overall, 35,800 Medicare beneficiaries were included in the sample for at least some time. NLTCS drew its sample from Medicare enrollment records for persons 65 years of age and older. A screener interview was administered to all beneficiaries. Based on responses to the screener, full interviews were conducted with persons who reported having at least one limitation in activities of daily living (ADLs) or in instrumental activities of daily living (IADLs).[1] Respondents lived in the community or in other facilities, most notably in nursing homes. The NLTCS collected detailed information on functional and cognitive status, health conditions, demographic characteristics of the family such as potential caregivers' education, race, and income, including sources of income and wealth.

The NLTCS was merged with data from other sources. First, data on all Medicare claims were merged with all individuals screened by NLTCS in any year (Manton et al. 1995). Each claim included information on diagnoses and amounts billed and paid by Medicare. In this study, we used Medicare claims information to document receipt of Medicare-covered rehabilitation services following the index hospital stay. Data on Medicare reimbursements for rehabilitation were only available for 1991 through 1995. To allow for a minimal time for follow-up, we restricted the sample to hospital admissions occurring during 1991–94. Dates of deaths for all NLTCS respondents were verified by using Medicare enrollment records. Data on other outcomes came from NLTCS interviews conducted during 1994.

For purposes of this analysis, we limited the sample in four other ways. First, we selected persons who were admitted to hospitals with primary diagnoses falling in the categories of diseases and disorders of the nervous system (MDC 1) and diseases and disorders of the musculoskeletal system and connective tissues (MDC 8). Second, for persons to be included, we had to have information from the NLTCS interviews conducted in 1989. These interviews provided demographic and financial information, and information on the person's health before the index health event occurred, as well as lagged values for outcome measures. Third, we excluded index hospitalizations that lasted more than 91 days. Fourth, the person had to have been discharged from the index hospital stay alive. That is, having rehabilitation after the hospital stay had to be an option. Although we observed many important demographic characteristics and details of household income prior to the shock and coexisting conditions at the time of the shock, we did not observe the severity of the shock. This was a source of omitted heterogeneity since persons with severe shocks died during the index admission. After applying these screens, we were left with 1493 observations.

4   EMPIRICAL SPECIFICATION

4.1   Overview

Our basic strategy was to estimate equations for (1) the probability of receipt of rehabilitation and the Medicare program rehabilitation cost for the individual, conditional on receipt, and (2) health outcomes with receipt of rehabilitation as the main explanatory variable with the total sample, and, for those who received rehabilitation, explanatory variables for receipt and the amount received, measured in terms of Medicare rehabilitation cost. In the health outcomes analysis for the whole sample, we accounted for endogeneity of receipt by using the generalized method of moments/ instrumental variables (GMM/IV) method. For the outcomes analysis conditional on receipt, we used a mixed strategy of GMM/IV and discrete factor analysis.

4.2   Dependent Variables

We used a binary variable to denote persons who received rehabilitation. We identified persons with Medicare claims for rehabilitation for such services rendered during the first six months (183 days) following the date of admission to the hospital immediately after the index event; that is, a stroke or hip fracture, or other condition within the two MDCs. Program cost was defined as total payments made by Medicare for rehabilitation services during this time period. Rehabilitation was received at up to four sites by any one patient: inpatient hospital; skilled nursing facility (SNF); home health; and outpatient. The binary took the value 1 if an individual

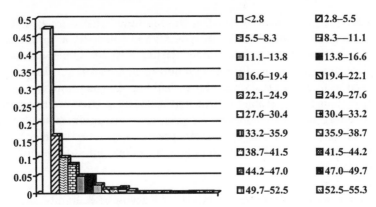

Figure 5.1 Frequency distribution of Medicare rehabilitation cost

received rehabilitation at any site at least once during the specified period. Rehabilitation claims were identified by variables specifying that the service being reimbursed by Medicare was for rehabilitation. For inpatient rehabilitation, this meant a claim identified an individual as being admitted to a rehabilitation unit, with an admission and discharge date for such a stay. SNF claims also had admission and discharge dates. Home health and outpatient rehabilitation claims specified the date of service receipt; if an individual had ten home health visits, there were ten claims.

We used the natural logarithm of real payments for rehabilitation from all sites during the six-month period as the measure of rehabilitation cost. We expressed such payments in 1994, using the Consumer Price Index, all items as the inflator. Eliminating zero values, the frequency distribution of such payments had a long right tail (Figure 5.1). Values ranged from $13 to over $50 000. (The extreme right tail payments ≥ $25 000 is not shown in the figure.)

We specified health outcome equations for the probability of death within 12 and within 24 months of the index admission and four outcome measures, conditional on the patient's survival to the interview following the admission, which occurred in 1994. Each equation had a binary dependent variable: living in the community as opposed to a nursing home; being cognitively aware; having fewer or the same number of limitations in activities of daily living as at the NLTCS interview before the index admission (in 1989); and having fewer instrumental activities of daily living than at the interview before the index admission.

The NLTCS measured cognitive functioning with a ten question Short Portable Mental Status Questionnaire (Pfeiffer 1975). We considered a person to be 'cognitively aware' if they answered seven or more questions correctly. Questions dealt with orientation in time (what is today's date?) and place (what is the name of this place?) and ability to perform simple calculations (count backward in threes starting with 20). Otherwise, or if a proxy respondent was used for a cognition-related reason, this binary was set equal to 0. The ADLs were: eating, bathing, dressing, moving around inside, toileting and getting in and out of bed. The IADLs were: preparing meals, doing laundry, shopping for groceries, managing money/paying bills, taking medicine and making telephone calls. As explained below, we used alternative techniques to deal with endogeneity of rehabilitation receipt and cost.

4.3   Explanatory Variables: Analysis of Receipt of Rehabilitation and of Medicare Program Cost

To gauge potential benefits from rehabilitation, we were able to measure demographic characteristics of the individual, diagnoses at the time of the index admission, and health, functional, and cognitive status at the NLTCS interview before the admission. The demographic characteristics were: age, gender, years of schooling completed, and race (white versus other).

Explanatory variables measured for the index hospital admissions were: a comorbidity index, patient intubated, patient paralyzed, and primary diagnosis, which fell into six mutually exclusive categories. We included a risk adjuster (comorbidity index) developed to forecast future payments on behalf of Medicare beneficiaries (DxCG 1996; Ellis et al. 1996). The comorbidity index classified patients on the basis of diagnoses contained in the index admission hospital claims record using ICD-9-CM diagnosis and procedure codes. Diagnoses other than the primary reason for the index admission were reflected in this index, which allowed for comparison of patients with divergent conditions in terms of future expected Medicare-financed resource use.

We also controlled for whether a person had a procedure code during the index admission that showed them to be intubated, which would suggest very substantial impairment during the index stay, and a variable equal to 1 if secondary diagnosis codes during the index admission showed paralysis. Intubation involves inserting a tube to assist respiration following complications, such as from pneumonia or chronic respiratory failure. Patients requiring this assistance during the index admission have a relatively poor prognosis, and therefore are less likely to be good candidates for rehabilitation (Horner et al. 1998). The six primary diagnostic categories were: pertrochanteric hip fracture; other hip fracture; other musculoskeletal (other MDC 8) disease or disorder; ischemic stroke;

hemorraghic stroke; and other nervous (other MDC 1) disease or disorder. Other (than pertrochanteric) hip fracture was the omitted reference group.

From the NLTCS interview before the index admission, we included variables for: marital status; total household income (converted to 1994 dollars); living in the community; being cognitively aware; number of limitations of activities of daily living; whether or not the person reported problems with bowel or bladder control; and whether or not the person was diagnosed with dementia. The dementia variable was a binary variable set equal to 1 if a person had an ICD-9-CM diagnosis of Alzheimer's disease, vascular dementia, or other dementia on at least one claim prior to the index admission (Cano et al. 1997; Newcomer et al. 1999).

We also included variables for whether or not the person had a child or children who had contacted the sample person within 30 days, measured at the interview, following the index admission. To the extent that rehabilitation substitutes for care provided by relatives, one would expect rehabilitation to be less likely for married individuals and for those with children, in particular where the children have an active relationship with the parent. Alternatively, marital status and children may influence the site of rehabilitation, making outpatient settings more likely.

Cost in part reflects availability of rehabilitation facilities. We included explanatory variables for the number of rehabilitation hospital beds per 1000 population in the primary sampling unit (PSU) in which the person lived and binary variables for whether or not the hospital at which the person was admitted at the time of the shock had a rehabilitation unit or had a contract with another organization to provide such services. PSUs are counties in rural areas or clusters of counties in urban areas. We included a wage index that is used by Medicare to determine the relative costliness of labor inputs in the hospital's area for payment purposes. Population density in the PSU is likely to be correlated with travel time, a determinant of health services use (see, for example, Folland et al. 1997, Chapter 6).

We also controlled for the teaching status of the hospital to which the person was initially admitted, and the average annual per capita (Medicare) cost (AAPCC) in the person's PSU. Following Taylor et al. (1999), we distinguished between major teaching and minor teaching hospitals, based on the hospital's resident-to-bed ratio. The median ratio for teaching hospitals was 0.097. We used this as the dividing line between major and minor. The omitted reference group was no teaching, defined as a hospital with no residents on its staff. The AAPCC reflects the intensity of care delivered to elderly persons in the geographic area. Presumably, where the AAPCC is high rehabilitation is more likely to occur.

Persons with higher income may be willing to pay more for better outcomes, or this may correlate with preferences expected to lead to higher demand for rehabilitation. In regression analysis with the probability of receipt of rehabilitation as the dependent variable, we included squared terms for some of the area variables. This was done to improve goodness of fit. Rehabilitation receipt and cost were endogenous variables in our analysis of health outcomes. Finally, we included a time trend equal to 1 for an index admission occurring in 1991, to 4 if it occurred in 1994.

4.4   Explanatory Variables: Health Outcomes

The health outcomes equations excluded explanatory variables for rehabilitation availability, the wage index, and the AAPCC. Although excludable for conceptual reasons, we performed specification tests to determine that these variables could be excluded (see below). In the equations for living arrangement, cognition and changes in functional status, we included lagged dependent variables measured at the NLTCS interview before the shock and a variable for the number of months from the date of the shock to the next NLTCS interview. Other things being equal, a longer recovery time should be associated with better health.

5   ECONOMETRIC STRATEGY

5.1   Overview

Conceptually, the decision to prescribe rehabilitation and, if prescribed, its amount, is endogenous to outcomes. More specifically, as mentioned above, persons who die or are extremely disabled are unlikely to benefit from rehabilitation and therefore are less likely to receive it. To deal with the endogeneity resulting from unmeasured heterogeneity of illness severity, we first used a GMM/IV estimator. Results for the health outcome equations containing the binary variable for rehabilitation appeared to be robust. However, GMM/IV estimates of the continuous measure of rehabilitation program cost were imprecise. A discrete factor analysis provided superior estimates and we report the results of those estimations.

5.2 Generalized Methods of Moments/Instrumental Variables

This method minimizes the expression below with respect to β:

$$q = (Y - h(X, \beta))'Z(Z'\Sigma\ Z)^{-1}Z'(Y - h(X, \beta))$$

where $\Sigma = E[(Y - h(X, \beta))(Y - h(X, \beta))']$, X is an $n \times k$ matrix of explanatory variables and Z is an $n \times l$ matrix of instruments with $l \geq k$. In our analysis, Y was the dichotomous rehabilitation variable and $h(X_i, \beta) = \Phi(X_i'\beta)$.

Davidson and MacKinnon (1993) provide a thorough discussion of GMM estimation and inference. The estimates have desirable asymptotic properties and the variance covariance matrix is given by

$$[G'Z(Z'\Sigma Z)^{-1}Z'G]^{-1}$$

where $G = -\partial h(X, \beta)/\partial \beta$. This variance covariance matrix is consistently estimated using a two step procedure described in Davidson and MacKinnon (1993) allowing for heteroscedasticity of unknown form.

We tested the validity of our overidentification restrictions by calculating the q-test from the GMM/IV estimator. A large test statistic for the identification restriction may imply either that the model is specified incorrectly, or the instruments are invalid. For all of our specifications reported here, we could not reject the null hypothesis that the model is overidentified.

5.3 Discrete Factor Analysis

When rehabilitation was measured as a continuous variable, we used a quasi-maximum likelihood estimator with discrete factor approximations. This estimator is identical to the one used in Picone et al. (1999). The models to be estimated had a binary dependent variable (health outcome measure) and a continuous endogenous explanatory variable (rehabilitation cost).

Our quasi-maximum likelihood estimator with discrete factor approximations has several advantages compared to traditional maximum likelihood and two-step estimators. Traditional maximum likelihood estimators to estimate our model would involve evaluating a bivariate integral, which is very expensive computationally. Two-step estimators as the ones described in River and Vuong (1988) are computationally attractive, but unreliable without very strong exclusion restrictions. (See Staiger and Stock 1997.)

The quasi-maximum likelihood estimator with discrete factor

approximations used in this study is well suited to correct for endogeneity caused by unmeasured explanatory variables in qualitative dependent variable models (see, for example, Goldman 1995 and Cameron and Taber 1998). It obviates the need to evaluate bivariate normal integrals, and Mroz (1997), in a Monte Carlo study, found that this estimator is more robust to deviations from normality and quality of instruments than two-stage methods.

To apply this method, we assumed that the error terms can be written as $u_1 = \alpha_1 v + \varepsilon_1$ and $u_2 = \alpha_2 v + \varepsilon_2$, where ε_1 and ε_2 are independently normally distributed and v is a univariate random variable with equation specific factor loading parameters α_1 and α_2. Thus the joint density function of u_1 and u_2 conditional on v can be written as:

$$f(u_1, u_2 \mid v) = \frac{1}{\sigma_1} \phi\left(\frac{u_1 - \alpha_1 v}{\sigma_1}\right) \frac{1}{\sigma_2} \phi\left(\frac{u_2 - \alpha_2 v}{\sigma_2}\right)$$

where σ_1 and σ_2 are the standard deviations of ε_1 and ε_2.

The discrete factor approximation method assumes that the distribution of v can be approximated by a discrete distribution, where $Pr(v = 0_k) = P_k \geq 0$ for $k = 1,...,K$ and $\Sigma P_k = 1$. The number of steps, K, the location parameters, η_k, and the probabilities, P_k, are called incidental parameters; they are estimated jointly with the other parameters describing the model. By letting K become large as the sample becomes large, this method can approximate any smooth distribution function relatively well. Using discrete factor approximations, the likelihood function associated with our model is given by

$$L = \prod_{i=1}^{N} \sum_{k=1}^{K} \frac{P_k}{\sigma_1} \phi\left(\frac{u_{1i} - \alpha_1 \eta_k}{\sigma_1}\right) \Phi(u_{2i} - \alpha_2 \eta_k)^{d_i} \left(1 - \Phi(u_{2i} - \alpha_2 \eta_k)\right)^{1-d_i},$$

where d_i is the binary outcome. This likelihood function only contains integrals of univariate normal densities and is therefore computationally less expensive than the maximum likelihood estimator. If the incidental parameters satisfy some regularity conditions the estimates obtained from this method are consistent (Lindsay 1983).

Because the number of points K, η_k and P_k are unknown, the maximization of the above likelihood function is numerically challenging. Heckman and Singer (1984) estimated η_k and P_k directly and used an iterative procedure to maximize the likelihood function with respect to the regular parameters of the model and the incidental parameters η_k and P_k. In this study, we used the method proposed in Mroz (1997). We parameterized η_k and P_k and then we maximized the likelihood function with respect to all the parameters of the model simultaneously (including the parameters describing η_k and P_k).[2] The location and scale of the distribution of v was not identified. Because both the rehabilitation and the outcome equations contained an intercept and we estimated both factor loading parameters α_1 and α_2, in our parameterization, η_k was restricted to be between 0 and 1 with $\eta_0 = 0$ and $\eta_k = 1$.

No standard theory exists regarding selection of the number of points of support, K, in a finite sample. Some studies have fixed the number of points of support in advance (Goldman 1995) while others add points of support until the likelihood fails to improve (Cameron and Heckman 1998, Heckman and Singer 1984). In this study, we followed the latter approach. We used Akaike's (1973) information criterion to decide on the number of points. According to this criterion, an additional point should be added if the maximized likelihood increases by more than three units for the first point and for more than two units for any extra point.

6 RESULTS

6.1 Descriptive Statistics

Overall, 51 percent of sample persons received some rehabilitation following the index hospital stay. Comparing mean probabilities of receiving rehabilitation by diagnosis, probabilities were higher for patients admitted for problems related to the musculosketetal system than for those admitted for problems of the nervous system (Table 5.1). Among musculoskeletal patients, persons admitted for hip fracture were more likely to have received rehabilitation than were those in MDC 8 admitted for other reasons. Similarly, stroke patients were more likely to have received rehabilitation than were other patients in the nervous system category.

On average, for those receiving any rehabilitation after the index hospital stay, the mean value of Medicare payments for rehabilitation within six months of index admission was $5968 (1994 dollars). But there was substantial variation in such payments. The standard deviation was larger than the mean, $7367. This dispersion reflected a long right tail (Figure 5.1). The minimum value for those with some rehabilitation was $13. The maximum was over $50 000. (Values in the upper tail are not shown in the figure.)

Table 5.1 Probability of receiving rehabilitation by diagnosis

Diagnosis	Probability
Nervous system	
Ischemic stroke	0.53
Hemorraghic stroke	0.52
Other	0.31
Musculoskeletal system	
Pertrochanteric hip fracture	0.70
Other hip fracture	0.75
Other	0.53

Variable means and standard deviations are presented in Table 5.2. Many sample persons fell in the 'oldest old' category. The mean age was 79 years with a standard deviation of over seven years. More persons were not married than married, most were female and white. Most reported that they had communicated with a child within 30 days of the 1989 NLTCS interview before the index admission. Fewer than one-tenth had been diagnosed with dementia.

6.2   Receipt of Rehabilitation

Older and more educated persons were more likely to have received rehabilitation (Table 5.3). Having more severe comorbidities at the index admission led to higher probability of receiving rehabilitation afterwards. Persons in the 'other hip fracture' category, the omitted reference group, were more likely to have received rehabilitation.   Persons who had been intubated during the index admission were less likely to receive rehabilitation, not surprising since such persons had a lower probability of surviving. Persons with any paralysis were more likely to get rehabilitation, suggesting that the marginal benefit for such persons is relatively high. Among variables describing functional and cognitive status at the interview before the index admission, having been cognitively aware and having lived in the community led to a higher probability of receipt of rehabilitation after the index admission.

Married persons were less likely to have received rehabilitation, suggesting that rehabilitation may be a partial substitute for informal care. This extends the Kramer et al. (1997) finding that those receiving rehabilitation in a skilled nursing facility were more likely not to be

Table 5.2 Means and standard deviations

Variable	Mean	SD
Dependent		
Rehabilitation	0.51	0.50
Rehabilitation $		
Death within 12 months	0.21	0.41
Death within 24 months	0.29	0.45
Live in community – after	0.81	0.39
Cognitively aware – after	0.30	0.46
ADLs same or better – after	0.54	0.50
IADLs same or better – after	0.36	0.46
Explanatory		
Age	79.4	7.55
Married	0.44	0.50
Male	0.34	0.47
Education (yrs)	9.67	2.36
White	0.93	0.26
Income ('0000$)	1.77	0.87
Comorbidity index	1.95	2.81
Intubated	0.012	0.11
Paralysis	0.052	0.22
Alzheimer's disease	0.074	0.26
ADLs – before	0.68	1.47
Cognitively aware – before	0.23	0.42
Lived in community – before	0.94	0.23
Had contact with children within 30 days of interview – before	0.73	0.44
Had problems with bowel or bladder – before	0.050	0.22
Major teaching hospital	0.15	0.36
Minor teaching hospital	0.11	0.32
Hospital has rehab.	0.73	0.45
Hospital has contract for rehab.	0.044	0.20
Population density	0.56	0.79
Rehab. beds/1000 pop.	7.95	15.8
Wage index ('000)	9.75	1.68
AAPCC	3.45	0.83

Table 5.3 Determinants of probability of receipt of rehabilitation and Medicare program cost for rehabilitation conditional on receipt

Variable	Probability		Cost	
Age	0.013[b]	(0.0052)	0.018[b]	(0.0083)
Married	−0.17[b]	(0.082)	−0.0071	(0.13)
Male	−0.064	(0.078)	−0.074	(0.13)
Education (yrs)	0.045[a]	(0.016)	−0.0046	(0.025)
White	0.043	(0.14)	−0.20	(0.23)
Income ('0000$)	−0.0024	(0.0044)	0.077	(0.065)
Comorbidity index	0.037[a]	(0.013)	0.054[a]	(0.020)
Intubated	−0.93[b]	(0.39)	1.31	(0.93)
Paralysis	0.74[a]	(0.17)	0.76[a]	(0.23)
Dementia	−0.12	(0.14)	−0.0049	(0.22)
Pertrochantric hip fracture	−0.20	(0.18)	0.24	(0.22)
Other musculoskeletal	−0.55[a]	(0.14)	−0.34	(0.18)
Ischemic stroke	−0.75[a]	(0.16)	0.40	(0.22)
Hemorraghic stroke	−0.52[b]	(0.26)	−0.54	(0.39)
Other nervous	−1.21[a]	(0.15)	−0.20	(0.21)
Had contact children within 30 days – before	0.15	(0.10)	–	–
Cognitively aware – before	0.20[b]	(0.10)	−0.050	(0.14)
Lived in community – before	0.78[a]	(0.22)	1.06[a]	(0.38)
ADLs – before	0.051	(0.037)	0.053	(0.053)
Had problems with bowel/ bladder – before	0.057	(0.17)	0.15	(0.26)
Major teaching hospital	0.15	(0.10)	−0.019	(0.16)
Minor teaching hospital	−0.066	(0.11)	0.16	(0.18)
Hospital has rehab.	0.095	(0.088)	−0.11	(0.14)
Hospital has contract for rehab.	0.17	(0.18)	0.40	(0.28)
Population density	−0.16[a]	(0.062)	0.12	(0.11)
Rehab. beds/1000 pop.	−0.0069	(0.0047)	0.0090[a]	(0.0034)
(Rehab. beds/1000 pop.)^2	0.00011	(0.00007)	–	–
Wage index	0.41[b]	(0.20)	0.076	(0.042)
Wage index^2	−0.000015	(0.000009)	–	–
AAPCC	−0.014	(0.31)	0.60	(0.47)
AAPCC^2	0.0043	(0.041)	−0.10	(0.061)
Trend	0.065	(0.041)	0.18[a]	(0.065)
Constant	−4.31[a]	(1.14)	3.32[a]	(1.25)
			$R^2 = 0.14$	
			$R^2 (C) = 0.11$	
	$N = 1493$		$N = 760$	

Notes
[a] Significant at the 1% level (two-tail test).
[b] Significant at the 5% level (two-tail test).

married or not to have a willing and able caregiver. Having had children with whom the sample person had been in contact before the index admission did not have a statistically significant impact on the probability of receipt. However, the sign on the coefficient was positive and appreciably larger than its standard error. The role of children is complex. Perhaps rather than substituting for informal care, having children to act as advocates leads to pressures on health caregivers to take advantage of Medicare's rehabilitation benefit.

Among explanatory variables defined for the person's PSU, people in higher population density areas were less likely to have received any rehabilitation. By contrast, F-tests revealed that higher wage rates in an area led to a higher probability of receipt of rehabilitation. None of the measures of rehabilitation availability had statistically significant impacts. The coefficient for the time trend indicates a secular trend in the probability of receiving rehabilitation during the first half of the 1990s. Likelihood ratio test results demonstrated significance of the entire set of exclusion restrictions at $\alpha = 0.01$.

6.3   Rehabilitation Medicare Program Cost

Some of the same explanatory variables influenced Medicare spending for rehabilitation among those who received some rehabilitation. Age, the cormorbidity index, and paralysis had positive effects. Greater rehabilitation hospital bed availability in the PSU increased Medicare spending for rehabilitation. This is plausible since hospital-based rehabilitation is relatively costly (Kramer et al. 1997).

6.4   Effects of Receipt of Rehabilitation on Health Outcomes

Using probit, persons who received rehabilitation after the index hospital stay were more likely to live for a year after the index health event occurred (Table 5.4). Living for two years was more likely, but being cognitively aware, and having the same number or fewer limitations in activities of daily living and in instrumental activities of daily living at the 1994 NLTCS interview were all less likely if the persons had had rehabilitation. None of the latter results were statistically significant at the 5 percent level or better, but the results for ADLs and IADLs were nearly so.

When we controlled for endogeneity with GMM/IV, signs on the coefficients reversed in the analysis of mortality. For persons who had had rehabilitation, death at one and at two years was more likely. This change suggests that persons at high risk for death were less likely to receive

Table 5.4 Effects of rehabilitation receipt on health outcomes

Dependent variable	Estimator	Coefficient	Std. error
Death within 12 months	Probit	−0.18[b]	0.085
	GMM/IV	0.45	0.84
Death within 24 months	Probit	−0.092	0.081
	GMM/IV	0.18[a]	0.72
Live in community – after	Probit	0.030	0.11
	GMM/IV	0.85	0.87
Cognitively aware – after	Probit	−0.044	0.11
	GMM/IV	−1.23	1.04
ADLs same or better – after	Probit	−0.17[c]	0.10
	GMM/IV	2.06	1.96
IADLs same or better – after	Probit	−0.26	0.14
	GMM/IV	−0.17	0.64

Notes
Endogenous variable was a binary equal to 1 when a person received some rehabilitation.
[a] Significant at the 1% level (two-tail test).
[b] Significant at the 5% level (two-tail test).
[c] Significant at the 10% level (two-tail test).

rehabilitation, a finding in line with descriptive findings for the effect of intubation (negative) and living in the community in 1989 (positive) on receipt of rehab. When we controlled for endogeneity, the negative signs disappeared.

For cognitive and functional status, conditional on surviving to the next NLTCS interview, we only observed a sign reversal for ADLs same or better. This result implies that receipt of rehabilitation is productive in terms of improved ability to perform such activities. However, the coefficient is not statistically significant at conventional levels.

6.5   Effects of Rehabilitation Spending on Health Outcomes

For those who received rehabilitation, we tested the effect of the amount of rehabilitation spending on the health outcomes. The results are listed in Table 5.5. Our discrete factor model with one point of support yielded probit results, unadjusted for unobserved factors. We added points of support to account for the unmeasured heterogeneity. Applying Akaike's criterion led us to four points of support for the IADL-same-or-better outcome and three points of support for each of the other five outcome

Table 5.5 Effects of rehabilitation amount on health outcomes

Dependent variable	Estimator	Coefficient	Std. error	Likelihood function	Points
Death within 12 months	Probit	−0.044	0.038	−1673.89	1
	Discrete factor	−0.047	0.128	−1629.88	3
Death within 24 months	Probit	−0.044	0.036	−1718.18	1
	Discrete factor	−0.079	0.125	−1674.12	3
Live in community – after	Probit	−0.068	0.050	−1243.34	1
	Discrete factor	0.128	0.148	−1209.77	3
Cognitively aware – after	Probit	0.032	0.043	−1288.36	1
	Discrete factor	−0.109	0.137	−1255.13	3
ADLs same or better – after	Probit	−0.153[a]	0.043	−1154.84	1
	Discrete factor	−0.0302	0.126	−1125.5	3
IADLs same or better – after	Probit	−0.050	0.058	− 746.31	1
	Discrete factor	0.103	0.253	− 713.15	4

Note: Sample included those persons receiving some rehabilitation; the endogenous variable was cost of rehabilitation received.

measures. We rejected the null hypothesis of no unmeasured heterogeneity in each of the six estimations.

For all outcomes assessed, the intensity of rehabilitation was endogenous to the outcome. In only one case was there a significant finding for rehabilitation intensity, decreasing the probability of ADLs being the same or better in a probit estimation. However, this result did not hold when unobserved factors were included. After accounting for unmeasured heterogeneity, there were no significant findings for intensity of rehabilitation on mortality, living in the community, cognition, or activity limitations. Rehabilitation was not productive at the margin after appropriately controlling for unmeasured variables. These unobserved factors should have led to systematic selection of persons who are more likely to improve or to survive to receive more intensive rehabilitation.

Table 5.5 only reports the rehabilitation intensity coefficients for the six outcomes to focus on the key results. Many of the remaining coefficients were statistically significant and intuitively clear. For example, one-year mortality rates rose significantly with age, being male, living in the community in 1989, and with the comorbidity index. The probability of death within one year of the hospital discharge was significantly reduced by being married, by recovering from an 'other musculoskeletal' shock and by being treated at a major teaching hospital.

Age was statistically significant in four of the six outcome estimations, increasing the probability of mortality at one and at two years after release from the hospital, decreasing the probabilities of living in the community in 1994, and of having the same or fewer ADL limitations. The number of ADLs in 1989 was negatively related to living in the community and being cognitive aware in 1994, but was positively related to having the same or fewer ADLs and IADLs in 1994. Recovery from an ischemic stroke made it less likely that a person lived in the community or had the same or fewer ADLs or IADLs in 1994. The only factor that was significant for all six outcomes was the comorbidity index, reducing the probability of the favorable health outcome in each case.

7 DISCUSSION

Rehabilitation services are among the fastest growing types of services in the Medicare program. Understanding whether or not such care is productive at the margin is of great policy and clinical significance. Overall, we found that rehabilitation is not productive in terms of improved health. Our research was based on a national sample for the United States, and we controlled for unmeasured heterogeneity. We found that there is little effect of rehabilitation beyond selection. This is an average marginal effect. Such care may be productive for certain types of elderly patients.

We did not attempt to investigate this more detailed issue for two reasons. The first was lack of sufficient statistical power to identify variations in subgroups of Medicare beneficiaries. Second, patient type is not a criterion for Medicare coverage of rehabilitation services. Thus from the vantage point of public policy, more, rather than fewer, aggregate effects are relevant.

Findings from previous studies are conflicting. The literature to date shows some impact on mortality among stroke patients and less often on other outcomes. For hip fracture, the results overall do not indicate that rehabilitation is productive. Generalization is made difficult because of variation in methodologies, for example, controls for selection into rehabilitation to isolate selection from treatment effects and in study samples. Most past research on this topic has been based on localized samples, generally much smaller than ours.

For stroke, there is some evidence that rehabilitation is effective but, even here, the evidence is conflicting. A review by Cifu and Stewart (1999) of the medical literature from 1950 to 1998 summarized 79 articles examining relationships between rehabilitation interventions and functional outcome after stroke. Two findings are noteworthy. First, functional status at admission to rehabilitation had a strong relationship to outcome. Second, intensity of rehabilitation services was weakly associated with improved functional status after stroke. Flick (1999) contradicted this second point, concluding that several studies demonstrate benefits from physical therapy, occupational therapy, and speech therapy in chronic stroke patients. An analysis of ten randomized controlled trials found a significant reduction in mortality for patients in specialized stroke units (Langhorne et al. 1993). A meta-analysis found moderate functional improvements in stroke units relative to usual care, especially for younger patients – younger than the persons in our sample (Ottenbacher and Jannell 1993).

For hip fracture, the evidence on the effects of rehabilitation leads to a more pessimistic conclusion. Early studies suggested no benefits of intensive hospital rehabilitation (Jette et al. 1987), but more recent evidence implies that more intensive rehabilitation leads to better outcomes (Gerety et al. 1989; Bonar et al. 1990; Zuckerman et al. 1992). In a localized study, Levi (1997) reported no difference in older women's ability to care for themselves within six months of the fracture, depending on where they received their posthospital care.

The most comprehensive study of the effect of rehabilitation on outcome measures was conducted by Kramer et al. (1997), who examined outcomes and cost of 518 randomly selected patients with hip fractures and 485 patients with stroke. For stroke, patients admitted for more intensive rehabilitation of the type provided by hospital-based rehabilitation facilities were more likely to return to the community and to recover from limitations in activities of daily living. Following hip fracture, outcome improvements were due to selection effects (endogeneity) instead of treatment effects. Kramer and coauthors (1997) concluded that, for hip fracture patients, based on outcomes, admission to the more intensive rehabilitation programs provided by hospital-based facilities was not worth the extra cost to Medicare. The Kramer et al. study was based on a broader sample (92 hospital-based rehabilitation facilities and 92 units based in skilled nursing facilities in 17 states) than most research on this topic which has been typically based on single-site reports. However, their sample only included persons who received rehabilitation in an inpatient setting (either a hospital or a skilled nursing facility). Limiting the sample to persons receiving rehabilitation in a hospital or nursing home yields findings that cannot generalize to rehabilitation provided in all settings.

In spite of hip fracture and stroke being commonly rehabilitated conditions, half of our stroke sample did not receive rehabilitation; nor did 20 percent of the hip fractures. Focusing on those receiving some rehabilitation in the hospital or nursing home produces a different type of selection bias than that associated with choice of site of rehabilitation, which the Kramer paper dealt with.

The use of claims data potentially allowed for a larger and more nationally representative sample than one based on data collected from facilities. However, because we did not obtain data abstracted from medical records, expressly for research rather for administrative purposes, we lacked measures of shock severity. For example, some stroke victims may have been admitted in a coma and discharged with serious impairments. Other stroke victims may have been relatively unimpaired. The discrete factor approach is specifically designed to cope with omitted heterogeneity.

Medicare spending in the United States is increasing at a pace far above the growth in prices and incomes (McClellan 2000). To cope with such expenditure growth and to improve resource allocation, it will be necessary to conduct rigorous research to learn more about the marginal benefits of various medical interventions. To achieve meaningful savings in program outlays, some reductions in quantity of services provided to program beneficiaries will be necessary (Fuchs 2000). In this study, we found that rehabilitation was not productive at the margin, implying that this deserves further scrutiny by the Medicare program. We suspect that analysis of other types of services using the analytic approaches used in this study will reveal other areas in which Medicare spending is not particularly productive with the ultimate goal of improving resource allocation of public monies.

NOTES

1. ADLs are very personal activities such as eating, dressing and bathing. IADLs refer to less personal activities such as doing laundry.
2. Because the likelihood function has multiple local optima, we used a grid of over 100 separate starting values.

REFERENCES

Akaike, H. (1973), 'Information theory and an extension of the maximum likelihood principle', in B. Perov and C. Csaki (eds), *Second International Symposium on Information Theory*, Budapest: Akademiai Kiado, pp. 267–81.

Bacon, W.E. (1996), 'Secular trends in hip fracture occurrence and survival: age and sex differences', *Journal of Aging and Health*, **8**(4):

538–53.

Bonar, S.K., M.E. Tinetti, M. Speechley and L.M. Cooney (1990), 'Factors associated with short- versus long-term skilled nursing facility placement among community-living hip fracture patients', *Journal of the American Geriatrics Society*, **38**: 1139–44.

Brainsky, A., H. Glick, E. Lydick, R. Epstein, K.M. Fox, W. Hawkes, T.M. Kashner, S.I. Zimmerman and J. Magaziner (1997), 'The economic cost of hip fractures in community-dwelling adults: a prospective study', *Journal of the American Geriatrics Society*, **45**: 281–7.

Broderick, J.P., S.J. Phillips, J.P. Whisnant, W.M. O'Fallon and E.J. Bergstrahlh (1989), 'Incidence rates of stroke in the eighties: the end of the decline of stroke', *Stroke*, **20**: 577–82.

Cameron, S.V. and C. Taber (1998), 'Discount rate bias in the returns to schooling', unpublished manuscript, Northwestern University.

Cameron, S.V. and J.J. Heckman (1998), 'Life cycle schooling and dynamic selection bias: models and evidence for five cohorts', *Journal of Political Economy*, **106**: 262–3.

Cano, C., K.D. Hennessy, J.L. Warren and J. Lubitz (1997), 'Medicare part a utilization and expenditures for psychiatric services: 1995', *Health Care Financing Review*, **18**: 177–93.

Chan, L., T.D. Koepsell, R.A. Devo, P.C. Esselman, J.K. Haselkorn, J.K. Lowery and W.C. Stolov (1997), 'The effect of medicare's payment system for rehabilitation hospitals on length of stay, charges, and total payments', *New England Journal of Medicine*, **337**(14): 978–83.

Cifu, D.A. and D.G. Stewart (1999), 'Factors affecting functional outcome after stroke: a critical review of rehabilitation interventions', *Archives of Physical Medicine and Rehabilitation*, **80**: S35–S39.

Cooney, L.M. (1997), 'Do we understand the true cost of hip fractures?', *Journal of the American Geriatrics Society*, **45**: 382–3.

Cooper, R., C. Sempos, S.C. Hsieh and M.G. Kover (1990), 'Slowdown in the decline of stroke mortality in the United States, 1978–1986', *Stroke*, **21**: 1274–9.

Davidson, R. and J.G. Mackinnon (1993), *Estimation and Inference in Econometrics*, New York: Oxford University Press.

Dombovy, M.L., J.R. Basford, J.P. Whisnant and E.J. Bergstralh (1987), 'Disability and use of rehabilitation services following stroke in Rochester, Minnesota, 1975–1979', *Stroke*, **18**: 830–6.

DxCG Inc. (1996), *DxCG Software Version: 02e (Medicare) Program Documentation and User's Manual*, Walham, MA: DxCG.

Ellis, R.P., G.C. Pope, L.I. Iezzoni, J.Z. Ayanian, D.W. Bates, H. Burstin and A.S. Ash (1996), 'Diagnosis-based risk adjustment for Medicare capitation payments', *Health Care Financing Review*, **17**: 101–28.

Flick, C.L. (1999), 'Stroke rehabilitation. 4. Stroke outcome and psychosocial consequences', *Archives of Physical Medicine and Rehabilitation*, **80**: S-21–S-26.

Folland, S., A.C. Goodman and M. Stano (1997), *The Economics of Health and Health Care*, Upper Saddle River, NJ: Prentice Hall.

Fuchs, V.R. (2000), 'Medicare reform: the larger picture', *Journal of Economic Perspectives*, **14**(2): 57–70.

Gerety, M.B., V. Soderholm-Difatte and C.H. Winograd (1989), 'Impact of prospective payment and discharge location on the outcome of hip fracture', *Journal of General Internal Medicine*, **149**: 2237–41.

Goldman, D. (1995), 'Managed care as a public cost-containment mechanism', *RAND Journal of Economics*, **26**: 277–95.

Health Care Financing Review (1998), 'Trends in Medicare inpatient hospital and post-acute non-hospital benefit payments', Statistical Supplement.

Heckman, J. and B. Singer (1984), 'A method for minimizing the impact of distributional assumptions in econometric models for duration data', *Econometrica*, **52**: 271–320.

Horner, R.D., R.J. Sloane and K.L. Kahn (1998), 'Is use of medical ventilation a reasonable proxy indicator for coma among Medicare patients hospitalized for acute stroke?', *Health Services Research*, **32**(6): 841–59.

Jette, A.M., B.A. Harris, P.D. Cleary and E.W. Campion (1987), 'Functional recovery after hip fracture', *Archives of Physical Medical Rehabilitation*, **68**: 735–40.

Koval, K.J. and J.D. Zuckerman (1994), 'Functional recovery after fracture of the hip', *Journal of Bone Joint Surgery Annals*, **76A**: 751–8.

Kramer, A.M., J.F. Steiner, R.E. Schlenker, T.B. Ellertsen, C.A. Hrincevich, D.A. Tropea, L.A. Ahmad and D.G. Eckhoff (1997), 'Outcomes and costs after hip fracture and stroke', *Journal of the American Medical Association*, **277**(5): 396–404.

Langhorne, P., B.O. Williams, W. Gilchrist and K. Howie (1993), 'Do stroke units save lives?', *Lancet*, **342**: 395–8.

Lee, A.J., J. Huber and W.B. Stason (1996), 'Poststroke rehabilitation in older Americans: the Medicare experience', *Medical Care*, **34**(8): 811–25.

Levi, S.J. (1997), 'Posthospital setting, resource utilization, and self-care outcome in older women with hip fracture', *Archives of Physical Medicine and Rehabilitation*, **78**: 973–9.

Lindsay, B. (1983), 'The geometry of mixture likelihoods: a general theory', *Annals of Statistics*, **11**: 86–94.

Manton, K.G., E. Stallard and L. Corder (1995), 'Changes in morbidity and chronic disability in the U.S. elderly population: evidence from the 1982, 1984, 1989 national long-term care surveys', *Journal of Gerontology and Social Sciences*, **50B**: S194–S204.

McClellan, M. (2000), 'Medicare reform: fundamental steps', *Journal of Economic Perspectives*, **14**(2): 21–44.

Mroz, T. (1997), 'Discrete factor approximations in simultaneous equation models: estimating the impact of a dummy endogenous variable on a continuous outcome', mimeo, University of North Carolina, Chapel Hill.

Newcomer, R., T. Clay, J.S. Luxenberg and R.H. Miller (1999), 'Misclassification and selection bias when identifying Alzheimer's disease solely from Medicare claims records', *Journal of the American Geriatrics Society*, **47**: 215–9.

Ottenbacher, K.J. and S. Jannell (1993), 'The results of clinical trials in stroke rehabilitation research', *Archives of Neurology*, **50**: 37–44.

Pfeiffer, E. (1975), 'A short portable mental status questionnaire for the assessment of organic brain deficit in elderly patients', *Journal of the American Geriatrics Society*, **23**: 433–41.

Picone, G., F.A. Sloan, S.-Y. Chou and D.H. Taylor (1999), 'Does high hospital cost imply higher quality of care?', unpublished manuscript.

River, D. and Q. Vuong (1988), 'Limited information estimators and exogeneity tests for simultaneous probit models', *Journal of Econometrics*, **39**: 347–66.

Schlenker, R.E., A.M. Kramer, C.A. Hrincevich and T.B. Eilertsen (1997), 'Rehabilitation costs: implications for prospective payment', *Health Services Research*, **32**(5): 651–68.

Sloan, F.A., D.H. Taylor and G. Picone (1999), 'Costs and outcomes of hip fracture and stroke,1984 to 1994', *American Journal of Public Health*, **89**(6): 935–7.

Staiger, D. and J. Stock (1997), 'Instrumental variables regression with weak instruments', *Econometrica*, **65**: 557–86.

Taylor, D., D. Whellan and F. Sloan (1999), 'Effects of admission to teaching hospitals on cost and quality of care: evidence from Medicare', *New England Journal of Medicine*, **340**(4): 293–9.

US Department of Health and Human Services (1995), 'Post-stroke rehabilitation', Clinical Practice Guideline, Agency for Health Care Policy and Research, ACPHR Pub. No. 95-0662, May.

US Medicare Payment Advisory Commission (1998), 'Hospitalization and post-acute care utilization', in *Report to Congress: Context for a Changing Medicare Program*, Washington, DC: US Government Printing Office, pp. 89–114.

Wolf, P.A., R.B. D'Agostino and P.A. O'Neal (1992), 'Secular trends in stroke incidence and mortality: the Framingham Study', *Stroke*, **23**(11): 1551–5.
Zuckerman, J.D., S.R. Sakales, D.R. Fabian and V.H. Frankel (1992), 'Hip fractures in geriatric patients: results of an interdisciplinary hospital care program', *Clinica Orthopedics*, **274**: 213–25.

6. Do investments in child education and nutrition improve adult health? Evidence from Indonesia

Paul Gertler and Jennifer Zeitlin

1 INTRODUCTION

Large declines in fertility and mortality are causing the populations of many developing countries to age rapidly (Kinsella 1988; World Bank 1995a). As a result of this shift in the population age structure, these countries will soon be confronted with the health problems of large cohorts of elderly. Concurrent decreases in rates of infectious diseases also contribute to this health transition in which adult health concerns will become higher priority areas for health policy (Feachem et al. 1992).

The economic and social implications of an aging population are important since adult ill health has direct productivity losses (World Bank 1991; Strauss and Thomas 1995), imposes indirect costs on families coping with adult ill health (Over et al. 1992), and places large demands on health care systems. In particular, treating the chronic illnesses associated with aging is more expensive than addressing the acute infectious illnesses associated with younger populations. In addition, formal institutions that provide financial support for the elderly such as social security and health insurance cover only a small fraction of the elderly in most developing countries (Martin 1989; Ju and Jones 1989; World Bank 1995b). In the absence of these institutions, families will be responsible for the financial and social consequences of adult ill health.

Despite its relevance to policy and in contrast to child health, little is known about the socioeconomic determinants of adult health in developing countries. Of particular interest is the question we address in this chapter: the impact of education and health investments in childhood and on later health. Understanding how the large secular shifts in educational attainment and childhood nutrition and health in developing countries will affect adult health is important for predictions about the health status of future generations. If higher educational levels and improved health at younger ages are associated with better health outcomes later in life, this may mitigate predictions about levels of morbidity and mortality in the next generation of elderly. These links between childhood and adulthood also imply that policies to improve adult health cannot neglect educational and health investments for children. Considering the longer-term health benefits of investments in education also provides a broader perspective for evaluating the benefits of educational policies. These benefits are traditionally measured as increases in market productivity. Yet education influences many other aspects of welfare by improving basic capabilities (Sen 1982), such as good health.

Studies from Western Europe and the United States find that education and child health are significant determinants of adult health (Adler et al. 1993; Elo and Preston 1992; Machenbach et al. 1997; Smith and Kington 1997). The posited mechanisms underlying these associations vary, but multiple processes are most likely to be involved (Lichtenstein et al. 1992). Illnesses in childhood, such as respiratory tuberculosis, hepatitis B, and acute rheumatic fever, have a direct impact on the risk of mortality and ill health in adulthood, while poor childhood nutrition is linked to an elevated risk of cardiovascular disease (Elo and Preston 1992). Education affects later health by influencing occupational choices and thus exposure to health risks and income levels as well as behavioral choices such as diet, smoking, and use of preventive health services (Adler et al. 1993; Machenbach et al. 1997).

Investigating the link between socioeconomic factors and adult health status is a challenging undertaking because of the complexities of determining causality and measuring health status. Establishing causal relationships is particularly difficult for measures of wealth, since ill health has a direct impact on current earning capacity and may hide a cumulative negative effect of ill health on resource accumulation (Smith and Kington 1997). This problem is minimized in analyses that focus on childhood investments since by definition these are not affected by health status in adulthood.   However, other unobservable endowments, such as family background characteristics and genetic endowments, still make it difficult to establish causality. As first discussed in the wage literature, individuals from better family backgrounds are likely to earn higher wages (and be healthier), independently of what they learn in school because of the greater investments they receive during childhood (Strauss and Thomas 1995). At the same time, individuals from more advantaged family backgrounds are more likely to complete a higher level of schooling. If family background characteristics are not taken into consideration, the estimate of the impact of schooling will be biased upwards. The same arguments apply to measures of the impact of childhood health status on adult health outcomes – better health status in childhood can reflect a range of different influences linked to family background and genetic endowments.

Measuring health status is the second challenge facing researchers, especially in developing countries. The absence of reliable civil registration systems makes it impossible to replicate the methodological approaches of studies from developed countries, which link mortality outcomes to individual characteristics. A commonly used approach is surveys of self-reported morbidity.[1] Most of this work, however, finds that individuals with higher levels of education report more illness. In a review of the self-reported morbidity literature, Hill and Mamdani (1989) conclude that these results are due to reporting bias rather than real effects. Better-educated individuals tend to report more minor problems than do less educated individuals. Minor illnesses, which are endemic in poorer, less educated populations, are often not reported as health problems since they are perceived to be part of the normal health state.

The most informative studies have focused on mortality and indeed find large impacts of education on longevity.[2] However, mortality tells us little about the health of the individuals who survive. In a review of the literature on adult health in developing countries, Feachem et al. (1992) focus almost exclusively on mortality. Morbidity is discussed in Chapter three, which is entitled 'Limited Data and Methodological Uncertainty.'

One study to overcome these data limitations used self-reported indicators of physical functioning to measure adult health and showed that these measures did not suffer from the same reporting bias as self-reported morbidity (Strauss et al. 1994). Using data from Jamaica, the authors found education to be a significant and important predictor of better health status for both males and females, and found the effects to be stronger for younger adults.

We investigate the link between investments in education and nutrition in childhood and the impact on adult health using the Indonesian Family Life Survey (IFLS), a multipurpose household survey conducted in 1993. The IFLS is a random sample of about 7000 households representing approximately 85 percent of the Indonesian Population (Frankenberg and Karoly 1995). The IFLS collected validated self-reported measures of physical functioning abilities and adult anthropometric measurements from which we construct indicators of chronic energy deficiency and obesity. The IFLS also collected information on the characteristics of the parents and siblings of adults. These characteristics allow us to control for family background in the analysis.

We begin the analysis by describing the institutional context of the study setting. Next, we describe the measures of health status, then we specify an economic model of human capital investment based on Grossman (1972) that provides an empirical specification. The next section describes the data and presents the results of the empirical models; these results are discussed in the concluding section.

2   THE STUDY SETTING

Indonesia is a particularly rich setting for this research. It is the fourth most populous country in the world with tremendous cultural and economic diversity. Indonesia has the tenth largest elderly population in the world, and the elderly comprise a rapidly increasing share of its population. Between 1971 and 1985 the total population of Indonesia increased by 39 percent, while the population over 65 increased by 88 percent, and the population over 75 increased by 109 percent. In 1990, 6.4 percent of Indonesians were aged 60 or older with a ratio of 1.1 females to every male. The percent elderly is expected to increase to 7.3 percent by 2000 and to 14.1 percent by 2030 (World Bank 1995a).

Over the last 20 years the living standards of Indonesians have improved dramatically. Though economic growth has been impressive with an average real per annual capita growth rate of 3.9 percent over the last 15 years, per capita incomes are still low, at $US880 per year in 1996 (Asian Development Bank 1997). Indonesia has also seen remarkable improvements in health status. Between 1970 and 1991 the total fertility rate of Indonesia decreased from 5.5 to 3.0, life expectancy at birth rose from around 48 years to 60 years, and infant mortality fell by about 35 percent, and child mortality decreased 68 percent to 111 per thousand (World Bank 1995b). Similarly, there have been commensurate gains in education and in controlling population growth. Enrollment rates of children in primary schooling have increased from 60 percent in 1971 to 94 percent in 1985, and total fertility rates have fallen from 5.6 in 1970 to 3.0 in 1990 (World Bank 1995b).

Indonesia has invested heavily to develop a comprehensive government-operated health care delivery system. Recent investments have focused on the primary care network. A wide range of primary care services are available from government health centers, including curative outpatient and limited inpatient treatment; maternal and child health care services; nutrition services; family planning services; community health education and outreach; and dental treatment. By 1991, there was at least one health center and several sub-centers in each of Indonesia's 3400 sub-districts. A network of government-operated hospitals at the district, provincial and central levels backs up Indonesia's large primary care system. Despite the large increase in government spending on health care, however, Indonesia's health care expenditures remain low relative to those of its neighbors (World Bank 1995b). In 1990, annual expenditures on health care from both public and private sources were only about $12 per person which amounted to about 2 percent of GDP.

Few individuals in Indonesia are covered by health insurance other than the implicit insurance provided through the almost free public health care system; on average, user fees at public facilities amount to 5 percent of average costs (World Bank 1995b). While the public health care system provides extensive primary care services, its hospital care is more limited. Moreover, many individuals opt to pay out of pocket for higher quality private sector services as over half of all utilization is provided by the private sector (Gertler and Molyneaux 1996). About 10 percent of the population are covered by health insurance provided to civil servants. However, this insurance only covers utilization of public facilities and, therefore, the benefit to the individual is only to cover the small user fees. An additional 4 percent of the population are covered by health insurance offered through employers, but this insurance typically has capped benefits, minimizing absenteeism from minor illnesses but not paying the costs of major illness (Dow and Gertler 1997). Similarly, there is limited disability insurance as there is no government program, over two-thirds of workers are self-employed, and few firms provide extensive sick leave.

3 MEASURING ADULT HEALTH STATUS

3.1 Issues and Methods

Measuring adult health is a challenging task for both conceptual and methodological reasons. Mortality data, the most commonly used analytic tool for describing adult health status, does not portray the levels of health and disability among individuals who are still alive. Yet this information is essential for health planners and may better measure the levels of well-being within a population. Reported morbidity provides information on acute, readily perceived illnesses, but not other health problems such as hypertension or anemia, unless previously diagnosed. Even clinical evaluations of health status show considerable discrepancy with individuals' own perceptions of their health state (Murray and Chen 1992). There is no clear answer to these conceptual dilemmas, except to acknowledge that health has many dimensions. Each indicator when well constructed can be considered a valuable measure of health.

Of more concern for analyses of the determinants of health status are the biases linked to measurement of health indices. In particular, the reporting bias linked to self-reported or proxy reported morbidity data makes it difficult to differentiate between determinants of reporting behavior and those of underlying health status. Studies of reported illness tend to find higher levels of morbidity among wealthier and more educated individuals (Hill and Mamdani 1989; also see studies by Murray and Chen 1992; Over et al. 1992; and Schultz and Tanzel 1992). Other approaches, such as using facility based statistics or health service utilization patterns, are seriously flawed because of the selection bias associated with the decision to seek care. Data on mortality are free from these types of selection bias, but accurate measurement of mortality rates is difficult in countries without adequate registration systems. Moreover, mortality misses many of the dimensions of health associated with morbidity, especially those that are not life threatening.

This analysis uses three approaches to measuring adult health. The first approach is based on measures of physical functioning (or activities of daily living (ADL) measures) and the second uses anthropometric measurements of weight and height to define the prevalence of chronic energy deficiency and obesity. We also include a self-assessment of general health status. Although general health questions have been criticized for their sensitivity to financial incentives and individual motivations in the literature on health and retirement in the United States (Bound 1991; Stern 1989), they have been found to be good predictors of future mortality (Idler and Kasl 1991). In an Indonesian context, where disability benefits are not widespread, financial incentives to define oneself as disabled may be less important. The link between these measures of health status and mortality has not been assessed in a developing country context, however.

Physical functioning measures are based on individuals' self-ratings of ability to engage in specific activities. These assessments are then combined to create scores capturing various dimensions of physical functioning. Initially developed for studying levels of disability among the elderly, these measures are used increasingly to study the health status of all adults. Physical functioning measures have been tested extensively for reliability (consistency between tests and interviewers) and validity (consistency between individual assessments of different skills). In the United States and South-East Asia, they have been found to be reliable and individual assessments have a high degree of internal consistency (Andrews et al. 1986; Guralnik et al. 1989; Jitapunkul et al. 1994; Ju and Jones 1989; Ware et al. 1980). These measures also appear to be less sensitive to reporting bias. In an analysis of ADL data from Jamaica, Malaysia and Bangladesh, Strauss et al. (1994) found that physical functioning measures were not positively correlated with education levels. A positive association between better health and higher socioeconomic status has been found in the United States (Strauss et al. 1994).

Health status can also be measured using data on nutritional state. Adequate energy intakes are essential for maintaining health and productivity. Long-term deprivation leads to chronic energy deficiency (CED), defined as 'a steady state at which a person is in energy balance although at a "cost" either in terms of risk to health or as an impairment of function and health' (James et al. 1988, p. 969). CED has been associated with a greater risk of illness, lower physical activity levels, and low birth weight babies (see, for example, Deolalikar 1988; Durnin 1994; Ferro-Luzzi et al. 1992; Garcia and Kennedy 1994; Immink and Viteri 1981; Kennedy and Garcia 1994; Kusin et al. 1994).

In research on children, body weight and height are commonly used to define nutritional state. For adults, however, the criteria for defining under-nutrition are less well defined and attempts to develop reference standards for CED are recent. Definitions of CED can be based on energy intake, expenditure, therapeutic tests, or a 'state of the body' which is not compatible with an acceptable level of function and health. The International Dietary Energy Consultative Group adopted this last approach, using body mass index (weight (kg) divided by height (m) squared) to develop criteria for defining CED (Ferro-Luzzi et al. 1992; James et al. 1988). Based on reviews of population studies of body mass index in the developed and developing world and existing studies of the impact of BMI on productivity and illness, they defined CED as a BMI of under 18.5 with the following grades: grade I: 17–18.5, II: 16–16.99, III < 16. Initially, a measure of physical activity level (PAL) was associated with these cut-off points, but that additional criterion did not improve identification of CED (Ferro-Luzzi et al. 1992). It should be noted that although body weight and height are 'objective measures', there is not yet a clear consensus on the definition of cut-off points for determining CED and this definition is still evolving.[3]

In these analyses, we also include a measure of obesity defined as a BMI greater or equal to 25 in accordance with Ferro-Luzzi et al. (1992). Severe obesity has long been known to have a detrimental affect on health (Mann 1974; Van Itallie 1979) and moderate obesity has been linked with higher morbidity and mortality (Larsson et al. 1981; Manson et al. 1995). The prevalence of obesity in developing countries, in tandem with other risk factors for cardiovascular disease, is increasing with potentially serious consequences for adult health in the future (INCLEN 1992).

Unlike the patterns observed in studies of obesity in the developed world, the prevalence of obesity tends to be positively associated with more education and higher incomes in developing countries (INCLEN 1994; Popkin et al. 1993; Sichieri et al. 1994; Sobal and Stunkard 1989).[4] While education and increasing income levels can have beneficial influences on health because of access to more and better quality foods, better hygiene and sanitation, and better medical care, they are also associated with the adoption of unhealthy behaviors such as high fat and alcohol intake, smoking and decreased exercise.

3.2   Descriptive Statistics

This analysis uses five different measures of adult health: a general health question, an index of intermediate functioning, an index of basic functioning and chronic energy deficiency, as defined by a BMI less than 18.5. We also include obesity, defined as a BMI of 25 or more. Table 6.1 describes these health measures and displays sample statistics for males and females.

The self-reported measure of general health has four possible responses: very healthy, somewhat healthy, somewhat unhealthy and unhealthy. For these analyses, individuals defining themselves as unhealthy are grouped together. The index for intermediate skills includes self-assessment of the ability to carry a heavy load 20 meters, to walk for 5 kilometers and to draw water from a well. Basic skills include the ability to stand up from sitting in a chair, to dress without help, and to go to the bathroom without help. Responses are: easily, with difficulty, and unable to do it, coded as 1, 2 and 3, respectively. Factor analysis was used to select appropriate questions and verify the internal consistency of the indices. As part of this process, several questions in the health module were excluded from the functioning indices. These were ability to sweep the floor, ability to bow or squat, and ability to stand from sitting on the floor. The factor analyses identified two clear groups which could be interpreted as moderate limitations (those questions chosen for the intermediate functioning score) and severe limitations (those chosen for the basic functioning score). The other questions were not consistently associated with either of these factors.

The selected questions for the functioning scores were combined in accordance with the following algorithm developed for the RAND Medical Outcome Study:

$$Function = \left[\frac{\text{Actual score} - \text{Lowest possible score}}{\text{Highest possible score} - \text{Lowest possible score}} \right] \times 100$$

Table 6.1 reports descriptive statistics for these measures and Table 6.2 presents associations between the health measures to verify the validity of these measures. All the health measures, with the exception of obesity, are highly correlated. Individuals who report themselves to be unhealthy are much more likely to report limitations in intermediate and basic functioning. The prevalence of CED is also higher among individuals reporting poor health or physical functioning limitations.

4   A CONCEPTUAL FRAMEWORK

In this section we specify a behavioral model of family investments in the health of family members. We use that model to motivate the empirical specification from which we will examine the socioeconomic determinants of health. The framework is a standard utility maximizing model in which families allocate resources between investments in health and non-health goods and services. Health is not purchased directly but rather is produced through a health production function. The health production function is the technological process that transforms inputs such as nutrition, medical care, and time use into health status. The investments are also constrained by individual and household resources.

We use the conceptual framework to motivate and specify reduced-form empirical models.

4.1   The Health Production Function

In order to identify the factors that directly affect health status, we first describe the biomedical technical relationship between investments and outcomes. Following Grossman (1972), health can be thought of as a form of human capital. An individual's health stock at any point in time is determined by an initial genetic endowment, subsequent behavioral choices (for example, nutrition, medical care, smoking, exercise), and exogenous shocks from the public health environment (for example, contracting cancer from toxic waste).

Over a period of time the change in an individual's health status is determined by a health production function. The health production function makes explicit the mechanism that transforms inputs consumed

Table 6.1 Measures of adult health, Indonesian Family Life survey, 1993

I General health question	Male	Female
% Very healthy	15.4%	14.0%
% Healthy	72.4%	72.8%
% Unhealthy	11.5%	12.7%
% Very unhealthy	0.6%	0.6%
N	5584	6774
II Intermediate functioning score	Male	Female
Carry a heavy load 20 meters		
Easily (1)	93.8%	88.3%
With difficulty (2)	3.3%	6.8%
Unable to do it (3)	3.0%	5.0%
Walk for 5 km		
Easily (1)	89.9%	78.6%
With difficulty (2)	5.9%	11.8%
Unable to do it (3)	4.2%	9.6%
Draw a pail of water from a well		
Easily (1)	96.2%	93.8%
With difficulty (2)	1.9%	3.2%
Unable to do it (3)	1.9%	3.1%
Average *score**	*4.9 (16.7)*	*9.5 (21.3)*
N	5584	6768
III Basic functioning score	Male	Female
Stand from a chair without help		
Easily (1)	98.4%	97.3%
With difficulty (2)	1.0%	1.9%
Unable to do it (3)	0.6%	0.8%
Dress without help		
Easily (1)	99.0%	98.7%
With difficulty (2)	0.5%	0.5%
Unable to do it (3)	0.6%	0.8%
To go to the bathroom without help		
Easily (1)	98.8%	98.4%
With difficulty (2)	0.6%	0.9%
Unable to do it (3)	0.6%	0.7%
Average *score**	*0.9 (8.0)*	*1.3 (9.3)*
N	5573	6765
IV Anthropometry	Male	Female
Average weight (kgs)	54.1 (9.2)	48.3 (9.4)
Average height (meters)	1.6 (.06)	1.5 (0.6)
Average BMI	21.0 (3.0)	21.7 (3.7)
% CED < 18.5	18.8%	17.8%
% Obese ≥ 25	10.3%	18.0%
N	5219	6295

Note: * Average score defined in text on page 116.

Table 6.2a Association between health measures, males

	% Poor health	% With IFS > 0	% With BFS > 0	% CED	% Obese
Self-reported health*					
Good health	–	5.4	0.7	16.3	10.3
poor health		52.7	9.6	32.5	8.1
Inter function score (IFS)					
no limitation	6.4	–	0	16.0	10.2
any limitation	57.1		16.1	36.22	9.0
Basic function score (BFS)					
no limitation	11.0	0	–	18.0	10.1
any limitation	64.4	100		32.2	10.0
Body mass index					
Overweight	9.8	9.9	1.7	–	–
Normal	10.0	8.5	1.4		
CED	21.5	22.0	3.0		

Table 6.2b Association between health measures, females

	% Poor health	% With IFS > 0	% With BFS > 0	% CED	% Obese
Self-reported health*					
good health	–	16.6	1.3	16.1	18.8
poor health		68.9	13.4	29.6	15.8
Inter function score (IFS)					
no limitation	5.3	–	0	15.4	18.2
any limitation	38.5		12.3	26.0	19.3
Basic function score (BFS)					
no limitation	11.7	21.0	–	17.6	18.4
any limitation	60.9	100.0		25.8	18.0
Body mass index					
Obese	11.2	23.9	2.7	–	–
Normal	11.2	19.5	2.4		
CED	21.7	33.2	4.0		

Note: * Good health includes those reporting being healthy and very healthy and poor health includes those reporting being unhealthy and very unhealthy.

during that period into health. Some of the inputs are chosen, such as food (nutrition), medical care, and time use (exercise). The disease environment is partially determined by a household's choices of sanitation, waste disposal, and water source. Other inputs are exogenous to the household, such as the portion of the disease environment that is determined by the public health and sanitation infrastructure.

The productivity of inputs not only depends on biological mechanisms, but also on individual and household characteristics such as education, age, gender and family background. For example, better-educated households may be better able to follow a recommended medical treatment and thus obtain greater improvements in health from medical services.

Finally, the change in health status over a period of time is likely to depend on the stock of health at the beginning of the period. For example, a frail individual's health may depreciate faster than a robust individual's health. The productivity of inputs may also depend on health stock. Individuals who are frail may be more susceptible to unhealthy disease environments. The efficacy of medical care depends on the type and severity of the illness and general health status.

Formally, the addition to individual i's health stock or health production function is:

$$H_t = H\!\left(H_{t-1}, X_{ht}, \tilde{u}_{ft}, \tilde{u}_{ct}, \varepsilon_t\right)$$ (6.1)

where health H_t is individual i's health stock at the end of period t, X_{ht} is a vector of chosen inputs invested in health during period t, u_{ft} is a vector of individual and household (family) characteristics, $\tilde{u}_{ct}$ is a vector of community characteristics – including environment, public infrastructure, and quality of medical care – and ε_t is unobserved individual, household and community shocks to health.

Specifying the health production function as conditional on the previous period's health has two implications. First, the productivity of health inputs depends on current health status. For example, surgery is more likely to be successful in more robust individuals. Second, since the health production function is conditioned on the previous period's level of health stock, only current input choices affect health at the end of the period. The previous period's health stock represents all investments and unobserved shocks up to period t and for the initial genetic endowment.[5]

4.2   Integration With an Economic Model of Household Behavior

While the health production function captures critical information, it is in practice very difficult to estimate. Estimation of the parameters of the production function is not trivial and requires detailed information on the choice of all inputs. In addition, since these choices are simultaneously determined with the outcome, H_t, an identifying instrument, such as a price, is required for each input included in the production function (Rosenzweig and Schultz 1983). There are few data sets which can meet these requirements.

In addition, we believe that health status cannot be captured by a single measure, but rather has many dimensions. In the extreme, each dimension may have its own production function. The specifications that appropriately capture the underlying biological mechanisms of all these relationships are not at all clear (in contrast to child growth or to certain childhood illnesses such as diarrhea). Even if we were confident as to functional form, estimating adult health production functions would require an enormous amount of data, which are not available or feasible to collect. We consequently take the approach of estimating the reduced form determinants of those health outcomes that relate measures of health status to long term constraints.

To derive the reduced forms we make the standard economic assumption that households are making decisions rationally by maximizing their overall welfare as they define it; given their resources, the information available to them, their beliefs and the underlying health and sanitation environment. This assumption provides the mechanism by which those individual and household behaviors, the X_{ht}s, which directly affect health, are decided. The reduced form equations for health status are then derived from this behavior, taken together with the underlying health production, income and time constraints.

Assume that a household maximizes the expected value of a weakly separable quasi-concave utility function, and that the utility function in each period, U_t, is a function of a vector of commodity consumption goods, X_{et} (which may include some purchased health inputs, X_{ht}, for example cigarettes and food), a vector of health stocks of each family member, H_t, and a vector of family members' leisure time, ℓ_t:

$$\max E(U) = E(U_1, U_2, \ldots, U_t, \ldots, U_T) \qquad (6.2)$$

where $U_t = U(X_{et}, H_t, l_t; \hat{u}_{ft})$. Preferences may be affected by household characteristics, u_{ft}, some of which, such as education, are also arguments of the health production function.

This specification implies that many inputs into the production of health, such as medical care, are not directly valued in and of themselves, but rather are valued indirectly through the health they produce. Other inputs in the production of health, such as food and housing, may be valued indirectly through the health they produce and directly as consumption goods.

Household allocation decisions, however, are constrained by available time and resources as well as by the health production function. In each period, the household faces a budget constraint: current wealth, W_t, is simply the present value of wealth left over from the previous period plus the excess of income over expenditure, namely savings:

$$W_t = W_{t-1} + (1 + r_t)(Y_t - P_t X_t)$$ (6.3)

where Y_t is household income (earned and unearned including transfers), P_t is a vector of prices, r_t is a real annual interest rate and X_t is comprised of goods which enter the utility function, plus a vector of current health inputs. Across years, interest rates may vary or constraints on borrowing may result in imperfect smoothing of consumption.

An additional constraint is placed on the household's choice by characteristics of available medical services. The distance of medical care providers from the household and the time that households have to wait once they have arrived at facilities imposes a fixed time cost on the consumption of medical services. Therefore the price of medical services includes both the monetary price and the opportunity cost of time spent in obtaining the care.

4.3   The Reduced Form

Solving the system generates a set of first order necessary conditions leading to a set of commodity and health demand functions. These demand for health input functions depend on lagged health stock and household wealth (both of which are endogenous in this dynamic model), and exogenous individual, household and community characteristics:

$$X_{ht} = X(H_{t-1}, W_{t-1}, u_{ft}, u_{ct}, \varepsilon_t)$$ (6.4)

where u_{ft} is the complete set of household characteristics, both u_{ft} and u_{ft}, and u_{ct} is the union of the vector of community characteristics in the health production function and the price vector.

Substitution of the health input demand functions into the health production function yields the health demand function:

$$H_{ht} = \tilde{H}(H_{t-1}, W_{t-1}, u_{ft}, u_{ct}, \varepsilon_t)$$ (6.5)

By conditioning on lagged health status, we could use equation (6.5) to examine the transition from the previous health stock of health to the current stock — that is, the effect of current individual, household and community characteristics on changes in health.[6] We could also examine important interactions between health status and other characteristics to test hypotheses such as whether the impact of education is larger for healthier individuals or whether the impact of improvements in medical care quality or having medical care insurance has a larger impact on individuals in generally poor health.

However, equation (6.5) is not useful for examining the long-run effects of childhood investments on health later in life. In particular, we miss the effect of education and height on lagged health. Therefore, we solve equation (6.5) recursively to obtain the reduced form health production function:

$$H_t = H\left(H_0, W_0, \mu_f, \mu_c, \varepsilon\right) \qquad (6.6)$$

where the subscript 0 refers to the initial period (of adulthood) endowments, and μ_f is a vector of family-level constraints and μ_c is a set of constraints at the community-level since time 0. An important implication of this conceptualization is that measures of health stock are a function of past as well as current values of the constraints.

The reduced form relates current health to current and past constraints. On entering adulthood, individuals and households have physical and human capital that can be used to generate resources for investment in health and other consumption. Since income is determined together with health, we model the initial endowments of physical and human capital that determine subsequent choices.

By focusing on the effects of constraints we are able to investigate the consequences of childhood investments on subsequent adult health. Both W_0 and H_0 represent endowments of investments of parents in their children or in other words the circumstances under which children enter adulthood. In particular, we are able to examine the returns of parents' investments in their children's education, and child health and nutritional investments as proxied height. Moreover, we are able to control for other forms of family background by using parental and sibling characteristics. Community level variables are measured using a community fixed effect.

The reduced-form model in equation (6.6), however, does not distinguish the pathways through which childhood investments affect adult health. They could have a direct effect as well as influence choices of health inputs such as diet and medical care, and they could have an income effect by raising economic productivity and therefore wealth.

5   THE EMPIRICAL MODELS

5.1   Data and Specification of Models

The conceptual model developed above is used to explore the impact of childhood investments in education and health on adult health in Indonesia using data from the Indonesian Family Life Survey. This multipurpose household survey was conducted in 1993 and collected complete information from 7039 households in 321 enumeration areas randomly selected from 13 Indonesian provinces (Frankenberg and Karoly 1995). Respondents from each household were the head of household and spouse as well as any member over 50 and his or her spouse. For one quarter of all households, another member of the household between 15 and 49 years of age and their spouse was randomly chosen. The sample used for this analysis includes all respondents over 20 who completed the health questionnaire; proxy respondents were not permitted for this module of the IFLS. Nine percent of the women and 11 percent of the men had missing health data. The age cutoff at 20 was selected to ensure that a majority of individuals had completed their education and that nutritional status measures were compatible over all ages. Because some young adults are still growing, they may have a lower weight for height that can not be interpreted as chronic energy deficiency.

Table 6.3 presents the age distribution of the sample. Because of age groupings around ten- and five-year intervals, we have chosen to use ten-year age categories that include these points. This approach avoids the artificial assignment of individuals at these peaks to one or another age group.   In line with the selected age groupings we define a younger and an older cohort using 48 years as our cutoff point. This cutoff is also close to the definition of senior respondents used in the IFLS survey (50 years).

The distribution of gender and age in this sample reflects the IFLS survey methodology: women tend to be younger, on average, as would be expected since both partners of a married couple were interviewed. At the same time, there are a greater number of women resulting from the focus on elderly household coresidents.

The primary variables of interest are education and height – the indicators of childhood investments in an individual's human capital. The profile of educational attainment for men and women is displayed in Table 6.4. On average, men are better educated than women, although

Table 6.3 Age distribution by gender

	Males all ages ($N = 5584$)	Females all ages ($N = 6774$)
20–27	9.2%	15.3%
28–37	28.6%	30.3%
38–47	24.2%	20.3%
48–57	18.4%	18.7%
58–67	13.1%	10.9%
68–77	5.3%	3.7%
78+	1.2%	0.9%
Average age (standard deviation)	44.3 (13.9)	41.8 (13.8)

Table 6.4 Education levels by age for males and females

	Males all ages ($N = 5584$)	Females all ages ($N = 6774$)	Males age < 48 ($N = 3461$)	Females age < 48 ($N = 4461$)	Males age ≥ 48 ($N = 2123$)	Females age ≥ 48 ($N = 2313$)
No schooling	15.0%	29.7%	8.2%	15.8%	26.1%	56.6%
Some primary	29.6%	29.5%	28.4%	32.9%	31.6%	22.9%
Completed primary	22.4%	18.8%	22.7%	22.7%	22.0%	11.1%
Some secondary	14.2%	10.7%	16.5%	13.3%	10.3%	5.8%
Completed secondary	12.9%	8.8%	17.2%	11.7%	5.9%	3.4%
Some university	5.9%	2.5%	7.0%	3.6%	4.1%	0.4%
Average years of education (standard deviation)	5.82 (4.32)	4.30 (4.12)	6.71 (4.23)	5.40 (4.08)	4.35 (4.05)	2.18 (3.30)

Table 6.5 Family background variables

Variables	Males		Females	
	Mean	**Std. dev**	**Mean**	**Std. dev**
Father's years of schooling	2.45	3.3	2.53	3.4
Mother's years of schooling	1.47	2.6	1.55	2.8
Father deceased	0.677	0.47	0.637	0.48
Mother deceased	0.493	0.50	0.455	0.50
Father's age, if alive	64.8	10.9	63.7	11.2
Mother's age, if alive	61.7	11.8	59.9	11.7
Number of siblings	3.61	2.4	3.59	2.4

these differences are more pronounced at older ages reflecting the progress in women's education in Indonesia (World Bank 1993). Men in the cohort aged 48 years and over have had twice as much education as women in the same cohort. In contrast, younger men have had about 25 percent more schooling than women of the same age. Schooling is entered in the empirical models in two ways: first as a series of dummy variables indicating the level of schooling completed and second as completed years of education.

Height is a measure of nutritional status in childhood, since full height is attained by the end of adolescence and fully determined at an earlier age. Height also captures healthiness in childhood more generally, since growth is affected by illness. As stated by Leo and Preston,   height can 'serve as a marker of what is potentially a very wide variety of events and conditions in childhood that affected both growth and the ability of an individual to resist disease and death'. In these models we introduce height in meters as a continuous variable.[7] The descriptive data on height in this sample was presented in Table 6.1 with the adult health measures.

One of the confounders of the association between human capital investments and health is that individuals with greater ability and better family connections are more likely to be tall and better educated. Therefore, the estimated coefficients may reflect these family background characteristics rather than returns to human capital investments. In these analyses, we control for family background using information on parental schooling, whether parents are still alive, their current age if they are still alive, as well as total number of siblings in the family. These variables represent a broad range of influences including wealth, genetic factors related to ability and health endowments, and behavioral inputs.

Family background characteristics are displayed in Table 6.5. Fathers

Table 6.6a Determinants of adult health measures, males over 20

	Self reported poor health		Intermediate function score		Basic function score		CED (BMI < 18.5)		Obese (BMI ≥ 25)	
Mean value of dependent variable	*(0.121)*		*(4.9)*		*(0.9)*		*(0.188)*		*(0.103)*	
Some primary school	0.010	—	−0.21	—	−0.72	—	−0.036	—	0.017	—
	(0.68)		(−0.29)		(−0.19)		(−2.11)		(1.25)	
Completed primary school	0.000	—	−0.70	—	−0.24	—	−0.035	—	0.041	—
	(0.01)		(−1.90)		(−0.58)		(−1.88)		(2.84)	
Some secondary school	−0.28	—	−1.39	—	−0.42	—	−0.35	—	0.099	—
	(−1.55)		(−1.56)		(−0.89)		(−1.65)		(5.90)	
Completed sec. and above	−0.038	—	−1.47	—	−0.29	—	−0.086	—	0.155	—
	(−2.12)		(−1.65)		(−0.53)		(−4.01)		(9.21)	
Years of schooling	—	−0.004	—	−0.126	—	−0.01	—	−0.005	—	0.012
		(−3.07)		(−2.05)		(−0.33)		(−3.44)		(10.51)
Age (F-stat)	46.6	46.3	143.3	146.5	5.63	5.94	49.8	50.7	12.4	12.0
EA FE (F-stat)	2.00	1.99	1.45	1.45	1.03	1.03	1.71	1.71	1.99	1.99
N	5584	5584	5584	5584	5573	5573	5512	5512	5512	5512

Table 6.6b Determinants of adult health measures, females over 20

	Self reported poor health		Intermediate function score		Basic function score		CED (BMI < 18.5)		Obese (BMI ≥ 25)	
Mean value of dependent variable	*(0.133)*		*(9.5)*		*(1.3)*		*(0.178)*		*(0.180)*	
Some primary school	−0.009	—	−1.56	—	−0.56	—	−0.040	—	0.060	—
	(−0.75)		(−2.23)		(−1.66)		(−2.94)		(4.49)	
Completed primary school	−0.008	—	−0.95	—	−0.74	—	−0.061	—	0.091	—
	(−0.55)		(−1.16)		(−1.88)		(−3.78)		(5.78)	
Some secondary school	−0.015	—	−2.05	—	−1.07	—	−0.034	—	0.103	—
	(−0.91)		(−2.05)		(−2.24)		(−1.70)		(5.34)	
Completed sec. and above	−0.038	—	−1.19	—	−0.48	—	−0.016	—	0.077	—
	(−2.13)		(−1.14)		(−0.97)		(−0.74)		(3.76)	
Years of schooling	—	−0.003	—	−0.082	—	−0.05	—	−0.001	—	0.006
		(−1.93)		(−1.07)		(1.26)		(−0.82)		(4.30)
Age (F-stat)	39.2	42.0	169.9	188.0	13.4	15.0	41.8	52.7	15.7	16.5
EA FE (F-stat)	2.27	2.27	1.98	1.97	1.14	1.15	1.94	1.95	2.61	2.61
N	6774	6774	6768	6768	6765	6765	6696	6696	6696	6696

have an average of 2.5 years of education versus 1.5 for mothers. More fathers than mothers are no longer alive: about two-thirds versus about half. Differences in means between the male and female samples are due to the younger ages of the women in the sample. Average number of siblings is 3.6 for both male and female samples. Dummy variables are entered into models when family background characteristics are missing.

A number of different model specifications are estimated for each of the five dependent variables. We first investigate the relationship between schooling and health outcomes modeling education as a continuous and a categorical variable (Tables 6.6a and 6.6b); then we look at the impact of

Table 6.7a Expanded determinants of adult health measures, males over 20

	Self-reported poor health		Intermediate function score		Basic function score		CED (BMI < 18.5)		Obese (BMI ≥ 25)	
Some primary school	0.009	−0.007	−0.17	−0.25	0.01	0.01	−0.035	−0.030	0.017	0.016
	(0.57)	(0.49)	(−0.23)	(−0.35)	(0.25)	(0.02)	(−2.06)	(−1.76)	(1.24)	(1.18)
Completed primary school	0.005	0.003	−0.68	−0.73	−0.24	−0.26	−0.034	−0.026	0.041	0.039
	(0.32)	(0.16)	(−0.87)	(−0.93)	(−0.59)	(−0.64)	(−1.81)	(−1.42)	(2.81)	(2.69)
Some secondary school	−0.028	−0.035	−1.23	−1.29	−0.29	−0.31	−0.033	−0.024	0.098	0.093
	(−1.51)	(−1.86)	(−1.36)	(−1.40)	(−0.63)	(−0.66)	(−1.53)	(−1.10)	(5.85)	(5.49)
Completed sec. and above	−0.030	−0.040	−1.51	−1.52	−0.042	−0.38	−0.083	−0.073	0.154	0.144
	(−1.62)	(−2.04)	(−1.67)	(−1.61)	(−0.90)	(−0.79)	(−3.85)	(−3.26)	(9.12)	(8.21)
Height in meters	−0.179	−0.174	−10.82	−10.31	−1.14	−1.14	−0.139	−0.104	0.034	0.030
	(−2.24)	(−2.17)	(−2.79)	(−2.65)	(−0.58)	(−0.57)	(−1.54)	(−1.13)	(0.47)	(0.41)
Family background variables (F-stat)	—	1.04 ns	—	1.52 ns	—	0.68 ns	—	3.33 $p < 0.001$	—	0.72 ns
Age controls	Yes	Yes	Yes	Yes	Yes	Yes	Yes	Yes	Yes	Yes
Location controls	Yes	Yes	Yes	Yes	Yes	Yes	Yes	Yes	Yes	Yes
N	5224	5219	5224	5219	5212	5207	5512	5498	5512	5498

Table 6.7b Expanded determinants of adult health measures, females over 20

	Self-reported poor health		Intermediate function score		Basic function score		CED (BMI < 18.5)		Obese (BMI ≥ 25)	
Some primary school	−0.010	−0.006	−1.52	−1.50	−0.50	−0.51	−0.040	−0.032	0.060	0.056
	(−0.86)	(−0.53)	(−2.16)	(−2.11)	(−1.55)	(−1.57)	(−2.91)	(−2.38)	(4.45)	(4.12)
Completed primary school	−0.007	−0.002	−0.85	−0.74	−0.74	−0.78	−0.060	−0.054	0.091	0.086
	(−0.48)	(−0.14)	(−1.03)	(−0.89)	(−1.96)	(−2.02)	(−3.74)	(−3.28)	(5.72)	(5.36)
Some secondary school	−0.011	−0.001	−1.78	−1.52	−0.87	−0.92	−0.033	−0.022	0.102	0.093
	(−0.65)	(−0.08)	(−1.78)	(−1.46)	(−1.89)	(−1.93)	(−1.65)	(−1.06)	(5.26)	(4.66)
Completed sec. and above	−0.041	−0.031	−1.10	−0.57	−0.39	−0.42	−0.014	−0.005	0.075	0.065
	(−2.23)	(−1.53)	(−1.04)	(−0.49)	(−0.81)	(−0.79)	(−0.67)	(−0.55)	(3.65)	(2.89)
Height in meters	0.003	0.021	−6.37	−6.05	2.17	2.06	−0.064	−0.049	0.079	0.062
	(0.04)	(0.26)	(−1.39)	(−1.31)	(1.03)	(0.97)	(−0.72)	(−0.55)	(0.90)	(0.70)
Family background variables (F-stat)	—	1.50 ns	—	0.83 ns	—	0.95 ns	—	3.04 $p < 0.001$	—	2.24 $p < 0.01$
Age controls	Yes	Yes	Yes	Yes	Yes	Yes	Yes	Yes	Yes	Yes
Location controls	Yes	Yes	Yes	Yes	Yes	Yes	Yes	Yes	Yes	Yes
N	6510	6505	6510	6505	6501	6496	6696	6683	6696	6683

height and schooling and, finally, height, schooling and family background characteristics (Tables 6.7a and 6.7b). All of the models control for age and geographical location, defined as the 321 sampling units or enumeration areas used in the IFLS survey. Enumeration areas correspond to village of residence. By controlling for place of residence we eliminate confounding due to other environmental conditions associated with higher rates of schooling and better health.

All models are estimated by least squares with fixed effects for place of residence. For the binary dependent variables, this specification is simply a linear probability model. Models are estimated separately for males and females as Chow tests rejected pooling at conventional significance levels.

For our preferred model specification we have also obtained separate estimates for young (age < 48) and older adults (age 48 and over). There are two reasons for splitting the sample by age. The first is to investigate whether the effects of education and height on health diminish with age. For example, initial investments may produce diminishing returns with time or, alternatively, the quality of schooling may be lower for earlier cohorts, resulting in a smaller effect. The second reason is mortality selection. One of the main effects of greater human capital investments may be to improve survivorship. If so, then an older cohort is comprised of a selected group of better-educated and taller individuals. This selection effect would attenuate the magnitude of the education coefficients. While estimates of the model may be biased for the older sample, there is less likely to be mortality bias in the younger sample.

5.2   Estimation Results

The first set of models explores the relationship between education and health outcomes as reported in Tables 6.6a and 6.6b. The first row gives the mean of each dependent variable. The next five rows report the estimated coefficients on the education variables, and the following two rows report the F-statistic for the joint significance of the age and location (village) dummy variables. In all models, the age effects and the location effects are jointly significantly different from zero. In the interest of space we do not report the age and location coefficient estimate. However, the multivariate results indicate that health typically worsens with age in a pattern is consistent with the relationships indicated in the bivariate non-parametric regressions reported above. While location seems to matter, Hausman tests in many cases indicate that location is uncorrelated with the other right hand variables, so suggesting that random effects may not be biased.

These results indicate that better educated men and women are healthier. However, this relationship is not always linear, especially for women. With respect to self-reported ill health, individuals with secondary schooling are healthier. There is little difference in perceived health status between those who have primary schooling and those who have no schooling. In the intermediate functioning models, the importance of secondary education relative to primary education remains for men. However, women appear to get some intermediate function value from primary education. With respect to the more serious functional limitations, better-educated men do not seem to be healthier. However, women with primary education are significantly healthier. Lack of education is strongly correlated with chronic energy deficiency. Again, for men, the stronger effects are at the secondary level and for women they are at the primary level. Finally, better-educated men and women are more obese. For men, the prevalence of obesity rises linearly with education level and years of schooling. For women, any education is associated with a higher prevalence of obesity.

In Tables 6.7a and 6.7b we add height and family background variables. The age and location effects do not change and again are not reported in the tables. The addition of family background controls does not alter these results. In fact, when including height, family background controls are almost always jointly and individually insignificant, with the exception of chronic energy deficiency. The individual coefficients for the family background variables are not reported, but are available upon request. The addition of height slightly lowers the effect of education, but does not affect the basic pattern of results or precision. Interestingly, while taller males are significantly healthier, as measured by self-reported ill health and intermediate functioning, taller females are not.

One possible concern is that the results may reflect mortality selection – that is, better educated and taller individuals are more likely to survive. In order to investigate mortality selection, we split the sample into younger (less than 48 years old) and older cohorts (age 48 and older) and re-estimated the models. The younger cohort is less likely to suffer from mortality selection. The results are reported in Tables 6.8a and 6.8b. While the coefficients on education and height are somewhat lower for the younger cohort, the basic pattern of results does not change. The only significant change is that education matters only for the older cohort in the intermediate functioning score models for both males and females.

Finally, we report the estimated orders of magnitude of the impacts of education and height on health outcomes using the coefficients from Tables 6.7a and 6.7b. Overall, completing secondary education seemed to be most important for males and completing primary education seemed to be most important for females. Table 6.9 reports the percentage change in the measures of health outcomes associated with going from no schooling to completing secondary schooling for males and to completing primary education for females. Table 6.9 also reports the percentage change associated with a 10 cm increase in height.

Males who have completed primary school are 25 percent less likely to report being in poor health, have intermediate functioning scores that are

Table 6.8a Expanded determinants of adult health measures by cohort, males over 20

	Self-reported poor health		Intermediate function score		Basic function score		CED (BMI < 18.5)		Obese (BMI ≥ 25)	
Cohort	< 48	≥ 48	< 48	≥ 48	< 48	≥ 48	< 48	≥ 48	< 48	≥ 48
Mean value of dependent variable	0.07	0.21	1.5	10.3	0.7	1.2	0.12	0.30	0.11	0.09
Some primary school	−0.004	0.030	−0.00	−0.39	−0.15	0.01	−0.024	−0.017	0.008	0.013
	(−0.20)	(1.14)	(−0.01)	(−0.28)	(−0.26)	(0.01)	(−1.03)	(0.59)	(0.35)	(0.74)
Completed primary school	0.008	0.005	−0.43	−1.48	−0.37	−0.49	−0.033	0.003	0.040	0.032
	(0.37)	(0.15)	(−0.57)	(−0.91)	(−0.62)	(−0.80)	(−1.35)	(0.10)	(1.71)	(1.63)
Some secondary school	−0.037	−0.004	0.08	−4.48	0.038	−1.38	−0.025	−0.046	0.108	0.074
	(−1.71)	(−0.10)	(0.10)	(−2.11)	(0.06)	(−1.73)	(−0.96)	(−1.07)	(4.26)	(2.83)
Completed sec. and above	−0.036	−0.044	−0.54	−5.95	−0.38	−0.70	−0.066	−0.100	0.136	0.186
	(−1.69)	(−1.05)	(−0.67)	(−2.61)	(−0.60)	(−0.81)	(−2.55)	(−2.19)	(5.44)	(6.64)
Height in meters	−0.092	−0.349	−4.04	−20.1	−3.21	1.88	−0.005	−3.53	−0.012	0.152
	(−1.07)	(−2.09)	(−1.27)	(−2.23)	(−1.27)	(0.56)	(−0.05)	(−1.97)	(−0.12)	(1.39)
Family background variable	No	No	No	No	No	No	No	No	No	No
Age controls	Yes	Yes	Yes	Yes	Yes	Yes	Yes	Yes	Yes	Yes
Location controls	Yes	Yes	Yes	Yes	Yes	Yes	Yes	Yes	Yes	Yes
N	3222	2002	3222	2003	3215	2002	3339	2173	3339	2173

Table 6.8b Expanded determinants of adult health measures by cohort, females over 20

	Self-reported poor health		Intermediate function score		Basic function score		CED (BMI < 18.5)		Obese (BMI ≥ 25)	
Cohort	< 47	≥ 47	< 47	≥ 47	< 47	≥ 47	< 47	≥ 47	< 47	≥ 47
Mean value of dependent variable	0.09	0.22	4.9	18.3	0.8	2.2	0.13	0.30	0.20	0.16
Some primary school	−0.004	−0.014	−1.04	−3.31	−0.57	−0.57	−0.026	−0.016	0.056	0.041
	(−0.39)	(−0.56)	(−1.40)	(−2.11)	(−1.39)	(−0.91)	(−1.50)	(−0.62)	(2.78)	(2.07)
Completed primary school	0.011	−0.062	−0.30	−4.47	−0.81	−0.98	−0.024	−0.115	0.080	0.085
	(0.66)	(−1.89)	(−0.37)	(−2.12)	(−1.77)	(−1.16)	(−1.26)	(−3.40)	(3.61)	(3.24)
Some secondary school	0.012	−0.061	−0.46	−4.38	−0.66	−1.67	−0.010	−0.070	0.081	0.138
	(0.66)	(−1.61)	(−0.48)	(−1.81)	(−1.25)	(−1.73)	(−0.43)	(−1.75)	(3.16)	(4.45)
Completed sec. and above	−0.031	—	0.159	—	−0.11	—	−0.000	—	0.063	—
	(−1.61)		(0.16)		(−0.20)		(−0.00)		(2.35)	
Height in meters	0.054	−0.001	−2.14	−11.2	2.36	5.02	−0.002	−0.097	0.056	0.120
	(0.55)	(−0.00)	(−0.48)	(−1.02)	(1.01)	(1.14)	(0.02)	(−0.56)	(0.47)	(0.89)
Family background variable	No	No	No	No	No	No	No	No	No	No
Age controls	Yes	Yes	Yes	Yes	Yes	Yes	Yes	Yes	Yes	Yes
Location controls	Yes	Yes	Yes	Yes	Yes	Yes	Yes	Yes	Yes	Yes
N	4319	2191	4319	2186	4313	2191	4165	2531	4165	2531

Table 6.9 Estimated effects of completed schooling and height on health

Males	% Change from no schooling to completed secondary school	% Change from increasing height by 10 cm
Poor health	−24.8**	−14.8***
Intermediate function score	−31.0*	−22.1***
Basic function score	−4.7	−12.7
Chronic energy deficiency	−38.8***	−5.5
Obese	149.5***	3.3
Females	% Change from no schooling to completed primary school	% Change from increasing height by 10 cm
Poor health	−5.3	0.2
Intermediate function score	−0.9	−6.7
Basic function score	−56.9**	16.7
Chronic energy deficiency	−33.7***	−2.8
Obese	50.6***	3.4

Notes
* Significantly different from zero at the 0.1 level.
** Significantly different from zero at the 0.05 level.
*** Significantly different from zero at the 0.01 level.

31 percent higher, and are 39 percent less likely to have chronic energy deficiency. However, they are 150 percent more likely to be obese. Males who are 10 cm taller are 15 percent less likely to report poor health and have intermediate functioning scores 22 percent lower. Females who have completed primary schooling have basic functioning scores that are 57 percent lower and are 34 percent less likely to have chronic energy deficiency. However, they are 51 percent more likely to be obese. Height does not seem to be associated with better health for females.

6   CONCLUSIONS

Our results show that better educated Indonesians are healthier as measured by self-reported health status, physical functioning and prevalence of chronic energy deficiency. However, better education is strongly associated with obesity for both men and women. Education has an impact for younger and older adults, although the results are stronger for the older cohort. This contradicts our initial hypotheses that the returns to education might diminish with age or time or be stronger among younger adults who may have received a better quality education. It is possible that these differential effects reflect mortality selection or just plain cohort differences. The results also indicate that men seem to benefit only from secondary education, while women benefit more from primary education than secondary. In addition, nutrition investments in children's health, as measured by height, appear to be correlated with better health later in life for men, but not for women.

Since future cohorts of elderly subjects are better educated and taller, our results suggest that future cohorts may suffer from a different mix of health problems than the current cohort. More specifically, the results suggest that future cohorts are less likely to suffer from malnutrition and physical functioning problems, but more likely to suffer from illnesses associated with obesity.

These results suggest that there may be a gender difference in the importance of the pathways through which human capital investments affect health. In this model, education affects health both indirectly through its impact on wages and wealth and directly by increasing the technical and allocative efficiency of the production of health. Education may also be a signaling mechanism for the selection of a spouse and thus be a predictor of household characteristics. One explanation for the observed differences between men and women may be that secondary education and height give men an advantage in labor markets, but do not do so for women. In contrast, efficiency effects could be more important for women. Improved efficiency in the production of health, which could be associated with primary schooling, may be more pronounced for women since they are most often the targets of health education campaigns and are generally responsible for caring for their family's health. This explanation would be consistent with results from the literature on parental education and child health in developing countries (Caldwell 1989; Cleland 1990).

These analyses also show that better educated Indonesians are more likely to be obese. Other studies from the developing world have also reported positive associations between education and obesity (INCLEN 1994; Popkin et al. 1993; Sichieri et al. 1994). These results are important for predicting future health trends if younger cohorts of better educated individuals are more likely to adopt unhealthy behaviors which increase the risk of cardiovascular diseases, diabetes and cancer. How the negative effects of increased education and prosperity counter-balance the positive effects seen with the other indicators of health status is an important question to explore further.

The association of education with the prevalence of obesity again raises the question of how educational investments affect health and, additionally, whether these processes can be modified by health policy. The public health environment may be of particular importance in creating efficiency effects. In industrialized countries, at least for women, the prevalence of obesity is inversely associated with education (Sobal and Stunkard 1989). These inverse associations are partially explained by better comprehension of public health information and a subsequently greater awareness of the health risks associated with a poor diet.

In these analyses, the addition of selected family background variables did not weaken the effects of education on health, suggesting that human capital investments do have an effect on health, independently of family endowments. However, the social support system provided by the extended family as measured by income transfers and physical proximity to family could be an important determinant of health. A future avenue of research will be to explore how social support networks and intergenerational transfers affect health. This question is key in an aging population where the family is a primary source of support for the elderly.

NOTES

[1] See, for example, Wolfe and Behrman (1984), Rosenzweig and Schultz (1985), Behrman and Wolfe (1989), Over et al. (1992), and Schultz and Tanzel (1992). A few of the studies have investigated specific diseases, such as malaria, and are better able to measure illness (Castro and Mokate 1988; and Fernandez and Sawyer 1988).

[2] See Feachem et al. (1992) for a review of this literature.

[3] See discussion in James and Francois (1994); arguments against in Durnin (1994) and Immink and Viteri (1981); and the results of Manson et al. (1995).

[4] In developed societies, there is an inverse relationship between obesity and socioeconomic status for women and an inconsistent relationship for men and children (Sobal and Stunkard 1989).

[5] It is possible that the lag structure may be more complicated. With our data we will have to assume this more simple form. However, where possible we will test the importance of this assumption.

[6] However, the estimation of equation (6.5) is more demanding on the data because it requires measures of health status in at least two periods.

[7] We also considered models which included a dummy variable indicating whether the individual was in the bottom quartile of the height distribution. The qualitative pattern of the results did not change. These results are available upon request.

REFERENCES

Adler, N.E., W.T. Boyce, M.A. Chesney, S. Folkman and S.L. Syme (1993), 'Socioeconomic inequalities in health', *JAMA*, **269**(24): 3140–5.

Andrews, G., A. Esterman, A. Braunack-Mayer and C. Rungie (1986), *Aging in the Western Pacific*, Manila: World Health Organization Regional Office of the Western Pacific.

Asian Development Bank (1997), *Asian Development Outlook 1996 and 1997*, Manila: Asian Development Bank.

Berhman J. and B. Wolfe (1989), 'Does schooling make women better nourished and healthier? Adult sibling random and fixed effects estimates for Nicaragua', *Journal of Human Resources*, **24**(4): 644–63.

Bound, J. (1991), 'Self-reported versus objective measures of health in retirement models', *Journal of Human Resources*, **26**(1): 106–38.

Caldwell, J.C. (1989), *The Causes of Demographic Change*, Madison: University of Wisconsin Press.

Castro, E. and K. Mokate (1988), 'Malaria and its socioeconomic meaning: the study of Cunday in Colombia', in A. Herrin and P. Rosenfield (eds), *Economics, Health and Tropical Disease*, Manila: University of the Philippines, School of Economics.

Cleland, J. (1990), 'Maternal education and child survival: further evidence and explanations', in J. Caldwell et al. (eds), *What We Know About Health Transition: The Cultural, Social and Behavioral Determinants of Health,* Canberra: Health Transition Centre, Australian National University.

Deolalikar, A. (1988), 'Nutrition and labor productivity in agriculture: estimates for rural south India', *Review of Economic Statistics*, **70**: 406–13.

Dow, William and Paul Gertler (1997), 'Private health insurance and public expenditures in Indonesia', mimeo, Santa Monica, CA: RAND.

Durnin, J.V. (1994), 'Low body mass index, physical work capacity and physical activity levels', *European Journal of Clinical Nutrition*, **48** (Suppl 3): S39–43; discussion S43–4.

Elo, I.T. and S.H. Preston (1992), 'Effects of early-life conditions on adult mortality: a review', *Population Index*, **58**(2): 186–212.

Feachem, R., T. Kjellstrom, C. Murray, M. Over and M. Phillips (eds) (1992), *The Health of Adults in the Developing World*, Oxford: Oxford University Press.

Fernandez, R. and D. Sawyer (1988), 'Socioeconomic and environmental factors affecting malaria in an Amazon frontier area', in A. Herrin and P. Rosenfield (eds), *Economics, Health and Tropical Disease*, Manila: University of the Philippines, School of Economics.

Ferro-Luzzi, A., S. Sette, M. Franklin and W.P.T. James (1992), 'A simplified approach of assessing adult chronic energy deficiency', *European Journal of Clinical Nutrition*, **46**: 173–86.

Frankenberg, E. and L. Karoly (1995), *The 1993 Indonesian Familiy Life Survey: Overview and Field Report*, Santa Monica, CA: RAND

Corporation.

Garcia, M. and E. Kennedy (1994), 'Assessing the linkages between low body mass index and morbidity in adults: evidence from four developing countries', *European Journal of Clinical Nutrition*, **48** (Suppl 3): S90–6; discussion S97.

Gertler, Paul and Jack Molyneaux (1996), 'The effect of medical care prices on utilization and health outcomes: experimental results', mimeo, Santa Monica, CA: RAND.

Grossman, M. (1972), 'On the concept of health capital and the demand for health', *Journal of Political Economy*, **80**(2): 223–55.

Guralnik, J., L. Branch, S. Cummings and J.D. Curb (1989), 'Physical performance measures in aging research', *Journal of Gerontology*, **44** (5): M141–6.

Hill, A. and M. Mamdani (1989), *Operational Guidelines for Measuring Health Through Household Surveys*, London: Centre for Population Studies, School of Hygiene and Tropical Medicine, University of London.

Idler, E. and S. Kasl (1991), 'Health perceptions and survival: do global evaluations of health status really predict mortality?', *Journal of Gerontology: Social Sciences*, **46**(2): S55–65.

Immink, M.D.C. and   F.E.Viteri (1981), 'Energy intake and productivity of Guatemalan sugarcane cutters: an empirical test of the efficiency wage hypothesis', *Journal of Development Economics*, **9**: 273–87.

INCLEN (1992), 'Risk factors for cardiovascular disease in the developing world. A multicentre collaborative study in the International Clinical Epidemiology Network (INCLEN). INCLEN Multicentre Collaborative Group', *Journal of Clinical Epidemiology*, **45**(8): 841–7.

INCLEN (1994), 'Socio-economic status and risk factors for cardiovascular disease: a multicentre collaborative study in the International Clinical Epidemiology Network (INCLEN). The INCLEN Multicentre Collaborative Group', *Journal of Clinical Epidemiology*, **47**(12): 1401–9.

James, W.P.T., A. Ferro-Luzzi and J.C. Waterlow (1988), 'Definition of chronic energy deficiency in adults: report of a working party of the International Dietary Energy Consultative Group', *European Journal of Clinical Nutrition*, **42**: 969–81.

James, W.P.T. and P. J. Francois (1994), 'The choice of cut-off point for distinguishing normal body weights from underweight or "chronic energy deficiency" in adults', *European Journal of Clinical Nutrition*, **48**(Suppl 3): 179–84.

Jitapunkul, S., P. Kamolratanakul and S. Ebrahim (1994), 'The meaning of activities of daily living in a Thai elderly population: development of a new index', *Age & Ageing*, **23**(2): 97–101.

Ju, A. and G. Jones (1989), *Aging in ASEAN and Its Socio-economic Consequences,* Singapore: Institute of South Asian Studies.

Kennedy, E. and M. Garcia (1994), 'Body mass index and economic productivity', *European Journal of Clinical Nutrition*, **48**(Suppl 3): 45–55.

Kinsella, K. (1988), *Aging in the Third World*, US Bureau of the Census, International Population Reports Series P-95, No. 79, Washington, DC: GPO.

Kusin, J.A., S. Kardjati and U.H. Renqvist (1994), 'Maternal body mass index: the functional significance during reproduction', *European Journal of Clinical Nutrition*, **48**(Suppl 3): 56–67.

Larsson, B., P. Bjorntop and G. Tibblin (1981), 'The health consequences of moderate obesity', *International Journal of Obesity*, **5**: 81–116.

Lichtenstein, P., J.R. Harris, N.L.Pedersen and G.E. McClearn (1992), 'Socioeconomic status and physical health, how are they related? An empirical study based on twins reared apart and twins reared together', *Social Science & Medicine*, **36**(4): 441–50.

Machenbach, J.P., A.E. Kunst, A.E.J.M. Cavelaars, F. Groenhof and J. J.M. Geurts (1997), 'Socioeconomic inequalities in morbidity and mortality in western Europe', *The Lancet*, **349**(7): 1655–9.

Mann, G.V. (1974), 'The influence of obesity on health', *New England Journal of Medicine*, **291**: 178–85, 226–32.

Manson, J. E., W.C. Willett, M.J. Stampfer, G.A. Colditz, D.J. Hunter, S. E. Hankinson, C.H. Hennekens and F.E. Speizer (1995), 'Body weight and mortality among women', *The New England Journal of Medicine*, **333**(11): 677–85.

Martin, L. (1989), 'Living arrangements of the elderly in Fiji, Korea, Malaysia and the Philippines', *Demography*, **16**(4): 627–43.

Murray, C.J.L. and L.C. Chen (1992), 'Understanding morbidity change', *Population and Development Review*, **18**(3): 481–503.

Over, M., R. Ellis, J. Huber and O. Solon (1992), 'The consequences of adult ill-health', in R. Feachem, T. Kjellstrom, C. Murray, M. Over and M. Phillips (eds), *The Health of Adults in the Developing World*, Oxford: Oxford University Press, pp. 161–207.

Popkin, B.M., G. Keyou, F. Zhai, X. Guo, H. Ma and N. Zohoori (1993), 'The nutrition transition in China: a cross-sectional analysis', *European Journal of Clinical Nutrition*, **47**(5): 333–46.

Rosenzweig, M.R. and T.P. Schultz (1983), 'Estimating a household production function: heterogeneity, the demand for health inputs, and their effects on birth weight', *Journal of Political Economy*, **91**: 723–46.

Rosenzweig, M.R. and T.P. Schultz (1985), 'The demand for and supply of births: fertility and its life-cycle consequences', *American Economic Review*, **75**(5): 992–1015.

Schultz, T. Paul and Aysit Tanzel (1992), *Measurement of Returns to Adult Health: Morbidity Effects on Wage Rates in Cote d'Ivoire and Ghana*, New Haven, CT: Yale University.

Sen, A. (1982), 'Equality of what?', in *Choice, Welfare and Measurement*, Cambridge, MA: The MIT Press, pp. 353–69.

Sichieri, R., D.C. Coitinho, M.M. Leao, E. Recine and J.E. Everhart (1994), 'High temporal, geographic, and income variation in body mass index among adults in Brazil', *American Journal of Public Health*, **84**(5): 793–8.

Smith, J.P. and R. Kington (1997), 'Demographic and economic correlates of health in old age', *Demography*, **34**(1): 159–70.

Sobal, Jeffery and Albert J. Stunkard (1989), 'Socioeconomic status and obesity: a review of the literature', *Psychological Bulletin*, **105**(2): 260–75.

Stern, S. (1989), 'Measuring the effect of disability on labor force participation', *Journal of Human Resources*, **24**(3): 361–95.

Strauss, John, Paul J. Gertler, Omar Rahman and Kristin Fox (1994), 'Gender and life-cycle differentials in the patterns and determinants of adult health', *Journal of Human Resources*, **28**(4): 791–837.

Strauss, John and Duncan Thomas (1995), 'Human resources: empirical modeling of household and family decisions' in J. Behrman and T.N. Srinivasan (eds), *Handbook of Development Economics*, Amsterdam: North Holland, pp. 1883–2023.

Van Itallie, T.B. (1979), 'Obesity: adverse effects on health and longevity', *American Journal of Clinical Nutrition*, **32**: 2732–3.

Ware, J., A. Davies-Avery and R. Brook (1980), *Conceptualization and Measurement of Health Status for Adults in the Health Insurance Study: Vol VI, Analysis of Relationships Among Health Status Measures*, Santa Monica: RAND Corporation.

Wolfe, B. and J. Behrman (1984), 'Determinants of women's health status and health care utilization in a developing country: a latent variable approach', *Review of Economics and Statistics*, **56**(4): 696–703.

World Bank (1991), *World Development Report, 1991. Indonesia Poverty Report*, Washington, DC: World Bank.

World Bank (1993), *World Development Report, 1993. Investing in Health*, Washington, DC: World Bank.

World Bank (1995a), *Averting the Old Age Crisis*, Washington, DC: World Bank.

World Bank (1995b), *Indonesia: Public Expenditure, Prices and the Poor*, Washington, DC: World Bank.

PART III

Health Care Utilization

7. China's urban health insurance reform experiment in Zhenjiang: cost and utilization analyses

Gordon G. Liu, Renhua Cai, Schumarry Chao, Xianjun Xiong, Zhongyun Zhao and Eric Wu

1 INTRODUCTION

China has been reforming its centrally planned economy since the late 1970s. The economic reform has led to enormous changes in many sectors including the health care system (Cretin et al. 1990; Henderson et al. 1994; Hsiao 1984; Hu 1988; Liu et al. 1994, 1999; World Bank 1993, 1996; Yip and Hsiao 1997). For nearly five decades, the Chinese government has provided its urban employees with publicly funded primary care through two major health programs: the Government Insurance Program (GIP), and the Labor Insurance Program (LIP). GIP pays for the health care services of all government employees, their dependants, veterans, educators, and college students. LIP covers the employees and retirees of the state-owned enterprises, as well as their dependants. Some collective-owned enterprises also provide their employees with a full or partial health care coverage benefit following the LIP approach.

As China's growing economy takes a market-oriented direction, both GIP and LIP are threatened by three fundamental problems for the insured: low coverage, poor risk pooling, and the lack of incentives and accountability for economic efficiency and quality of care. First, GIP and LIP cover no more than 50 percent of the total urban population. Currently, there are about 360 million people living in urban areas. Second, both GIP and LIP are institution-based insurance plans, pooling disease risks only within each institution. Third, GIP and LIP reimburse health care providers through traditional fee-for-service models, producing few incentives and cost sharing responsibilities for both patients and providers. As a result, neither patients nor providers are motivated to have concern regarding cost and health outcomes in the use of health care resources (moral hazard).

In attempting to reform the existing urban health care system, in 1994 the Chinese central government initiated a community-based health insurance plan. This plan then has been used as an experiment in two middle-sized cities, Zhenjiang and Jiujiang, each having a population of over 2.5 million. The pilot experimental model and its difference from GIP and LIP are described in detail elsewhere (Yuen 1996; Yip and Hsiao 1997; Liu et al. 1999). Fundamentally, the new insurance plan differs from GIP and LIP in several aspects as follows. First, as an insurer, it pools together all citywide employers and employees under a single insurance entity, aiming to maximize the population disease risk-pooling capacity. This universal coverage policy is also intended to minimize the problem of adverse selections. Under this policy, all people working in public institutions and state-owned enterprises within the city are mandated to participate in the experiment. Also included are disabled army veterans, retired cadres, college students, Chinese workers employed under joint ventures, and some employees of private enterprises.

Second, the new plan has three financing tiers: individual Medical Savings Accounts (MSAs), out-of-pocket deductibles, and the Social Insurance Account for all subscribers. For the individual MSAs, the employee contributes 1 percent of his or her salary to his or her named account. The employer contributes 10 percent of the employee's salary, of which 4 percent goes to the individual MSAs for those under the age of 45 or 6 percent for those above 45, with the remaining portion for the Social Insurance Account. When seeking care, individuals are charged first through their MSAs, followed by an out-of-pocket payment of up to 5 percent of his or her annual salary as a deductible. Any expenses exceeding the deductible are then covered by the Social Insurance Account, coupled with a decreasing co-payment schedule. The primary goal of the three-tier payment policy is to create demand-side incentives for cost consciousness while risk pooling against catastrophic diseases.

Third, health care providers are all subject to the approval of their service contracts by the city Social Security Bureau in order to participate in the new plan. Providers must comply with an agreed fee schedule and other financing arrangements, and are subjected to audits from the Bureau. There are also some pre-determined financial arrangements between the insurer and providers. For example, a prospective budget is agreed on between the appointed facility and the insurer. The budget consists of several components: the payment for inpatient services based upon the previous year's average per diem cost, average length of stay and the number of admissions; and the payment for outpatient services based on the previous year's average cost per outpatient visit and the number of visits. Fee schedules, drugs formulary, and other guidelines are also employed based upon budgeted contracts.

Following the pilot experiment, China has taken a few further steps in reforming its urban health care system. In 1996, similar experiments were extended to 57 other cities. In 1998, the State Council determined to reform the rest of the urban sector following the basic guidelines of the experimental framework. Under the government agenda, the nationwide reform is expected to take place in all urban sectors by the end of 1999. Facing such an enormous challenge, China needs to address a wide array of critical issues concerning the reform. Among others, a major concern with the reform is whether the reform model can contain health care cost without compromising the overall quality and equity of care. To date, only the pilot experiment in Zhenjiang city has established a valuable database based on a series of annual surveys of the insured and providers. Given its uniqueness and predominant influence over the national reform, the Zhenjiang experiment provides invaluable information and observations for assessing China's urban health care reform.

There were a few previous studies that described the overall performance, impacts, and lessons of the pilot experiment at an aggregate level   (Jiangsu Province Bureau of Health 1996; Song 1997; World Bank 1993, 1996; Yip and Hsiao 1997; Yuen 1996). Most of these studies suggested that the experimental plan in Zhenjiang is successful in terms of cost savings in the short run. Yet there was a major remaining issue as to how the cost savings were obtained. In particular, it was questioned to what extent the cost savings were really due to any significant reduced utilization rates of various services (Yip and Hsiao 1997).

Using data from the 1995 survey at individual level, Liu et al. (1999) presented an explanatory analysis of the experiment. This was the first study on the experiment that was conducted in the context of an econometric framework. This study accorded with previous findings that the experimental model in Zhenjiang contained the total health care cost during the first post-reform year. As to the causes of the cost savings, Liu et al. showed that these were strongly associated with the reduced utilization rates of various services, especially of the hospital admissions and length of stay (LOS) per admission. As noted by the authors, however, this study was based on only one year's observation of the experiment. Thus the reliability and robustness of the study's findings were quite limited. For instance, it is likely that some people may have perceived the new health insurance plan to be less generous than GIP and LIP. Such a perception could then have induced people to 'stock up' on health care before moving into the new plan (Newhouse 1993; Long et al. 1998). This stock-up issue, in fact, did become an actual concern in 1994 for the city government of Zhenjiang. Nonetheless, the one-year database could contain some observations that may lead to some degree of over-estimation of the cost savings attributed to the experiment.

The present study, commissioned by the China Ministry of Health, presents a further assessment of the Zhenjiang experiment using the multiyear survey data series from 1994 through 1996. Two major policy issues are to be investigated in the study: (1) whether the experimental plan is more effective in containing overall health cost inflation, as a result of its enhanced cost containment mechanisms including prospective budgeting, Medical Savings Accounts, fee schedules, prescription guidelines, and consumer co-payments; and (2) whether the experimental plan may have altered the utilization of various services including outpatient care, inpatient care, emergency care, and use of expensive medical facilities. The first question is to address whether the new plan is more efficient than GIP and LIP in terms of cost savings, while the second question is to determine the main driving forces for any significant cost savings.

In the next section the study's analytical framework and database are discussed. The following section presents the major empirical findings from the estimated models. After that is a discussion on the explanations and implications of the findings, and the final section concludes the study.

2   DATA AND MODELING

2.1   Data

Data for this study were derived from a series of annual surveys at the individual level conducted in the city of Zhenjiang. Starting with a baseline survey in December of 1994, three similar surveys followed subsequently in 1995, 1996, and 1997. Zhenjiang is located in Jiangsu province and includes a county, three towns, and two districts. It has a population of 2.6 million, of which 525 000 are urban residents. Prior to the reform, the GIP covered 78 887, and LIP covered 360 004 individuals.

The baseline data were collected in 1994, comprising 10 376 individual observations. An important feature of the baseline survey is that most cost and utilization variables were collected for both 1993 and 1994. In the 1995 survey there were 14 745 observations, also containing variables for 1995 and partly for 1994. The 1996 survey includes about 10 000 observations. There are eight groups of variables in the survey series, including (1) demographic characteristics; (2) health status in the two-week period immediately prior to the survey; (3) inpatient care; (4) health status in the one-month period immediately prior to the survey; (5) annual utilization of outpatient visits, inpatient visits, emergency visits, usage of certain medical facilities; (6) chronic disease and disability; (7) annual medical expenditure and income; and (8) people's opinions on the new health plan.

2.2 Modeling

To document the year-specific responsiveness of health care costs and utilization to the transition of the health care system in the Zhenjiang experiment, an attempt was made to employ a multivariate econometric model that captured the effects of the experiment, while controlling for the effects of all other confounding factors. This was necessary partly because the series of annual survey databases for the study was not for the same panel of individuals. As a result, individuals could be different in different years in terms of socioeconomic characteristics and health behaviors. In addition, the study distinguishes the impact of the reform on the probability of obtaining care from that on the quantity of care for a given time period. This consideration is based on the grounds that the former is mainly a patient-driven event while the latter is more likely to be determined by both the patients and the providers. To accomplish the research tasks, this study derived an analytical framework from the two-part model (TPM) (Duan et al. 1983; Newhouse 1993; Short et al. 1997). The TPM assumes that health care users and non-users follow different distributions with regard to their demand for health care. Accordingly, the use of health care was modeled in a two-step process: whether or not to use care; and how much to use, given that care was to be used. More formally, the model was specified for individual i:

$$I_i = \alpha_{95} D_{95i} + \alpha_{96} D_{96i} + X_i A_{Xi} + \varepsilon_i \quad i = 1,...N \qquad (7.1)$$

$$M_i\big|_{I_i=1} = \beta_{95} D_{95i} + \beta_{96} D_{96i} + Z_i B_{Zi} + \eta_i\big|_{I_i=1} \quad i = 1,...N_1 \qquad (7.2)$$

Where I_i is a dummy variable being 1 for users (N_1), and 0 for non-users (N_0), and M_i measures the amount of health care expenditures or utilization rates. D_{95} and D_{96} are dummy variables measuring the reform-induced effects for 1995 and 1996, respectively. X_i and Z_i are row vectors of observed confounding variables that could also influence the individual's use of care, A_{Xi} and B_{Zi} are column vectors of coefficients to be estimated, and ε_i and η_{1i} are error terms which capture the effects of unobserved factors.

In the model system, equation (7.1) estimates the likelihood of obtaining care by all individuals (N). Conditional on using medical care ($I_i = 1$), equation (7.2) identifies the quantity of medical care use by medical users only (N_1)). As noted earlier, the two equations reveal quite different behaviors and consequences in the determination of health care use. The probability function mainly indicates patient behavior in seeking care and may shed light on access to care, while the conditional utilization function shows both patient and health care providers' roles in the use of health care recourses.

In estimating the net impact of the experimental health plan in contrast to the previous GIP and LIP, several critical issues must be taken into account. One of which is the 'stock up' effect, referring to the hypothesis that people may 'stock-up' on the use of care before leaving a more generous plan for a less generous one (Long et al. 1998; Newhouse 1993). Presumably, people in Zhenjiang would perceive the new plan to be more restrictive and accountable. To minimize such a possible 'stock-up' effect in 1994, cost and utilization measures in 1993 were incorporated into the 1994 baseline measurement. In particular, two dummy variables were defined being 1 respectively for 1995 and 1996, and 0 jointly for 1993 and 1994. The two year-dummy variables included in the analytic model capture the net year-specific impact of the reform. Considering the non-longitudinal nature of the study database, the model was specified to include a set of non-system individual variables (X_i and Z_i) including age, sex, marital status, education, chronic disease status, occupation, and assigned providers for regular visits.

With respect to the statistical distributions of the error terms in equations 7.1 and 7.2, a logistic distribution was assumed for the probability function of obtaining care. Given the use of care, a log normal distribution was employed to estimate the conditional cost functions. For utilization analysis, a Poisson distribution was used to model the discrete outcome variables including outpatient visits, inpatient admissions, emergency visits, LOS per admission, and expensive medical facility use.

3   EMPIRICAL RESULTS

3.1   Expenditure Analysis

We first reveal some socioeconomic characteristics of the individuals included in this analysis. A total of 44 345 individuals were examined, of which 35 032 turned to be health care users (defined as those who used any care during any years from 1993 through 1996). The nonusers as a whole tended to be younger, at age 34, while users were aged 40 on average. Average annual income, measured in RMB ($1 = 8.3 RMB), was higher for the users at 4459 RMB in 1993/94, 5208 RMB in 1995, and 5595 RMB in 1996, than for the nonusers at 4143 RMB in 1993/94, 4935 RMB in 1995, and 5369 MRB in 1996. In terms of annual health expenditure among the users, the data show this was 541 RMB in 1993/94, 400 RMB in 1995, and 566 RMB in 1996. From the descriptive statistics, it appears that the reform experiment resulted in a decrease in total health expenditures for the first post-reform year, but failed to sustain the decreasing trend in the following year. This observation prompted a critical concern regarding the sustainability of the experimental model in containing costs. The following TPM analysis provides more in-depth investigation of this and other issues.

Results of the total expenditure analysis are given in Table 7.1. As shown by the coefficients of D95 and D96, the experimental plan led to significant increases in the probability of seeking care for both 1995 and 1996, as compared to 1993/94 ($p < 0.01$). Conditional on using any health care services during the study period, the individuals were found to consume 26 percent less health expenditure in 1995 than in 1993/94 ($p < 0.01$). As indicated in the above descriptive statistics, however, this downward change was reversed in 1996 when total expenditure went up. That is, the experimental plan effectively reduced health care expenditure for the first post-reform year, but not in the second year. This result raised a challenging question as to whether the re-increased health care spending pattern in 1996 was due to the system failure or any external policy shocks. Among the possible causes of the incident, a particular policy shock seemed to play a crucial role. This policy shock occurred in April through August of 1996, when local health care providers were given an unusual flexibility in prescribing and billing for reimbursement. This temporary policy was an attempt to accommodate increasing pressures for easing the cost control policies under the new health insurance scheme. Given such a policy shock, it seemed to be normal to anticipate a significant increase in annual health care spending in 1996.

To test the policy shock hypothesis, the TPM expenditure model was re-examined using one-month expenditure data. The rationale for estimating the one-month health expenditure data is that since the one-month surveys were conducted during November every year, the policy shocks that occurred during the middle of 1996 should have had no effect on the individuals' consumption patterns in November. The results of the one-month model are in Table 7.2. As expected, in the logistic probability

Table 7.1 General health care expenditure models

	Probability model (logistic)		Conditional expenditures model (semi-log)	
	Odds ratio	Pr > χ^2	β coefficient	Pr > |T|
Intercept			2.197	< 0.01**
D95	1.614	< 0.01**	−0.255	< 0.01**
D96	2.574	< 0.01**	0.163	< 0.01**
Other variables controlled in the model	Age, sex, marriage, education, income, chronic disease status, job status, and designated health care provider			
Pr > F			< 0.01**	
Pr > χ^2		< 0.01**		
Observations		44 345	35 032	

Note: ** Probability < 0.01; Pr > χ^2, based upon the statistic of −2 log L.

Table 7.2 One-month health care expenditure models

	Probability model (logistic)		Conditional expenditures model (semi-log)	
	Odds ratio	Pr > χ^2	β coefficient	Pr > |T|
Intercept			2.635	< 0.01**
D95	1.462	< 0.01**	−0.491	< 0.01**
D96	1.444	< 0.01**	−0.420	< 0.01**
Other variables controlled in the model	Age, sex, marriage, education, income, chronic disease status, job status, and designated health care provider			
Pr > F			< 0.01**	
Pr > χ^2		< 0.01**		
Observations		33 459	10 439	

Note: ** Probability < 0.01; Pr > χ^2, based upon the statistic of −2 log L.

function, the one-month expenditure model agrees with the annual expenditure model that people were more likely to seek care in a given month under the experimental plan ($p < 0.01$). In the conditional expenditure function, the results are strongly supportive of the anticipation that the individual total expenditures decreased consistently after the reform in 1995 (49 percent) and 1996 (42 percent), both of the reductions are highly significant ($p < 0.01$).

Furthermore, we looked into changes in inpatient care expenditures in response to the reform (Table 7.3). In contrast with the increased probability of seeking general care as shown in the above total expenditure models, the likelihood of seeking inpatient care by the

Table 7.3 Inpatient care expenditure models

	Probability model (logistic)		Conditional expenditures model (semi-log)	
	Odds ratio	$Pr > \chi^2$	β Coefficient	$Pr > |T|$
Intercept			4.713	< 0.01**
D95	0.842	< 0.01**	0.035	0.504
D96	0.809	< 0.01**	0.093	0.139
Other variables controlled in the model	Age, sex, marriage, education, income, chronic disease status, job status, and hospital type			
$Pr > F$			< 0.01**	
$Pr > \chi^2$		< 0.01**		
Observations		46 817	1824	

Note: ** Probability < 0.01; $Pr > \chi^2$, based upon the statistic of –2 log L.

general population decreased significantly in both 1995 and 1996 ($p < 0.01$). And among those who used inpatient services, the hospital expenditures per admission did not change significantly before and after the reform.

3.2   Utilization Analysis

Given the expenditure model results that the experimental insurance plan resulted in substantial cost savings, the next question is what drove the cost savings. The question has particularly been raised as to whether the cost savings were primarily due to significant reduced utilization of primary care services, or to the decreased use of expensive diagnosis and treatment facilities (Yip and Hsiao 1997). To determine this issue, we examined year-specific changes in five utilization measures: outpatient visits, inpatient admissions, emergency visits, LOS per admission, and use of expensive technology instruments. Liu et al. (1999) presented some preliminary results based on 1995 data, suggesting that the reduced utilization of primary services seemed to play a major role in explaining the cost savings. Results below provide further evidence on this issue.

Tables 7.4 to 7.8 show the results from various utilization models based on five utilization measures. Basically, the results are very consistent with the implications from the expenditure analysis models. First, among the general population the likelihood of seeking outpatient visits increased in both 1995 and 1996 ($p < 0.01$). Among outpatient users, the annual number of outpatient visits decreased by 10 percent in 1995 ($p < 0.01$),

Table 7.4 Utilization models – annual outpatient visits

	Probability model (logistic)		Conditional utilization model (Poisson)		
	Odds ratio	$Pr > \chi^2$	β coefficient	$Pr > \chi^2$	change %
Intercept			0.050	0.566	
D95	1.617	< 0.01**	–0.106	< 0.01**	–0.101
D96	2.740	< 0.01**	0.239	< 0.01**	0.270
Other variables controlled in the model	Age, sex, marriage, education, income, chronic disease status, job status, and designated health care provider				
$Pr > \chi^2$	< 0.01**				
Observations	46 808			34 018	

Note: ** Probability < 0.01; $Pr > \chi^2$, based upon the statistic of –2 log L.

Table 7.5 Utilization models – annual inpatient admissions

	Probability model (logistic)		Conditional utilization model (Poisson)		
	Odds Ratio	$Pr > \chi^2$	β Coefficient	$Pr > \chi^2$	change %
Intercept			–0.114	0.583	
D95	0.842	< 0.01**	–0.043	0.157	–0.042
D96	0.809	< 0.01**	–0.010	0.783	–0.010
Other variables controlled in the model	Age, sex, marriage, education, income, chronic disease status, job status, and designated health care provider				
$Pr > \chi^2$	< 0.01**				
Observations	46 817			2127	

Note: ** Probability < 0.01; $Pr > \chi^2$, based upon the statistic of –2 log L.

Table 7.6 Utilization model – length of stay per admission

	Inpatient days model (Poisson)		
	β Coefficient	$Pr > \chi^2$	change %
Intercept	1.444	0.002	3.238
D95	–0.175	< 0.01**	–0.160
D96	–0.255	< 0.01**	–0.225
Other variables controlled in the model	Age, sex, marriage, education, income, chronic disease status, job status, and designated health care provider		
Observations	1702		

Note: ** Probability < 0.01; $Pr > \chi^2$, based upon the statistic of –2 log L.

Table 7.7 Utilization models – annual emergency visits

	Probability model (logistic)		Conditional utilization model (Poisson)		
	Odds ratio	$Pr > \chi^2$	β coefficient	$Pr > \chi^2$	change %
Intercept			0.050	0.566	
D95	0.854	$< 0.01**$	–0.104	$< 0.01**$	–0.099
D96	0.919	0.047*	–0.015	0.714	–0.015
Other variables controlled in the model	Age, sex, marriage, education, income, chronic disease status, job status, and designated health care provider				
$Pr > \chi^2$	$< 0.01**$				
Observations	46 817		4452		

Note: ** Probability < 0.01; $Pr > \chi^2$, based upon the statistic of –2 log L.

Table 7.8   Utilization models – expensive medical facility use

	Probability Model (Logistic)		Conditional Utilization Model (Poisson)		
	Odds Ratio	$Pr > \chi^2$	β Coefficient	$Pr > \chi^2$	change %
Intercept			0.050	0.566	
D95	0.892	0.144	–0.070	0.382	–0.067
D96	1.019	0.828	–0.021	0.812	–0.021
Other variables controlled in the model	Age, sex, marriage, education, income, chronic disease status, job status, and designated health care provider				
$Pr > \chi^2$	$< 0.01**$				
Observations	46 778		958		

Note: ** Probability < 0.01; $Pr > \chi^2$, based upon the statistic of –2 log L.

but increased by 27 percent in 1996, as compared to the pre-reform level. This upward trend in 1996 was well expected, in light of the middle-year policy shock discussed above.

As to inpatient care utilization among the general population, the likelihood of being admitted to a hospital decreased sharply in both 1995 and 1996 ($p < 0.01$). Among those who were ever hospitalized, the annual number of admissions per patient remained constant before and after the reform. Interestingly, however, the average length of stay (LOS) per admission reduced sharply by 16 percent in 1995 ($p < 0.01$) and by 22 percent in 1996 ($p < 0.01$).

Changes in emergency care visits follows a similar pattern as that of inpatient care. The likelihood of seeking emergency visits was lower after the reform in 1995 ($p < 0.01$) and in 1996 ($p < 0.05$). Annual emergency visits per user decreased by 10 percent in 1995. In 1996, however, these were no different from the pre-reform level. In contrast, for the use of expensive technologies which were defined to include CT, MRI, color-doppler, x-ray, and b-ultrasound, the study finds no evidence for any significant changes in terms of either the probability of using the facilities among the general population, or the quantity of utilization among users.

4   DISCUSSIONS AND IMPLICATIONS

The central finding established in the study is that the experimental community-based insurance model is more efficient in containing total health care cost as compared to LIP and GIP, the two existing primary health programs for urban employees. Both the expenditure and utilization analyses provided consistent evidence for the effectiveness of the experimental health plan in achieving the overall cost savings. In attempting to explain the determinants of the cost savings, several explanations seem to provide great insights and also offer some important policy implications.

First, the experimental plan produced a strong substitution effect between outpatient care and inpatient care. Initial evidence for such a substitution effect was from the expenditure analysis suggesting that after the reform the likelihood of using all care and outpatient care increased, while the likelihood of inpatient care use decreased. The utilization analyses enhanced the observation that to a large extent outpatient care was substituted for inpatient and emergency care in terms of annual utilization rates. Moreover, the decreased LOS per admission after the reform further helped establish the substitution effect. Nonetheless, the substitution effect appeared to play a major role in accomplishing the cost savings under the reform experiment. From international experience, the concept of substituting outpatient care for inpatient care has been widely advocated in health professions. Yet empirical studies are somewhat inconclusive as to how the use of outpatient care versus inpatient care would respond to changes in health insurance policies (Davis and Russel 1972; Elnicki 1976; Freiberg 1979; Phelps 1992).

Second, the experimental plan seemed to yield positive impact on improving access and equality of care. This observation, while not based on any formal analysis, can be seen from the structure of the TPM estimates. For instance, on the one hand, the probability function indicated an increased likelihood of seeking care by the general population after the reform. On the other hand, among those who accessed care, the quantity of care was reduced (except for the external policy shock effect in 1996). A direct implication from this finding is that more people obtained care, indicating improved access care among the general population after the reform. Moreover, utilization among users decreased, suggesting a more equal distribution of care among the general population. It must be noted, however, that equality does not equate with equity. The latter defines distribution of care on the basis of needs, and thus it remains to be explored in further research.

Third, the experimental plan resulted in substantially reduced utilization of inpatient care in terms of admissions and length of stay per admission, and emergency care services. Changes in the use of expensive facilities were not significant in response to the reform. An implication of these findings is that the use of specific medical facilities was not particularly elastic to the policy change, whereas the structural changes in the use of outpatient care versus inpatient care and emergency care seemed to be rather responsive. Since there were substantial total cost savings accomplished by the new plan, it appears that cost containment strategies in general may be more effective when focusing on the efficient allocation of types of care as the first line, as opposed to managing the use of specific medical technology facilities.

5   CONCLUDING REMARKS

This study carried out an evaluation analysis of the new health insurance plan experimented in Zhenjiang based on a multiyear survey database at the individual level. The analysis focuses on a major financing issue of the reform experiment: whether the experiment could contain health care costs. It concluded that the experimental plan is significantly more efficient in the use of health care resources than LIP and GIP, the two major health care programs for urban employees in China before the reform. The study also sheds light on the likelihood that the reform has led to some progress in other areas including access to care and equality of utilization.

This study has left a number of areas for future research. First, the study was designed in a pre- and post-reform fashion to evaluate various impacts of the experimental plan. Due to data limitations, the model was unable to explicitly include non-experimental individuals to serve as a control group. While efforts were made to control for changes in individual characteristics in modeling the experimental impact, the results should be read with caution as the reform dummy variables could capture the reform effect as well as other non-reform confounding factors. Future research may consider revising the model by including a population group that did not experience the experiment but was compatible to the experimental groups in terms of population characteristics and environmental conditions.

Second, while the study concentrated on the pre- and post-reform changes in a large spectrum of aspects from cost containment, it did not address the distributional effects of these changes among different cohorts of people due to income, occupation, job status, or education. More specifically, given the identified overall benefits from the reform, the current study provides no information on who benefited and who did not, and how large might be the difference. In fact, the distributional impact of the reform is of great concern for both the government and the public. Information on the distributional impact therefore should help policy makers better identify and implement effective instruments in making the health care system more equitable, accessible, and efficient. A recent study by Liu et al. (2001) extended the analysis on equity issues with the reform experiment.

Third, this study focused on the overall health care financing and alignment of incentives to control cost and utilization, evaluating implications of the financing model on utilization. Little has been revealed on the risk variations for different diseases, and individual characteristics, as well as the relative value (cost–benefit) of health services including pharmaceuticals towards the overall cost savings and health outcomes as the reform platform for plan design and coverage for services. For example, a good risk analysis of the diseases and institutional arrangement across individuals may provide quite useful insights into both curative and preventive strategies in order to reduce the future risk of catastrophic events. In addition, the data will be valuable in policies driving the supply and distribution of provider resources.

Fourth, while it found cost savings and reduced utilization in health care services in the post-reform period, the study did not go as far as explaining what specific features of the reform led to the changes. In other words, it remains unknown whether and how the changed cost and utilization were attributable to which of the new model instruments such as MSAs, cost sharing, essential drug formulary, or prospective payment schemes. The study is thus limited in its ability to draw policy implications on the effectiveness of the considered policy instruments in cost containment.

Another limitation of the study is the lack of health outcomes assessment due to data limitations. While this study has implied an improvement in equity of using care, it is far from clear how the reform has really changed the whole spectrum of population health outcomes.

From the economics perspective, many would agree that whether one health care system is superior to the other should depend on an important criterion – efficiency; that is, which system would achieve better population health outcomes for a given budget. Following this notion, it would be insufficient to carry out an adequate assessment of the best health care model without data on population health outcomes.

Finally, it is worth noting that while the study indicated the cost-saving effect of substituting outpatient care for inpatient care induced by the new plan, the substitution alone without further investigation might not be sufficient to accomplish the long-term goal of sustainable cost-effective quality care through the reform. In the US, for example, cost containment measures implemented by managed care plans were found to be effective in changing the use of health services to having more office visits and preventive care, less use of inpatient services and expensive procedures, and reduced length of stay. These changes seemed to result in notable cost savings in the short run. In the long run, however, the cost-saving benefits have seldom been sustainable as more costly services were shifted to outpatient settings. Therefore, as a policy implication, a trend in substituting outpatient care for inpatient care alone may not convey much instrumental information for cost containment strategies. Instead, a more effective approach should focus on the cost effectiveness of service-specific treatment protocols, regardless of whether these are in outpatient or inpatient settings, in order to improve the overall efficiency of allocating and utilizing health care resources.

REFERENCES

Cretin, S., N. Duan, A.P. Jr. Williams, X.Y. Gu and Y.Q. Shi (1990), 'Modeling the effect of insurance on health expenditures in the People's Republic of China', *Health Services Research*, **25**: 667–85.

Davis, K. and L.B. Russel (1972), 'The substitution of hospital outpatient care for inpatient care', *Review of Economics and Statistics*, **LIV**: 109–120.

Duan, N., W. Manning, C.N. Morris and J.P. Newhouse (1983), 'A comparison of alternative models of the demand for medical care', *Journal of Business and Economic Statistics*, **1**: 115–26.

Elnicki, R.A. (1976), 'Substitution of outpatient for inpatient hospital care: a cost analysis', *Inquiry*, **XIII**: 245–61.

Freiberg, L. Jr. (1979), 'Substitution of outpatient care for inpatient care: problems and experience', *Journal of Health Politics, Policy and Law*, **3**: 479–96.

Henderson, G., J. Akin, L. Zhiming, S. Jin, H. Ma and K. Ge (1994), 'Equity and the utilization of health services: report of an eight province survey in China', *Social Science and Medicine*, **39**: 687–99.

Hsiao, W.C. (1984), 'Transformation of health care in China', *New England Journal of Medicine*, **310**: 932–6.

Hu, T.W. (1988), 'Diffusion of western medical technology in China since the economic reform', *International Journal of Technology Assessment in Health Care*, **1**: 345–58.

Jiangsu Province Bureau of Health (1996), *Zhenjiang Employee Medical Insurance System Reform Studies*, Nanjing: Jiangsu, P. R. China.

Liu, G., R. Cai, Z. Zhao, P. Yuen, X. Xiong, C. Shumarry and B. Wang (1999), 'Urban health care reform initiative in China: findings from its pilot experiment in Zhenjiang City', *International Journal of Economic Development*, **1**(4): 504–25.

Liu, G., X. Liu and Q. Meng (1994), 'Privatization of the medical market in socialist China: a historic approach', *Health Policy*, **27**: 157–74.

Liu, G., Z. Zhao, R. Cai, T. Yamada and T. Yamada (2001), 'Equity in access to health care: assessing the urban health insurance reform in China', *Social Science and Medicine*, in press.

Long, S.H., M.S. Marquis and J. Redgers (1998), 'Do people shift their use of health services over time to take advantage of insurance?', *Journal of Health Economics*, **17**: 105–15.

Newhouse, J.P. (1993), *Free for All? Lessons from the RAND Health Insurance Experiment*, Cambridge, MA: Harvard University Press.

Phelps, C.E. (1992), *Health Economics*, New York: Harper Collins Publishers.

Short, P.F., B.A. Hahn, K. Beauregard, P.H. Harvey and M.L. Wilets (1997), 'The effect of universal coverage on health expenditures for the uninsured', *Medical Care*, **35**: 95–113.

Song, X. (1997), *Reform of the Medical Insurance System of Urban Workers and Staff Members in China*, Beijing: State Commission for Economic Restructuring.

World Bank (1993), *China: Long-term Issues and Options in the Health Transition*, Washington, DC: The World Bank.

World Bank (1996), *China: Issues and Options in Health Financing*, Washington, DC: The World Bank.

Yip, W.C. and W.C. Hsiao (1997), 'Medical savings accounts: lessons from China', *Health Affairs*, **16**: 244–51.

Yuen, P.P. (1996), 'Reforming health care financing in urban China', *International Journal of Public Administration*, **19**: 211–32.

8. Catastrophic illness policy and equity in delivering health care: empirical evidence from Taiwan

Jui-Fen Rachel Lu

1 INTRODUCTION

Equity is one of the most frequently discussed policy objectives in health care. Among various definitions of equity debated, most of the discussions have centered around 'equality of expenditure per capita', 'distribution according to need', 'equality of access', 'equality of choice sets' and 'equality of health' (Le Grand 1987; Mooney et al. 1991; Culyer and Wagstaff 1993). Equity concern is prominently featured in the health care discussion because of the uncertainty (uncontrollable factor) in the demand for health care and – as Culyer and Wagstaff (1993) put it in a more philosophical context – 'good health' is necessary for an individual to flourish as a human being. Therefore, equity in health care implies distributing health care so as to equalize health. However, the measurement of health is often subjective and controversial, hence most of the equity issues are discussed in the context of the delivery of health care.

Most of the research investigates equity in the delivery of health care with a focus on income-related equity, in particular, in the case of national health care program assessment (Le Grand 1978; Collins and Klein 1980; O'Donnell and Propper 1991; Wagstaff et al. 1991; van Doorslaer and Wagstaff 1992). In terms of equity in the delivery of health care, horizontal equity and vertical equity are often discussed. Horizontal equity is interpreted to mean that persons in equal need of medical care should receive the same treatment and vertical equity to mean that those in unequal need should be treated differently, which is less frequently discussed (Wagstaff et al. 1991). Income-related equity is a horizontal version of the distribution principles. The emphasis here is therefore to examine whether people in equal need of health care receive the same treatment, irrespective of their income levels.

Although whether people in equal need of health care have received the same treatment is frequently studied to examine the equity principle, the definition for 'need of health care' is still inconclusive. Culyer and Wagstaff (1993) have discussed four major definitions of need: need as initial health, need as capacity to benefit, need as expenditures a person ought to have, and need as expenditures required to exhaust capacity to benefit. Then Culyer and Wagstaff (1993) argued that the definitions of need in the literature are inadequate. It is obvious that the optimal goal of seeking health care is to achieve health. Hence, theoretically, the equity principle will be better examined in the context of equality of health. Nonetheless, the appropriate way of measuring health is still in the early stage of development. Therefore, currently most of the research is restricted to an assessment of equity in the distribution of health care (O'Donnell and Propper 1991). Given the constraint in equity measurement, this chapter adopts the definition of "equal treatment for equal need" in examining the catastrophic illness policy under the National Health Insurance program in Taiwan.

Under the National Health Insurance (NHI) program in Taiwan, 'need' for medical care is judged by the potential health expenditures (financial burden) in the context of catastrophic illness policy. The NHI law exempts patients with NHI-defined catastrophic illness from copayment requirement, for fear of the financial burden which this may impose. In this chapter, the author argues that the policy statement is erroneous based on the following reason. In terms of financial burden, patients with a NHI-defined catastrophic illness may not bear as much as those who do not fit into the categories. Hence, exempting patients from copayment requirements based on pre-determined disease categories is not equitable, not to mention the potential moral hazard problems from copayment exemption. The goal of this chapter is to provide a Taiwan example in examining the equity issue of the catastrophic illness policy under the National Health Insurance program.

The first section provides the rationale for copayment exemption and its equity implication. The case of the catastrophic illness policy under NHI in Taiwan is also presented. The data collected and analyses performed to investigate the equity implication of Taiwan's current catastrophic illness policy are then provided in the methodology section. Finally, the chapter is concluded with a discussion on the research constraints and the empirical evidence.

2 COPAYMENT EXEMPTION AND EQUITY IN HEALTH CARE

Through its risk-pooling mechanism, health insurance has provided financial protection and improved the access to health care for financially disadvantaged people. However, despite all the merits of the health insurance program, there are potential welfare losses that may ensue. Insurance lowers the prices that the patients encounter. When the price for medical services is less, patients have incentives to consume more medical services than are clinically deemed necessary. The phenomenon is characterized as 'moral hazard' (Feldstein 1999). In practice, the copayment requirement of the health insurance policies is designed to reduce the potential impact of moral hazard. Empirical evidence has demonstrated that the degrees of coinsurance rate will influence health care utilization rates (Manning et al. 1987). Research results from the Rand Health Insurance Experiment (HIE) have demonstrated that people in the free care plan (with zero coinsurance rate) have 30 percent higher admission rate and consume 45 percent more health care expenditures than people in the plan with 95 percent coinsurance rate (Newhouse 1993). However, no system is perfect. The down side of the copayment system also needs to be taken into consideration, that is, the potential access barriers which may arise as a result of a high amount of copayment for the financially disadvantaged group. Hence, to assure people with equal need for health care are treated equally, irrespective of income levels, the potential financial burden should be lessened for people who are financially disadvantaged. Copayment exemption for specific groups of people is a means that is often taken.

Some researchers have advocated that cost sharing should be income related to protect the access to care for the poor, further ensuring the equity principle (Feldstein 1971; Rice and Thorpe 1993). A previous study on families with catastrophic health care expenditures has examined the families with annual out-of-pocket expenditures exceeding 5, 10 and 20 percent of the family income, respectively (Wyszewianski 1986). The results have shown that although such families represent a small proportion of all families, and the out-of-pocket expenditures by those families may be modest. However relative to their family incomes, even these modest sums may still be financially burdensome. In the 1980s, three states, Main, Minnesota and Rhode Island offered state catastrophic health insurance programs to assist residents in meeting uncovered catastrophic expenses, where the cost sharing amount was related to income levels (Friedman et al. 1984). A study based on an annual survey conducted by the Bureau of Labor Statistics (BLS) indicated that 2.7

percent of full-time employees and their dependants have participated in health care plans with deductibles based on earnings (Rice and Thorpe 1993). Rice and Thorpe (1993) further proposed that the income tax system should be used to make up for any inequities.

When the Taiwan government first provided universal health coverage to the citizens of Taiwan in 1995, one of the cost containment measures taken was the copayment requirement. At the same time, BNHI also implemented a catastrophic illness policy which exempts the copayment requirement for people with a BNHI-defined catastrophic illness. BNHI released its list for catastrophic illnesses based on the assumption that patients with these specific categories of disease will incur higher expenditures, therefore should be exempted from copayment. Hence, the stipulation of copayment exemption is considered to assure the equity of delivering health care to the needy. However, the policy was implemented without the support of empirical evidence. Not only may it not achieve its goal of equity, but also it actually may violate the equity principle. The equity distribution can be examined in two dimensions; first, with data on household income, the researcher can investigate whether patients with BNHI-defined catastrophic illness are in fact relatively financially disadvantaged. Second, do patients with similar needs for health care (but not BNHI-released catastrophic illness) consume less health expenditure as BNHI assumed?   If not, the fact that this group of patients was not given copayment exemption will violate the equity principle (that is, they were not treated the same). Due to data limitation, this chapter is taking the second approach to examine the equity implication of the catastrophic illness policy. Before the method section, a brief background on Taiwan's National Health Insurance program and the evolution of the catastrophic illness policy are provided.

The Case of Taiwan

Taiwan inaugurated a national health insurance program on 1 March 1995, based on National Health Insurance Act enacted in September 1994. The NHI Act has three major objectives: to provide universal coverage and reasonable access to health care for every citizen; to control cost escalation at an affordable level; and to improve the quality of health care.

By design, the NHI program is a compulsory social insurance and is administered through a newly created governmental agency – the Bureau of National Health Insurance (BNHI). Since implementation, the NHI program increased the population under coverage from 57 percent in the pre-NHI period to 96 percent in 1997. The program also stressed the importance of cost containment by adopting a two-prong strategy, supply and demand, to control future health care expenditures (Hsiao and Lu 1995). On the supply side, the NHI law establishes a single-payer system with a global budget (the global budget is currently enforced on dentistry and Chinese medicine services only). BNHI also has intended to reform the current fee-for-service payment system by phasing in a new case payment method (pre-DRG) to pay for hospital stays. By the end of 1999, there were 50 selected procedures reimbursed on a case payment basis. On the demand side, the NHI program initiates a copayment requirement when the insured demand services, except for cases of NHI-defined catastrophic illness, births and preventive medicines. Nonetheless, NHI has also instituted a cap for out-of-pocket copayment which is set at NT$19 000 (US$585) per admission and NT$31 000 (US$954) annually for acute hospital care (length of stay less than 30 days). Once the out-of-pocket expenditures exceed the ceiling, NHI will require no copayment from the patients. Meanwhile, the insured have complete freedom of choice of providers. Quality assurance is indirectly addressed in the NHI Act. BNHI is required by law to organize a Health Services Review Committee to review and monitor the quality and quantity of care provided under the system.

The NHI program is financed through a 4.25 percent payroll tax. In 1998, the approved medical claims have consumed NT$256 billion (US$8.5 billion). Currently, the NHI expenditure is increasing at an average annual rate of 11 percent, which has outpaced that of premium income by 5–6 percent, since its establishment (Bureau of National Health Insurance 1999). In addition to inpatient services, the hospital sector provides a significant amount of outpatient services and in total accounts for 64 percent of NHI expenditure. Unlike most of the OECD countries, outpatient services contribute a substantial amount of NHI dollars (68 percent) to Taiwan's health care system.

Before the NHI program was in place, the NHI Preparatory Office proposed two definitions of 'catastrophic illness' as: (1) illness which will call for high medical expenditures; and (2) illness which requires lifelong treatment. All the local medical societies were requested to provide a potential list of illnesses, which will fit into the definitions. However, despite numerous meetings, no consensus was achieved. Finally, the NHI Preparatory Office issued a public announcement that listed 15 categories of illness as NHI-defined catastrophic illnesses and the policy went into effect on the same day as NHI was inaugurated.

The implementation of the catastrophic illness policy has aroused heated debate on the inclusion criteria. Subsequently, as of May 1998, the list was expanded to cover 31 categories of illness through eight revisions, as a result of mounting pressure from patient support groups and medical

Table 8.1 Number of valid catastrophic illness certificates issued by the end of 1997

Category of major illness / injury	Number of certificates issued	Number of cancellations	Number of valid certificates issued
1. Cancer requiring aggressive or long-term treatment	178 623	21 634	156 989
2. Congenital abnormality of coagulation factors	794	10	784
3. Severe hemolytic and hypoplastic anemia	1846	122	1724
4. Chronic nephrasthenia (uremia) requiring regular dialysis	30 796	3215	27 581
5. Generalized autoimmune syndrome requiring lifelong treatment	19 941	487	19 454
6. Chronic psychiatric disorder	80 253	1832	78 421
7. Congenital metabolic disease	4288	131	4157
8. Chronic cardiac, pulmonary, gastrointestinal, renal, neurological, and skeletal disorders and chromosomal abnormalities	26 685	809	25 876
9. Second degree burns covering more than 20% of the body or third degree burns covering more than 10% of the body, facial burns with concurrent eye, ear, nose, or throat dysfunction	2931	96	2835
10. Follow-up treatment after heart, kidney, or bone marrow transplant	1380	31	1349
11. Poliomyelitis, cerebral palsy, and neurological, muscular, skeletal, pulmonary complications in premature infants (where the degree of impairment is medium or higher)	8235	258	7977
12. Major trauma rated 16 or above on the severity scale	10 385	1259	9126
13. Patients requiring long-term use of a respirator due to respiratory failure	6537	1690	4847
14. Patients suffering from severe malnutrition due to major enterectomy, intestinal failure, or other chronic disease, already on a fully intravenous diet for more than 30 days, and still unable to obtain sufficient nutrition through an oral diet	604	100	504
15. Severe decompression sickness or aeroembolism caused by scuba diving or improper decompression and accompanied by respiratory, circulatory, or neurological complications, and requiring long-term treatment	72	—	72

Table 8.1 Number of valid catastrophic illness certificates issued by the end of 1997 (cont.)

Category of major illness / injury	Number of certificates issued	Number of cancellations	Number of valid certificates issued
16. Myasthenia gravis	1343	16	1327
17. Congenital immunodeficiency	258	7	251
18. Neurological, muscular, cutaneous, skeletal, cardiopulmonary, urological, or gastrointestinal complications due to spinal injury or myeleterosis (where the degree of impairment is medium or higher)	3713	159	3554
19. Occupational disease	6106	240	5866
20. Cerebrovascular accident (CVA/stroke)			
21. Multiple Sclerosis	178	7	171
22. Congenital muscular dystrophy	252	11	241
23. Congenital vesicular epidermolysis	31	2	29
24. Leprosy	573	36	537
25. Cirrhosis of liver	6755	1312	5443
26. Premature infants determined to have medium impairments three months after birth	78	9	69
27. Black foot disease	174	–	174
28. Acquired immunodeficiency syndrome	13	–	13
Grand total	392 844	33 473	359 371

Source: Lu, J.F. and Y.C. Chuang 'Analysis on the inpatient utilization patterns under National Health Insurance: the case of catastrophic illness', research report for Department of Health, 1998.

specialty societies. In total, there were 0.36 million valid catastrophic illness certificates issued by the end of 1997 (Bureau of National Health Insurance 1998). The most common cause was in the first category of cancer (44 percent) (Table 8.1).

According to the Rules for Catastrophic Illness Certificates (1994), the insured who have a catastrophic illness can apply for catastrophic illness certificates. All relevant medical services in the course of treatment are exempted from copayment requirements. The catastrophic illness certificate is granted based on the descriptions in the formal diagnosis statements issued by physicians, referenced by ICD-9-CM codes. However, there are six categories of catastrophic illness which lack ICD-9-CM code specifications.

Due to the broad coverage of catastrophic illness, the definitions declared by BNHI are not specific. Consequently, substantial variations in medical treatment and health expenditures are observed among various categories of patients. There are also cases where patients with certain diseases may have decreasing demands for medical treatment and become no different from any other patients, as their health status improves and stabilizes over time. Hence, the equity of copayment exemption design is under scrutiny. In response, on 1 January 1998, BNHI announced it would limit the valid period for catastrophic illness certificates to three years. The extension of the certificate can be granted provided there is a formal diagnosis statement issued by the physician.

In sum, catastrophic illness patients consumed NT$40 billion (US$1.2 billion) of NHI expenditures, 44 percent on outpatient services and 56 percent on inpatient services, in 1997. On average, patients with catastrophic illness are only 2 percent of the covered population, but absorb 17.2 percent of the total NHI expenditure.

3   METHODS

This research adopts the definition of 'equal treatment for equal need' as the definition of equity. To assess patients' need for health care, the DRG (Diagnosis Related Group) classification system is applied. DRG is a patient classification scheme which reduces thousands of ICD-9-CM codes into approximately 467 groups based on patients' patterns of resource consumption (Altman and Ostby 1991). Factors such as principal diagnoses, complications, comorbidity, age, and discharge status are taken into account as classification criteria. Hence, patients in the same DRG group are assumed to possess similar needs for health care. The health care expenditure (NHI payment and out-of-pocket payment) is then used as a proxy for treatment received as data on clinical treatment are difficult to obtain and compare. The research hypothesis to test is that patients with BNHI-defined catastrophic illnesses actually may not consume more health care resources than non-catastrophic illness patients who have similar disease severity. Therefore, the copayment exemption based on pre-determined disease categories does not serve the principle of equity.

The empirical evidence is gathered through constructing two comparative groups whose patients have similar diseases and need for treatment in the disease episode. However, one group of patients has diseases that are NHI-defined catastrophic illnesses and the other has diseases which are not on the NHI list. DRG was selected for two reasons: first, DRG's grouping system is based on principal diagnoses and other indicators for disease severity, hence can be used to proxy patients' needs for health care in the treatment process. Comparative groups selected accordingly will achieve meaningful comparisons. Second, Taiwan is in the process of phasing in DRG as a hospital payment method, so comparisons made based on DRG will have more relevant policy implications.

Data Collection

Linkou Chang Gung Memorial Hospital (CGMH) was selected as the study site for its representation and data availability. CGMH, totaling 7210 beds in four locations is the largest hospital chain in Taiwan, which owns two medical centers (Linkou-Taipei, Kaohsiung), one specialty hospital – Children's Hospital (Linkou), and one regional hospital (Keelung). The Linkou CGMH alone, operating 3600 beds, is the largest medical center in Taiwan. Almost all the catastrophic illnesses are considered as major diseases; hence the patients tend to seek care at major medical centers. Given the patient volume at Linkou CGMH, the researcher assumes that data obtained from CGMH should have fair representation. In addition, for research purposes, data on out-of-pocket payment (which is not reimbursed by NHI) are required for the analyses on estimating the financial burden on the insured. Only CGMH is willing to release its data on out-of-pocket payment.

The primary data source is 1996 inpatient claim data for catastrophic illness patients treated in Linkou CGMH, totaling 28 138 records. The sample selection process is depicted in Figure 8.1. To assure the completeness and accuracy of the data, four exclusion screening criteria were applied and 27 057 records were obtained. The four exclusion criteria were as follows: (1) cross-year inpatient records; (2) records with missing personal identification numbers; (3) records with zero hospital day; (4) records with inpatient expenditure less than NT$900 (US$27.7).

In order to assign the 27 057 inpatients records into 28 catastrophic illness categories, three diagnosis codes (principal, secondary and third diagnosis) on the records were screened again based on BNHI released ICD-9-CM codes for catastrophic illness through computer programming. However, there were 3982 records whose diagnosis codes could not be matched with the NHI-declared codes in the first pass. At the second stage, a senior ICD coding specialist was hired to review each of the 3982 records manually to evaluate its relevance to the NHI-defined catastrophic illness list. The specialist identified an additional 622 ICD-9-CM codes, which included relevant codes for initial care and aftercare in the treatment process of catastrophic illness. These codes actually fit into the

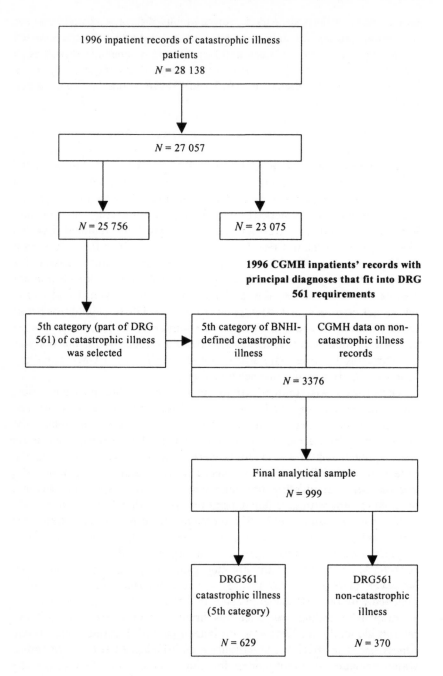

Figure 8.1 Sample selection

descriptions of the catastrophic illnesses but were not covered by the NHI-released list. Through the second pass, the number of unidentified records was reduced to 1301 and the sample then contained 25 756 records.

The analytical sample of 25 756 records was then analyzed to assist the selection of the DRG group for constructing two comparable groups. With the preliminary analyses performed, the in-house coding specialist was consulted on the selection of specific categories of patients. The specialist set out four screening criteria as follows: (1) precise disease descriptions; (2) appropriate number of cases at Linkou CGMH; (3) similar MDC (major diagnostic category); (4) similar DRG. As a result, the fifth category of patients with generalized autoimmune syndrome requiring lifelong treatment (including systemic lupus erythematosus, systemic sclerosis, vasculitis, etc.) was chosen. The principal diagnoses of the disease specified in the fifth category (15 ICD-9-CM codes) all fit into DRG561. Hence, out of the 25 756 records, the researcher gathered a sample whose diagnosis codes conformed to the 15 BNHI-defined catastrophic illness ICD-9-CM codes for the fifth category. Along with a separate dataset which contained the additional 240 ICD-9-CM codes of DRG561 (not NHI-defined catastrophic illness ICD-9-CM codes), a preliminary analytical sample for comparisons was constructed (N = 3376).

However, DRG 561 has specific requirements for secondary and third diagnoses, and non-surgical procedures to rule out inappropriate cases. For example, DRG561 is a medical DRG, hence any records with surgical procedures will be ruled out. After several screening paths, the final analytical sample of 999 records was collected. Among them, 629 records (506 patients) conformed to NHI-defined catastrophic illnesses and the remaining 370 records (321 patients) did not (Figure 8.1). Further, the overall financial burden of patients in these two groups was investigated by linking the outpatient expenditure in claims data as well as out-of-pocket expenditure (excluding copayment) for inpatient and outpatient services.

4   RESULTS

Within DRG561, patients with NHI-defined catastrophic illnesses are referred to as Group A (with 15 ICD-9-CM codes) and those whose admitting diagnoses do not conform to NHI definitions are therefore Group B (with 240 ICD-9-CM codes).

The distributions of length of stay and inpatient health expenditures

Table 8.2 Means of length of stay and inpatient expenditures of DRG561 records, 1996

DRG561	No. of records	Length of stay			Inpatient expenditures		
		Range	Mean (S.D.)	Coefficient of variation	Range	Mean (S.D.)	Coefficient of variation
Group A Catastrophic illness	629	1–65	** 10.33 (8.53)	0.83	88–19 929	1114 (1281)	1.15
Group B Non-catastrophic illness	370	1–94	** 12.48 (11.67)	0.93	38–13 930	1342 (1775)	1.32
Grand total	999						

Notes
Expenditures are in US dollars.
** Significant at $p < 0.01$ level.

were first examined on an individual record basis (Table 8.2). The results have shown that Group B has significant higher means for length of stay and inpatient expenditure. Moreover, compared to Group A, Group B possesses larger coefficients of variation in both lengths of stay and inpatient expenditure. It is obvious that there exists a pronounced variation in distributions for Group B. The researcher adopted Wilcoxon's rank sum test for statistical significance testing due to the distributions of data. Similar to any expenditure distributions, the overall distributions (either by patient records or by patients) are apparently skewed to the right as shown by a few extreme cases at the higher ends. Wilcoxon's rank sum test is one of the most frequently used distribution-free methods, which avoids unnecessary distributional assumptions.

To examine the overall health care expenditure incurred for each patient under study, the researcher aggregated the inpatient records by unique personal identification numbers and further located the outpatient expenditures as well as the out-of-pocket expenditures (Table 8.3). It has shown that Group B patients demonstrate a higher average age and higher proportion of males than those in Group A. Figure 8.2 compares the percentile distribution of the different types of expenditures to further demonstrate the differences in expenditure distributions between these two groups of patients. In terms of expenditure distributions, Group B is consistently higher than Group A except for self-pay outpatient services (Table 8.3, Figure 8.2). In particular, the differences in means of total

Table 8.3 *Means of length of stay and health expenditures of patients in DRG561, 1996*

DRG 561	No. of patients	Male (%)	Mean age	Length of stay Range	Length of stay Mean (S.D.)	Total inpatient expenditures	Total outpatient expenditures	Means Total out-of-pocket expenditures Inpatient	Outpatient	Total	Total NHI-paid expenditures Inpatient	Outpatient	Total	Grand total
Group A	506	28.8	**31.30 (22.51)	1–107	12.94 (12.49)	1608 (2017)	747 (1083)	223** (446)	121 (194)	258** (460)	1385 (1713)	712** (1063)	2095 (2072)	2353 (2369)
Group B	321	60.3	**40.80 (21.64)	1–111	14.43 (15.28)	2007 (3465)	752 (1454)	461** (1009)	103 (201)	486** (1013)	1547 (2849)	727** (1448)	2267 (3294)	2752 (3890)
Total	827													

Notes

Expenditures are in US dollars.

** Significant at $p < 0.01$ level.

171

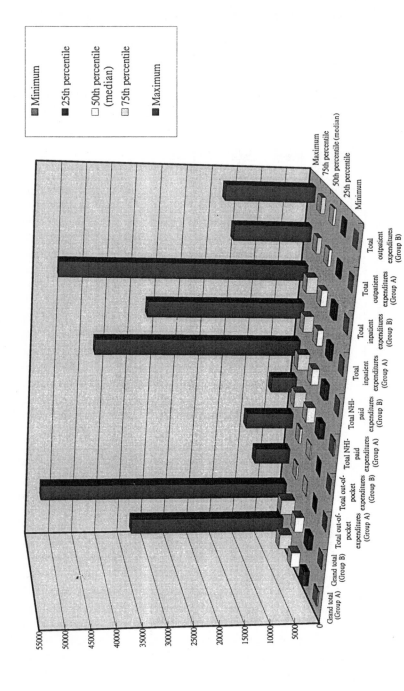

Figure 8.2 Percentile distribution of expenditures by two DRG561 groups, 1996

out-of-pocket and NHI-paid outpatient expenditures have reached statistical significance at a p-level of 0.01. The sources of variation are mainly from inpatient services for out-of-pocket expenditures. In general, the coefficients of variation are higher in Group B than in Group A. Nonetheless, Group A has a slightly higher readmission rate (1.25 admissions/patient) than Group B (1.15 admissions/patient) (Tables 8.2 and 8.3).

5   DISCUSSION AND CONCLUSION

Regardless of the consistently, though not all statistically significant, higher expenditure of patients in Group B than in Group A, a higher readmission rate is observed in Group A as opposed to Group B. It seems to suggest that the copayment exemption may have exerted some positive effects on catastrophic illness patients' access to health care, but whether it represents appropriate uses of health care resources requires future study.

In addition, there are a few issues which deserve further discussion:

1. Long-term effect is not observed with one single year data. BNHI has declared definitions of 'catastrophic illness' as (1) illness which will call for high medical expenditure; (2) illness which will require lifelong treatment. Hence, the research results would have been even more convincing if multi-year information had been available and the long-term trend in expenditures incurred had been studied. However, at the time of study, this research was limited to 1996 data, due to data availability and the young age of the NHI program.

2. Quality of ICD coding may have impact on classification results. The empirical study relies on ICD-9-CM coding quality of the claim data. If the coding is inaccurate, cases may be misplaced and wrongly analyzed. However, the in-house coding specialists at CGMH have routinely reviewed the quality of medical record coding. The errors should be minor, if any.

3. CGMH data may not cover all health care expenditure incurred for patients in the study sample. The limitation is well recognized. However, data on out-of-pocket expenditure is an essential piece of information to assess the financial burden, but is not available in a national database. Hence, considering data availability, the CGMH dataset is the researcher's best option. In addition, this study did not aim to establish a national standard (or a cutoff point) for catastrophic illness expenditures, but had the intention of comparing the financial burden incurred due to similar severity of diseases. Therefore, given the service volume, CGMH

data can still shed some important light on the equity issues explored in this chapter.

The NHI program in Taiwan was established with an emphasis on a self-financed mechanism (mainly financed through payroll tax); however, the welfare mission is still too important to be missed. It is designed so people with annual incomes below the official poverty level will obtain their coverage free of premiums. In addition, the NHI program has exempted specific groups of the insured from copayment requirements (such as catastrophic illness patients) to address its concern with the financially disadvantaged. In terms of the financial burden associated with illness, the NHI program has protected the insured from the major part of their medical care bills. Therefore, the potential financial burden which they may incur is really for out-of-pocket expenditure. In addition, the NHI program also has a ceiling for the out-of-pocket copayment for hospitalization services; in other words, the majority of the insured are well protected financially under the current program.

Two types of expenditure are examined in this research between two groups of patients with similar disease severity, one is the NHI-paid expenditure, and the second is the out-of-pocket expenditure which represent the direct financial stress on the patients. The study results have demonstrated that non-catastrophic illness patients (Group B) on average have consumed more health care resources than those with catastrophic illnesses (Group A). Although there is no substantial difference in NHI-paid expenditures between the two groups, on average, non-catastrophic illness patients spend nearly twice as much as patients with catastrophic illnesses in out-of-pocket expenditure. Yet the catastrophic illness patients are considered the disadvantaged, and consequently are exempted from copayment requirement. This is to say that the current catastrophic illness policy actually benefits the patients with less financial burden. Hence the purpose of lessening potential financial distress for the disadvantaged does not seem to be served.

The conventional wisdom often refers to 'catastrophic illness' as a high spending illness (such as long-term illness), which may deplete lifelong savings (Feenberg and Skinner 1994). Although Taiwan may have similar definitions, however, the decision on the inclusion criteria of catastrophic illness is constantly heatedly debated. The fact is that the current policy has caused political fights between the patient support groups and BNHI, as the patient support groups of various diseases have strongly and persistently lobbied for a specific disease to be included on the list.

Although income-related cost sharing may seem to be administratively sophisticated, the current catastrophic illness policy which exempts copayment based on pre-determined disease categories certainly creates a focal point for political fights. Most of all, the equity principle in distributing valuable health care resources is not achieved. Hence it is in the opinion of the author that copayment exemption based on annual medical expenses and the amount of cost sharing being income-related is a better alternative to protect the poor and serve the equity principle.

As the equity issue is well scrutinized in many countries in various contexts, this chapter presents a local example in Taiwan of addressing the equity concern in a national health insurance program. The research results may provide empirical evidence for future policy recommendation and further research will be needed to explore the income-related cost-sharing alternative.

ACKNOWLEDGEMENT

The author is grateful to the Administration Center, Chang Gung Memorial Hospital for providing the data, in particular, Mr. Yi-Chou Chuang for his generosity in releasing the data and Mr. Ying-Jen Hsu for extracting the datatapes.

REFERENCES

Altman, S.H. and E.K. Ostby (1991), 'Paying for hospital care: the impact on federal policy', in Eli Ginzberg (ed.), *Health Services Research: Key to Health Policy*, Cambridge, MA: Harvard University Press, pp. 46–68.

Bureau of National Health Insurance (1994), 'Rules for catastrophic illness certificates'.

Bureau of National Health Insurance (1998), '1997 national health insurance annual statistical report'.

Bureau of National Health Insurance (1999), '1998 national health insurance annual statistical report'.

Collins, E. and K. Klein (1980), 'Equity and the NHS: self reported morbidity, access and primary care', *British Medical Journal*, **281**: 1111–5.

Culyer, A.J. and A. Wagstaff (1993), 'Equity and equality in health and health care', *Journal of Health Economics*, **12**: 431–57.

Feenberg, D. and J. Skinner (1994), 'The risk and duration of catastrophic health care expenditure', *The Review of Economics and Statistics*, **76**(4): 633–47.

Feldstein, M.S. (1971), 'The high cost of hospitals – and what to do about it', *The Public Interest*, **48**: 40–54.

Feldstein, P.J. (1999), *Health Care Economics*, fifth edition, New York: Delmar Publishers.

Friedman, B., C. Ross and G. Misek (1984), 'On the surprisingly low cost of state catastrophic health insurance programs', *Journal of Risk and Insurance*, **51**(1): 31–48.

Hsiao, W.C. and J.F. Lu (1995), 'The political economy of health care reform: the case of Taiwan', working paper.

Le Grand, J. (1978), 'The distribution of public expenditure: the case of health care', *Economica*, **45**: 125–42.

Le Grand, J. (1987), 'Equity, health and health care', *Social Justice Research*, **1**: 257–74.

Manning, W.G., J.P. Newhouse, N. Duan, E. Keeler, A. Leibowitz and M.S. Marquis (1987), 'Health insurance and the demand for medical care: evidence from a randomized experiment', *The American Economic Review*, **77**(3): 251–77.

Mooney, G., J. Hall, C. Donaldson and K. Gerard (1991), 'Utilization as a measure of equity: weighing heat?', *Journal of Health Economics*, **11**: 199–205.

Newhouse, J.P. and the Insurance Experiment Group (1993), *Free for All? Lessons from the Rand Health Insurance Experiment*, Cambridge, MA: Harvard University Press.

O'Donnell, O. and C. Propper (1991), 'Equity and the distribution of UK national health service resources', *Journal of Health Economics*, **10**: 1–19.

Rice, T. and K.E. Thorpe (1993), 'Income-related cost sharing in health insurance', *Health Affair*, **12**(1): 21–39.

Van Doorslaer, E. and A. Wagstaff (1992), 'Equity in the delivery of health care: some international comparisons', *Journal of Health Economics*, **11**: 389–411.

Wagstaff, A., E. van Doorslaer and P. Paci (1991), 'On the measurement of horizontal inequity in the delivery of health care', *Journal of Health Economics*, **10**: 169–205.

Wyszewianski, L. (1986), 'Families with catastrophic health care expenditure', *Health Services Research*, **21**(5): 617–34.

9. Demand for supplemental health insurance and health care utilization in Taiwan

Shou-Hsia Cheng and Jung-Der Wang

1 INTRODUCTION

Health care reform is an ongoing process in almost every country. The provision of limited coverage and the implementation of cost-sharing requirements are common compromises reached between insurance carriers, government and health care recipients to provide affordable health care. The purchase of private supplemental insurance has emerged as a method to protect individuals from considerable out-of-pocket expense due to illness which is not covered by public insurance (Morrisey 1993). In 1995, the Taiwan government implemented a compulsory universal health insurance program which covers all citizens with a comprehensive benefits package. A cost-sharing mechanism was also instituted to reduce unnecessary use of health care services. Under the program, a co-payment is required for each physician visit and hospital admission. This study examined the demand for supplemental health insurance and investigated its effect on health care utilization after the implementation of the universal health insurance program in Taiwan.

2 SUPPLEMENTAL INSURANCE: EXPERIENCE/ STUDIES FROM OTHER COUNTRIES

The most popular supplemental insurance is the so-called Medigap program for the Medicare beneficiaries in the United States. The Medicare program for the elderly has various cost-sharing requirements and benefit limitations which may leave Medicare beneficiaries exposed to large out-of-pocket health care costs. In order to protect themselves against large potential losses, Medicare beneficiaries often purchase private supplemental coverage. Several types of supplemental insurance policies are available: (1) Medigap policies which typically provide coverage for hospital deductible and co-payments; (2) hospital indemnity policies which pay a fixed amount per day; (3) catastrophic disease policies which provide coverage for specific diseases such as cancer; (4) major medical coverage which is provided by employers to retired employees; and (5) policies which cover only specific services, such as pharmaceutical drugs (McCall et al. 1991). According to recent studies, the proportion of Medicare beneficiaries covered by supplemental health insurance ranges from 72 percent to 79 percent (Christensen et al. 1987; McCall et al. 1991; Morrisey 1993; Chulis et al. 1993; Vistnes and Banthin 1997).

The factors associated with the purchase of private supplemental insurance have been intensively investigated. Most reports have found that important determinants of private supplemental insurance include income, education, race, and self-perceived health status. Persons with higher incomes and a greater number of years of education were more likely to own private insurance (Rice and McCall 1985; Vistnes and Banthin 1997; Lillard et al. 1997; Bongers et al. 1997). However, the effect of health status on the purchase of private coverage was not conclusive. Several studies reported that adverse selection was found, meaning that persons with poor health would purchase more insurance (Wolfe and Goddeeris 1991; Browne and Doerpinghaus 1994; Ettner 1997). However, others suggested that there was no evidence of adverse selection (Christensen et al. 1987; Taylor et al. 1988; Lillard et al. 1997). Moreover, a recent study reported that Medicare beneficiaries with good health status were more likely to purchase private insurance than those in poor health. Researchers have also suggested that further investigation in this area is needed (Vistnes and Banthin 1997).

The effect of health insurance on the utilization of health care has been well documented (Manning et al. 1987; Cheng and Chiang 1997). The so-called moral hazard has been recognized by most researchers. The effect of private supplemental insurance also has a positive effect on health care utilization. A number of findings have suggested that the ownership of private insurance has significantly increased the use of health care services (McCall et al. 1991; Wolfe and Goddeeris 1991; Cartwright et al. 1992; Blustein 1995; Grana and Stuart 1996; Saag et al. 1998).

3   NATIONAL HEALTH INSURANCE IN TAIWAN

A universal health insurance program was implemented in Taiwan in

March, 1995. Enrollment in the National Health Insurance (NHI) is compulsory and the program covers all Taiwanese citizens. Three years after the implementation of NHI, the rate of enrollment reached 97 percent and the rate of hospitals and clinics under contract with the program reached 90 percent (Bureau of NHI 1998). The universal insurance program provides comprehensive coverage including physician visits, dental services, hospital admissions, emergency services, prescription drugs, and rehabilitation services through contracted clinics and hospitals. The payment system for health care providers is substantially fee-for-services based. A DRG-like prospective payment system is applied to about 50 diagnoses/procedures such as vaginal delivery and appendectomy. A detailed description of health care delivery in Taiwan has been previously reported (Peabody 1995; Chiang 1997).

The cost-sharing design in the NHI program differs for outpatient and inpatient services. A three-tier co-payment scheme is required for outpatient visits. Patients pay 50 NT dollars (about $1.5 US dollars) for a visit to the clinic physician. The fee for a visit to a small hospital is 100 NTD while that for a regional hospital or medical center is 150 NTD. In addition to the NHI co-payment requirement, clinics and hospitals in Taiwan charge a registration fee ranging from 50 NTD to 100 NTD for each visit. Therefore, a clinic may charge a patient a 100 NTD out-of-pocket fee for one visit, while a large hospital or medical center may charge 250 NTD for one visit. One purpose of the three-tier co-payment mechanism is to reduce the unnecessary use of outpatient care; the other is to encourage the use of physician services from primary care clinics rather than hospital outpatient departments. According to an NHI report, approximately 28 percent of patients received their physician services from hospitals' outpatient departments (Bureau of NHI 1998).

For inpatient services, a 10 percent co-payment of total hospital expense is required. However, in 1998, there was an out-of-pocket ceiling of 19 000 NTD for each hospitalization and a yearly ceiling for inpatient services of 31 000 NTD. Generally speaking, the financial burden on the patient from the cost sharing in the universal health insurance program is not heavy. Moreover, the NHI program provides special Catastrophic Illness Cards for persons with specific diagnoses or conditions such as cancer, renal failure, chronic psychiatric disorders, etc. There were 30 diagnoses and conditions for which individuals are eligible for Catastrophic Illness Cards in 1998. All co-payment requirements were waived for individuals holding a Catastrophic Illness Card.

Under Taiwan law, other insurance companies are not allowed to provide the same health care coverage as that included in the NHI program. However, in addition to the compulsory NHI program, people can obtain extra protection from supplemental health insurers. There are about 30 life insurance carriers in Taiwan, and approximately half of them are owned by international companies (Taipei Life Insurance Association 1997). Currently, there is no insurance policy designed specifically to share the out-of-pocket expense of the NHI program. Health-related coverage is available mainly as a supplement to life insurance policies. The most popular types of health-related coverage are catastrophic disease policies for cancer and hospital indemnity policies. Regrettably, there is no available data on the prevalence of private health insurance coverage, and even major insurance companies do not produce regular reports on the ownership of these policies.

To our knowledge, there has been no single study of the demand for supplemental health insurance or its effect on health care utilization after the implementation of the NHI program in Taiwan. It therefore remains unclear whether a need for extra protection via private insurance exists under compulsory universal health insurance and, if the demand exists, whether such insurance will affect the utilization of health care like Medigap. The purposes of this study were: (1) to determine the current demand for supplemental health insurance in Taiwan; and (2) to identify factors associated with the purchasing decision, including a test on the hypothesis of adverse selection; and (3) to investigate the effect of supplemental health insurance on health care utilization.

4   DATA SOURCE

Data used in this study came from a survey of a large-scale follow-up database establishment project. The project sought to develop a longitudinal database to collect information on income, occupation and health. At least five years of follow-ups will be carried out in the project, and the 1998 survey was the first. The health section of the database consists of data on personal health-related behavior, perceived health status, simple physical and mental measurements, insurance coverage, health care utilization, and job-related health problems.

Specific age groups were selected for various research purposes in the project. Households with residents with a birth year ranging from 1953 to 1957 were identified using an island-wide household database obtained from the Department of Internal Affairs, the Executive Yuan. Multiple stage random sampling with ten levels of urbanization strata was then carried out to select 2000 subjects for interview. A standardized face-to-face interview was conducted by well-trained interviewers. The interview was performed during August and September 1998. A total of 1925 individuals with ages ranging from 41 to 45 were successfully interviewed.

Because the status of supplemental health insurance ownership and health care utilization were used as two dependent variables in the study, individuals with missing values for these two variables were excluded from the analysis. Among the 1925 subjects who completed the interview, 50 persons who were not participating in the National Health Insurance program were excluded from the analysis. Another 13 individuals who had missing data for owing life insurance or for any inpatient or outpatient coverage were also excluded from the analysis. In all, a total of 1862 persons were included.

5   MODEL SPECIFICATION

To investigate the effect of insurance coverage on the use of health care services, the demand for health insurance must be determined. The demand for health insurance may be considered as a derived demand for health care. All citizens of Taiwan are required to participate in the universal health insurance program, therefore supplemental private insurance may not be considered necessary for many people. The economic models of demand for health insurance developed by Phelps (1973) provide a theoretical framework for identifying specific factors associated with this demand. In the Phelps model, an individual is assumed to be a utility maximizer who chooses to purchase the optimal level of health care and other goods given a budget constraint. The demand for insurance is a function of income, price of health care, the loading fee, expected loss due to illness, and other non-economic factors such as demographic factors and health status. Unfortunately, as in many other studies (McCall et al. 1991; Ettner 1997; Wolfe and Goddeeris 1991), loading fees and the expected loss are both difficult to measure in this kind of research and were therefore not included in our analysis.

In our analysis, individuals actually have to make two decisions: whether to purchase private insurance and how much health service to purchase. Our basic theoretical construct was derived from the work of Aday and Andersen (1974) and the empirical specifications are similar to other health services utilization studies (McCall et al. 1991; Cartwright et al. 1992; Grana and Stuart 1996; Saag et al. 1998). Utilization of health care is a function of need factors such as health status; enabling factors such as price of health services, and insurance coverage; and predisposing factors such as age, sex and education. Therefore, in our analyses the insurance equation had the same function as the utilization equation except that private insurance ownership was only included in the utilization equation. For the utilization analyses, a two-part model was adopted to first identify any use of health care via logistic regression analysis. The amount of utilization by those who use health care services was then examined using a logarithmic transformation of the number of the health care services received (Manning et al. 1987). We assumed there was a log-normal distribution of the error term in the second regression equation.

Although the information on supplemental insurance status and the use of health care services was gathered cross-sectionally, ownership of supplemental health insurance was treated as exogenous in the utilization model mainly because we found that need factors (that is, poor health or chronic conditions) had no effect on the purchase of supplemental health insurance. Therefore, a finding that people with supplemental insurance used more health care had low likelihood of being caused by sicker persons having more coverage. In addition, because the health-related coverage was only available as a supplement to life insurance policy in this series, it was unlikely that a person would buy the policy chiefly to obtain more coverage for health care services.

6   MEASUREMENT OF VARIABLES

The two dependent variables included in our analyses were the ownership of supplemental health insurance and health care utilization. Supplemental health insurance indicated that a person purchased private life insurance with some coverage for physician visits or hospital admissions. Health care utilization was composed of two variables, the first representing any use of health care services, the second representing the amount of use. Under the National Health Insurance program, every beneficiary has a health insurance card which is replaced every year. The insurance card has six cells on it for six visits to receive health care services. The provider puts a stamp on the card as a record each time a health care service is delivered. In each year, the initial card provided to the beneficiary is called the 'A card'. Within one year a person can apply for replacement cards (that is, B card or C card and so on.) after using up the six cells on the old one. During the interview process, the interviewers asked the interviewees to show their health insurance cards and recorded the card number and cell number. The amount of health care services used was then calculated by multiplying the card numbers and cell numbers. One stamp on the insurance card may indicate a physician visit, one emergency visit, or one hospital admission; therefore the intensity of services cannot be verified from the card alone.

Independent variables in this study mainly involved demographic characteristics and health status measurements. Age was calculated from the year of birth as recorded in the official household data files. Marital status was dichotomized into currently married and other status. Education was divided into junior high school (nine years or less), high school (ten to 12 years), and college or above (13 years or more). Perceived health was categorized into five groups: excellent, good, fair, poor, very poor; which were then combined into three groups of good, fair, and poor in subsequent analyses. An individual was considered to have a chronic condition if he or she had anyone of the following five diagnoses: hypertension, heart disease, diabetes mellitus, renal dysfunction, or stroke, and was currently taking medication for it. Smoking behavior indicates current smoker versus other status.

Employment status was used to represent whether a subject had either a full-time or part-time job in the past week. Income was defined as self-reported earnings from a job, assessed income or other non-job related income were not included. Therefore, a person without a job was considered to have zero income in our analyses. Owing to possible inaccuracies in measurement, income was dichotomized into high and low income groups with the high income group representing individuals with an income in the upper 20 percent of all subjects. Urbanization was also dichotomized into urban versus rural areas according to the degree of development in the area.

7 RESULTS

A total of 1862 subjects were included in the analyses. In the study sample, 37.6 percent of the subjects had no life insurance, 19.5 percent had life insurance without health-related coverage, and the remaining 42.9 percent had life insurance and health related coverage. The first two groups were merged into one category representing persons without supplemental health insurance. The basic characteristics of the sample are described in Table 9.1. The mean age of the sample was 43.6 years with a slightly higher proportion of females (51.8 percent). Approximately 88.6 percent of subjects were married. Fifty-one percent of subjects had spent nine years or less of school, 27.7 percent of them had graduated from high school and 21.2 percent of them had received a college or higher education. About 43.7 percent of subjects reported excellent or good health status, 40.6 percent were in fair health status, and 15.6 percent reported poor or worse health status. A total of 17.1 percent of subjects reported having chronic conditions and were taking medication at the time

Table 9.1 Socio-demographic characteristics of participants

Factors	N (%)	Supplemental health insurance	
		Yes (%)	No (%)
Total	1862 (100)	42.91	57.09
Age			
41 years old	376 (20.29)	44.95	55.05
42	350 (18.89)	44.29	55.71
43	356 (19.21)	41.85	58.15
44	378 (20.40)	39.95	60.05
45	393 (21.21)	44.27	55.73
Gender			
Male	897 (48.17)	47.94	52.06
Female	965 (51.83)	38.24	61.76
Marital status			
Married	1649 (88.56)	42.69	57.31
Others	213 (11.44)	44.60	55.40
Education			
9 years or less	948 (51.08)	35.13	64.87
10–12 years	514 (27.69)	48.44	51.56
13 years or higher	394 (21.23)	54.57	45.43
Chronic condition			
Yes	318 (17.08)	41.19	58.81
No	1544 (82.92)	43.26	56.74
Health status			
Good	814 (43.72)	43.49	56.51
Fair	757 (40.66)	43.86	56.14
Poor	291 (15.63)	38.83	61.17
Current smoker			
Yes	499 (26.80)	42.28	57.72
No	1363 (73.20)	43.14	56.86
Employment			
Working	1524 (81.85)	45.54	54.46
Unemployed	338 (18.15)	31.07	68.93
Earned income			
High	350 (18.80)	58.29	41.71
Other	1512 (81.20)	39.35	60.65
Urbanization			
Urban	1141 (61.28)	46.10	53.90
Rural	721 (38.72)	37.86	62.14

of the interview. A total of 81.8 percent of subjects had a job at the time of interview. Persons in the high income group had a minimum annual income of 756 000 NTD. About 61.3 percent of individuals lived in an urban area.

The association between socio-demographic factors and supplemental health insurance ownership is also listed in Table 9.1. A total of 42.9 percent of the subjects had some kind of supplemental health-related coverage. Males and persons with longer schooling years were more likely to have supplemental insurance. Subjects who were employed or had higher incomes were more likely to have supplemental health insurance. People living in urban areas had a higher proportion of supplemental health insurance coverage. Other factors such as marital status, perceived health, chronic condition, and smoking status were not significantly associated with the ownership of supplemental health insurance.

Table 9.2 shows the results of analysis using regression models. The first column indicates the decision to purchase at least one supplemental health insurance policy. Persons with fewer years of education were less likely to have private insurance with an odds ratio of 0.63. Employed persons and those in the higher income group were more likely to own supplemental insurance with an odds ratios of around 1.4. Current smokers were less likely to purchase supplemental health insurance. Health status and chronic condition showed no significant effect on the purchasing of supplemental insurance. These findings imply that adverse selection for supplemental health insurance purchasing might not exist among middle-aged persons under Taiwan's universal health insurance program.

Next, we examined the effect of supplemental insurance on health care utilization using a two-part model. Our findings show that supplemental health insurance did not significantly affect the probability or the amount of health care utilization. The most significant factors affecting health care utilization were health status and chronic condition. Persons with poor perceived health were more likely to seek health care services and used 51 percent more services than those with good health. The presence of a chronic condition was the most important predictor of the likelihood of using health services. Individuals with chronic conditions consumed 84 percent more services than those without chronic conditions. Male and married persons were less likely to use health care services. We also found that smoking status had a significant negative effect on the amount of health care used. The results of this study concerning the effects of health status, chronic condition, gender and marital status on health care utilization are consistent with previous studies.

Table 9.2 Estimated effects of each independent variable on the likelihood of supplemental insurance purchasing, any health service use, and on the number of health services used†

Factors	Private insurance O.R. (95% C.I.)	Probability of use O.R. (95% C.I.)	No. of times used ‡ % change (95% C.I.)
Private insurance (Yes = 1)	–	1.12 (0.98, 1.29)	2.55 (−6.66, 12.67)
Age	1.01 (0.97, 1.04)	1.05 (1.00, 1.10)	−0.88 (−3.99, 2.34)
Gender (Male = 1)	1.36 (1.20, 1.54) *	0.59 (0.50, 0.70) **	−9.76 (−19.68, 1.38)
Marital status (Married = 1)	1.14 (0.98, 1.33)	0.65 (0.53, 0.79) *	10.94 (−4.47, 28.83)
Education = 9 years or less	0.63 (0.54, 0.72) **	0.87 (0.71, 1.07)	15.74 (0.83, 32.87)*
Education = 10–12 years	0.96 (0.83, 1.10)	0.61 (0.50, 0.74) *	−2.11 (−15.02, 12.77)
Health status = Poor	0.97 (0.83, 1.13)	2.27 (1.74, 2.96) **	51.41 (31.43, 74.42)***
Health status = Fair	1.08 (0.94, 1.16)	1.42 (1.23, 1.63)	21.13 (9.50, 34.00)***
Chronic condition (Yes = 1)	0.95 (0.82, 1.09)	3.91 (2.92, 5.23) ***	83.93 (62.50, 108.19)***
Current smoker (Yes = 1)	0.77 (0.67, 0.87) *	0.75 (0.64, 0.89)	−16.07 (−26.07, −4.72)**
Employment (Yes = 1)	1.47 (1.28, 1.68) **	0.76 (0.63, 0.92)	6.93 (−5.73, 21.29)
Earning income (High = 1)	1.41 (1.23, 1.62) *	0.81 (0.67, 0.98)	2.48 (−10.87, 17.83)
Urbanization (Urban=1)	1.19 (1.08, 1.32)	0.69 (0.59, 0.80) *	−2.35 (−11.42, 7.64)
Intercept	–	–	–
Sample size	1848	1831	1553
Log likelihood X^2	86.76 (df = 12)	105.71 (df = 13)	–
Adjusted R^2	–	–	0.1267

Notes
† Natural log transformed number of health care services used.
* $P < 0.05$, ** $P < 0.01$, *** $P < 0.001$.
‡ For the dummy variables, these parameters show the effects on the dependent variables of a change in each variable from a value of 0 to 1. The reference group is: female, not currently married, college education or higher, in good health, without chronic condition, non-smoker, unemployed, not high income, living in a rural area, and without private insurance coverage.

186

8   DISCUSSION AND CONCLUSION

Before discussing our findings, the limitations of this study need to be addressed. Due to the specific need to perform long-term follow-up, our sample was limited to persons aged 41 to 45 years old. Findings from this particular age group may not be representative of other age groups. The supplemental health insurance coverage information was obtained from self-reported status rather than actual policy records. Thus the data may have been inaccurate since persons may have forgotten details about the actual contracts concerning supplemental medical coverage. Besides, as the health-related insurance was purchased as an add-on component to a life insurance, the results may not be comparable to other private health insurance studies. The measurement of health care utilization was not ideal in this study. Although the National Health Insurance Card revealed the actual number of visits conducted, outpatient and inpatient services could not be distinguished. Therefore the intensity of health care utilization could not be identified in the analysis.

Our findings indicate that the important determinants of supplemental health insurance purchasing are education, employment, income, and male gender. These findings are consistent with those of previous studies (Rice and McCall 1985; Vistnes and Banthin 1997; Lillard et al. 1997; Bongers et al. 1997). Besides, we found that smokers were less likely to purchase supplemental health insurance. It is well recognized that cigarette smoking is a risk factor for the development of disease. From the perspective of risk aversion, smokers tend to be less sensitive to possible risks. Especially, in our study, they had to buy the supplemental health insurance through a life insurance policy. On the other hand, they may hold a positive time preference, meaning that they weigh a present value much higher than a future one (Gafni and Torrance 1984). This may explain why smokers tend to be less interested in obtaining extra protection against future financial risks.

This study found little evidence to support the presence of an adverse selection effect. Persons with poor health status did not show a higher probability of purchasing supplemental health insurance than those with better health status. The implication of the finding has to be conservative because supplemental health coverage can be obtained only through a life insurance in Taiwan. Thus the measurement might not be sensitive enough to detect the effect. On the other hand, this finding is reasonable for the situation in Taiwan since the National Health Insurance program provides comprehensive benefit coverage for various health care services, and the magnitude of cost sharing is relatively small. Even for the 10 percent co-payment for inpatient services, there is a ceiling for out-of-pocket expenses. Therefore, the potential financial losses to NHI enrollees due to the need for health services are not as severe as those under the Medicare program in the United States. In particular, NHI Catastrophic Illness Card holders are waived from all co-payment requirements, so there is little incentive for these persons to purchase extra protection from private insurers. We also examined the demand for supplemental health insurance among the 50 persons who were not enrolled in the NHI program and found that the rate of having supplemental health insurance (46.9 percent) in this group was not significantly higher than that in the study group (42.9 percent).

The results of this study show that supplemental health insurance has a positive but not a statistically significant effect on the probability and the amount of health care utilization. One possible explanation for this finding is that health-related insurance policies are mainly purchased as protection against possible financial losses resulting from the treatment of catastrophic diseases like cancer or from hospital expenses, rather than for out-of-pocket co-payments for physician visits. Therefore the use of general health care services may not be affected by one's supplemental insurance status. Another possible explanation for the lack of significance is that our measurement of health care utilization may not have been sensitive enough to detect such a difference. Future studies based on health care expenditure or length of hospital stay are likely to yield more accurate results.

9 POLICY IMPLICATION

Under the universal health insurance program in Taiwan, the supplemental health insurance seems to have had a minimal and insignificant effect on the use of health care services. In the United States, the financial burden of the Medicare program is overwhelming. Medicare reform proposals mainly focus on cost containment. A cost-sharing policy has increased the demand for Medigap insurance. It has been argued that Medigap may not help to contain cost, or may even increase expenditures outside Medicare (Taylor et al. 1988; Cartwright et al. 1992). In Taiwan, the growth of health care expenditure is mainly dealt with by the Bureau of National Health Insurance, and the supplemental health insurance is much less influential.

However, raising the NHI's co-payment rates is currently on its reform agenda. The findings of this study may serve as baseline information for policy decision-makers and for future comparison. Future research which employs better quantitative measurement of private/supplemental health insurance ownership and more accurate measurements of health care utilization and spending may more accurately delineate the relationship between demand for private health insurance and its effect on health care utilization.

REFERENCES

Aday, L.A. and R. Andersen (1974), 'A framework for the study of access to medical care', *Health Services Research*, **9**: 208–20.

Blustein, J. (1995), 'Medicare coverage, supplemental insurance, and the use of mammography by older women', *New England Journal of Medicine*, **332**(17): 1138–43.

Bongers, I.M.B., J.B.W. van der Meer, J. van der Bos and J.P. Mackenbach (1997), 'Socio-economic differences in general practitioner and outpatient specialist care in the Netherlands: a matter of health insurance', *Social Science & Medicine*, **44**(8): 1161–8.

Browne, M.J. and H. Doerpinghaus (1994), 'Asymmetric information and the demand for Medigap insurance', *Inquiry*, **31**(4): 445–50.

Bureau of National Health Insurance (1998), *The 1997 National Health Insurance Annual Statistical Report*, Taipei: Bureau of NHI.

Cartwright, W.S., T.W. Hu and L.F. Huang (1992), 'Impact of varying Medigap insurance coverage on the use of medical services of the elderly', *Applied Economics*, **24**: 529–39.

Cheng, S.H. and T.L. Chiang (1997), 'The effect of universal health insurance on health care utilization in Taiwan: results from a natural experiment', *JAMA*, **278**: 89–93.

Chiang, T.L. (1997), 'Taiwan's 1995 health care reform', *Health Policy*, **39**: 225–39.

Christensen, S., S.H. Long and J. Rodgers (1987), 'Acute health care costs for the aged Medicare population: overview and policy option', *Milbank Quarterly*, **65**(3): 397–425.

Chulis, G.S., F.P. Eppig, M.O. Hogan, D.R. Walo and R.H. Arnett (1993), 'Health insurance and the elderly', *Health Affairs*, **12**(1): 111–8.

Ettner, S.L. (1997), 'Adverse selection and the purchase of Medigap insurance by the elderly', *Journal of Health Economics*, **16**(5): 543–62.

Gafni, A. and G.W. Torrance (1984), 'Risk attitude and time preference in health', *Management Science*, **30**: 440–51.

Grana, J. and B. Stuart (1996), 'The impact of insurance on access to physician services for elderly people with arthritis', *Inquiry*, **33**: 326–38.

Lillard, L., J. Rogowski and R. Kington (1997), 'Long-term determinants of patterns of health insurance coverage in the Medicare population', *The Gerontologist*, **37**(3): 314–23.

Manning, W.G., J. Newhouse, N. Duan, E. Keeler, A. Leibowitz and M.S. Marquis (1987), 'Health insurance and the demand for medical care: evidence from a randomized experiment', *American Economics Review*, **77**(3): 251–77.

McCall, N., T. Rice, J. Boismier and R. West (1991), 'Private health insurance and medical care utilization: evidence from the Medicare population', *Inquiry*, **28**: 276–87.

Morrisey, M.A. (1993), 'Retiree health benefits', *Annual Review of Public Health*, **14**: 271–92.

Peabody, J.W., J.C.I. Yu, Y.-R. Wang and S.R. Biskel (1995), 'Health system reform in the Republic of China: formulating policy in a market-based system', *JAMA*, **273**: 777–81.

Phelps, C.E. (1973), *Demand for Health Insurance: A Theoretical and Empirical Investigation*, Rand Pub. No. R-1054-OEO, Santa Monica, CA: The Rand Corporation.

Rice, T. and N. McCall (1985), 'The extent of ownership and the characteristics of Medicare supplemental', *Inquiry*, **22**(2): 188–200.

Saag, K.G., B.N. Doebbeling, J.E. Rohere, S. Kolluri, R. Peterson, M.E. Hermann and R.B. Wallace (1998), 'Variation in tertiary prevention and health service utilization among the elderly', *Medical Care*, **36**(7): 965–76.

Taipei Life Insurance Association (1997), *The 1996 Annual Report of Life Insurance, Republic of China*, Taipei: Taipei Life Insurance Association, pp. 14–22.

Taylor, A.K., P.F. Short and C.M. Horgan (1988), 'Medigap insurance: friend or foe in reducing Medicare deficits', in H.E. Frech III (ed.), *Health Care in America*, 1st edn, San Francisco: Pacific Research Institute for Public Policy, pp. 145–75.

Vistnes, J.P. and J.S. Banthin (1997), 'The demand for Medicare supplemental insurance benefits: the role of attitudes toward medical care and risk', *Inquiry*, **34**: 311–24.

Wolfe, J.R. and J.H. Goddeeris (1991), 'Adverse selection, moral hazard, and wealth effects in the Medigap insurance market', *Journal of Health Economics*, **10**(4): 433–59.

PART IV

Hospital Behavior

10. Cost shifting or sample selection: the case study of surgically treated workers' compensation back pain patients

Ya-Chen Tina Shih

1 INTRODUCTION

Cost shifting in health care is defined as the behavior of providers increasing their revenues from some payers to offset uncompensated care costs and lower net payments from other payers (Folland et al. 1997)[1]. In health economic literature, the term 'cost shifting' is often used as a descriptor for charging different prices to different groups[2]. Hospital cost shifting refers to the case that hospitals, in response to economic incentives and the pressure of cost containment, charge some insurance recipients more than the others.

Hospital cost shifting received a lot of public attention in the early 1980s in the United States when cost containment reimbursement mechanisms, such as the Tax Equity and Fiscal Responsibility Act (TEFRA) in 1982 and the Prospective Payment System (PPS) in 1984, were introduced in the Medicare program. Meyer and Johnson (1983)[3] examined the impacts of Medicare and Medicaid cost containment policies and claimed that doctors and hospitals would shift the unreimbursed costs to private sector payers. Ginsburg and Sloan (1984)[4] discussed the issue of cost shifting from the phenomenon of payment differentials across payers and concluded that these differentials had increased over time. Rosko and Broyles (1984)[5] hypothesized that the PPS, by not regulating all sources of payment, created an incentive for hospitals to transfer costs to nonregulated payers and empirically confirmed this hypothesis using hospital data from New Jersey, which was one of the states that had more mature experience in the prospective payment program before the phase-in of the DRG system. As private

193

payers also became more aggressive in implementing cost containment policies, discussions of hospital cost shifting to private payers in response to the PPS subsided. Recent studies of this topic have shifted the attention to workers' compensation recipients as possible 'victims' of hospital cost shifting.

The workers' compensation program was first introduced in the United States in 1908 for federal workers. In 1910, New York state enacted the first state workers' compensation program[6]. Workers' compensation is the first social insurance program in the US. It is a no-fault compensation system mandated in every state. The workers' compensation program requires employers to provide cash benefits, medical care, and rehabilitation services to their employees for work-related injury or illness[7]. Medical expenditures in this program increased by 151 percent between 1980 and 1987, compared with 102 percent for all insurance programs[8]. The percentage of medical care in workers' compensation benefits has also increased over time. Medical expenses accounted for 34 percent of workers' compensation benefits in 1985 and had increased to 40 percent by 1991[9]. Boden (1992)[10] attributed part of the fast-increasing workers' compensation medical costs to a lack of cost containment mechanisms in this program. For years, the provider fee schedule was the only cost containment mechanism used in workers' compensation.

Unlike workers' compensation, which lags behind in the effort to contain costs, most employment-based private insurance programs in the United States have aggressively sought ways to control their cost increases. Co-payments and deductibles are commonly used by these insurance programs, but cannot be used in workers' compensation due to legal restrictions. Other cost containment mechanisms commonly used include capitation, and gatekeeping responsibility delegated to primary care physicians. In the late 1980s, the 'last bastion of the open medical checkbook' was a nickname given to workers' compensation programs[11].

Whether workers' compensation programs were 'victims' of hospitals' cost shifting remains inconclusive in the literature. A recent study by the California Workers Compensation Institute (CWCI 1992)[12] found that among hospitalized back pain patients in California, there was no difference between hospital charges for those covered by workers' compensation and those covered by private health insurance. Zaidman (1990)[13] compared insurance claims between workers' compensation and Blue Cross in Minnesota and found that workers' compensation patients were charged higher than the Blue Cross patients. Baker and Kruger (1995)[14] used an inpatient sample constructed from Zaidman's Minnesota study and concluded that after controlling for baseline differences, workers' compensation patients were actually charged less than non-workers' compensation patients. However, when using both inpatient and outpatient claims data, the same study found that workers' compensation recipients were charged more. Another study using insurance claims data from California concluded that the observed charge differentials could be explained by a difference in service utilization patterns rather than price discrimination[15].

Most studies, except for Baker and Kruger (1995), agreed that disparities between insurance programs were greatest for treatments for which medical care providers had the most discretion. Back pain treatment falls into this category. Back pain is the most frequent item among all the workers' compensation medical claims. It is also the second most common ailment for adults seeking physician care in the United States. Back pain affects 5–14 percent of adults in the US each year; the estimated annual health care cost (direct and indirect) of back pain was $100 million[16] in 1989. Treatment for back pain can be categorized into two types: conservative versus operative. The conservative treatments include bed rest, traction, hot and cold therapy, drug therapies, manipulation, acupuncture, back supports, back schools, psychotherapy, and exercises. The operative treatments include microdiscectomy, automated percutaneous lumbar discectomy, chemonucleolysis, spinal fusion, facet blocks, lumbar decompression, and salvage spine surgery[17]. A wide variation of back pain treatments was observed in practice, especially with regards to whether to treat back pain patients surgically. Studies have shown dramatic geographic variations in back pain surgery rates internationally as well as within the United States[18, 19].

With the wide variations in back pain treatments, it is likely that different payers may develop different treatment protocols, and some may even design a protocol that yields substantial cost saving. For example, a payer (payer A) might encourage medical treatment of back pain in order to avoid the high cost associated with surgery. In that case, only very severe cases will be treated surgically, whereas the patient pool of surgical cases covered by another payer (payer B) that does not interfere with the choice of treatment will be composed of a mix of patients with different degrees of severity. Therefore, comparisons of surgical charges between payers A and B are likely to be biased because of the difference in patient mix. That is, it is not surprising to find that the average surgical charge of payer A is higher than that of payer B since the back pain conditions of patients covered by payer A are a lot worse than those covered by payer B. However, a conclusion of no charge differential may no longer be valid after taking into account the difference in patient mix. Specifically, if the comparison was made between patients covered by payer A and payer B with a similar level of severity, patients covered by payer B may actually be charged more since the previously discovered 'charge equality' was based on contrasting a sicker patient group (payer A) with a less sick group (payer B). The above example demonstrates that by overlooking the selection issues in treatment pattern across payers, findings from the previous studies may be biased. The objective of this study is to re-examine the hospital cost shifting issue in workers' compensation by taking into account the treatment pattern selections across payers.

2   METHOD

To examine the charge differences among surgically treated back pain patients whose claims were paid by employment-based or non-public payers; an intuitively straightforward approach is to regress hospital charges on a list of explanatory variables, including different sources of payment. Equation (10.1) demonstrates such model specification:

$$C_i = \beta'X_i + \alpha'P_i + \varepsilon_i \qquad (10.1)$$

where C_i is hospital charges for person i back pain visits;
$\quad X_i$ is a vector of explanatory variables other than payment sources;
$\quad P_i$ is a vector of binary variables representing each payment source;
$\quad \varepsilon_i$ is the error term; and
$\quad \beta'$ and α' are the regression parameters.

Then, using workers' compensation as the reference group for payers, regression coefficients α' will capture the charge differences between workers' compensation back pain patients and those covered by other payers, after controlling for explanatory factors other than payment sources. Therefore, α' can be used to test the hypothesis of hospital cost shifting to workers' compensation back pain patients. That is, if α' are significantly negative, the cost shifting hypothesis was supported empirically.

However, the above model specification may suffer from sample selection bias. Given the lack of consensus on back pain treatment in the medical community, patients with back pain conditions may be treated surgically or medically, depending on the severity of the conditions as well as factors such as the preference of patients, physicians or payers. Failure to recognize the possible selection issue associated with treatment choice could yield biased and inconsistent estimates of α', leading to incorrect conclusions and/or policy implications[20,21].

To explore possible sample selection biases introduced by a different preference for medical versus surgical management of back pain patients across payers, the Heckman[22] selection model was used. This model takes into account the censored structure in estimating the charge differences using only the surgical sample, and adds a probit model to account for the selection between medical and surgical treatment. Equation (10.2a) describes the censored portion of the Heckman model, whereas equation (10.2b) characterizes the selection process.

$$C_i = \beta'X_i + \alpha'P_i + \varepsilon_i \qquad if \quad Y_i = 1 \tag{10.2a}$$

$$Y^* = \gamma Z_i + \lambda'P_i + \mu_i \qquad \mu \sim N(0,1) \tag{10.2b}$$

$$
\begin{aligned}
Y &= 1 & if \quad Y^* &> 0 \\
Y &= 0 & otherwise & \\
Prob(Y = 1) &= \Phi(\gamma Z_i + \lambda'P) & & \\
(\mu, \varepsilon) &\sim N(0,0,1, \sigma_\varepsilon, \rho) & &
\end{aligned}
$$

where Φ represents cumulative normal distribution.

Heckman's two-stage estimation yields the following result:

$$E(C_i | C_i > 0) = \beta'X_i + \alpha'P_i + \rho \frac{\phi_i(\hat{\gamma}Z_i + \hat{\lambda}'P_i)}{\Phi_i(\hat{\gamma}Z_i + \hat{\lambda}'P_i)} \tag{10.3}$$

$\phi_i(\cdot)/\Phi_i(\cdot)$ in Equation (10.3) is the Mill's ratio. Consistent estimates of β' and α' are obtained from OLS estimation of equation (10.3)[20,21]. ρ, the regression coefficient associated with Mill's ratio, can be used to test selection bias. If ρ is significantly different from zero, then the hypothesis of no sample selection bias is rejected. It is worth mentioning that X, the explanatory variables in equation (10.2a), should be a strict subset of Z, the explanatory variables in equation (10.2b). That is, Z needs to contain at least one variable that affects selection (that is, surgical treatment) but does not have a partial effect on surgical charges[23]. Without meeting this exclusion restriction, Heckman's two-step estimation method is likely to suffer from collinearity problems, leading to high standard errors for the estimated parameters[24].

3   DATA SOURCE

Inpatient back pain patients were extracted from the 1995 Nationwide Inpatient Sample (NIS) data, Release 4. The 1995 NIS is part of the Healthcare Cost and Utilization Project (HCUP-3), sponsored by the Agency for Health Care Policy and Research (AHCPR). It contains an approximate 20 percent sample of US community hospitals, which was drawn from 19 states and included information on all inpatient stays from over 900 hospitals in 1995. The total number of records in 1995 NIS was about 6.7 million. Information provided in this data includes: patient demographics (age, gender, race), institutional characteristics (location, ownership, types, and so on), clinical (DRG, diagnoses, procedures, admission type, discharge status), expected primary and secondary payers, length of stays, admission/discharge dates, and total charges. For analytical convenience, the 1995 NIS also included two 10 percent sub-samples with proper sampling weights. This chapter constructed its inpatient back pain sample from a 10 percent NIS sub-sample. Three DRGs (DRG 214, DRG 215, and DRG 243) were used to identify back pain-related hospital admissions. Among the back pain DRGs, DRGs 214 and 215 are back pain hospitalization treated with surgical procedures, whereas DRG 243 refers to medical back pain procedures.

4   RESULTS

4.1 Descriptive Statistics

Table 10.1 summarizes the payer distribution of inpatient visits paid by employment-based or non-public insurance in the US. When all diagnoses were considered, workers' compensation payments only accounted for a small percentage of inpatient care utilization. However, when limited to back pain diagnoses only, a significant percentage of inpatient visits were paid for by workers' compensation. As shown in Table 10.1, out of all the hospitalized patients between age 18 and 65 in 1995, only 2.2% identified workers' compensation as the primary payer. More than 70% of hospital admissions were covered by two payers: other private insurance (44.4%), and HMOs and PHPs (26.1%). If limited to hospitalization with a back pain diagnosis, the top two payers were other private insurance (42.7%), and workers' compensation (21.9%). That is, a significant proportion of back pain hospital admissions were paid for by workers' compensation. Table 10.1 also describes the payer mix of surgical and medical admissions, respectively. Cases paid by workers' compensation accounted

Table 10.1 Distribution of payment sources, age 18–65, NIS, 1995 (percentages)

Payer	Whole sample	Back Pain sample	Surgical treatment	Medical treatment
Blue Cross	13.9	11.3	11.3	11.1
HMO, PHP	26.1	19.2	20.8	13.4
Other private insurance	44.4	42.7	41.2	48.0
Self-pay	13.4	4.9	3.0	11.8
Workers' compensation	2.2	21.9	23.7	15.7

Table 10.2 Back pain surgical percentage and charges by source of payment, age 18–65, NIS, 1995

Payer	Surgical treatment (%)	Surgical DRGs
Blue Cross	78.2	$ 9,262
HMO, PHP	75.1	$11,405
Other private insurance	84.5	$11,169
Self-pay	47.1	$13,665
Workers' compensation	84.2	$11,539

for 23.7% of all back pain related surgical admissions, compared with 15.7% of medical admissions. In addition, a higher representation in surgical admissions was also found in back pain hospitalizations paid by HMOs or PHPs. The opposite pattern (that is, higher payer percentage in medical cases than surgical cases) was found in back pain admissions with 'other private insurance' or 'self-pay' as the primary payer.

Table 10.2 compares the proportion of hospitalized back pain patients treated surgically across payer. Surgery procedures were more common among patients covered by workers' compensation (84.2%) and 'other private insurance' (84.5%), and were least common among self-pay patients (47.1%). In addition, average charges per surgical back pain admission were highest among self-pay patients ($13,665), followed by those covered by workers' compensation ($11,539), HMOs/PHPs ($11,405), other private insurance ($11,169), and Blue Cross ($9,262).

Table 10.3 compares the baseline differences in patients' and providers' characteristics between back pain related surgical admissions paid by workers' compensation and other payers. Mean total charges for surgically treated back pain hospitalizations paid by workers' compensation were $11,540, approximately $430 higher than that paid by other payment sources. The average length of stay (LOS) for workers' compensation admissions was slightly lower (2.9 versus 3.0 days), though a paired *t*-test indicated that the difference in LOS was not statistically significant. Workers' compensation surgical patients were on average younger (41.1 versus 44.7 years). Compared with surgical back pain admissions not covered by workers' compensation, a significantly higher proportion of male patients (73.8% vs. 54.0%) and white patients (73.4% vs. 69.5%) was found among those paid by workers' compensation.

In general, the distributions across hospital size and ownership types were compatible between the two groups. A smaller proportion of surgically treated back pain patients covered by workers' compensation (34.1% vs. 41.4%) were admitted to teaching hospitals. Compared with back pain related surgical admissions paid by other payers, a higher proportion of workers' compensation admissions was observed in the South (38.4% vs. 35.2%) and in the West (23.9% vs. 18.4%), whereas a lower proportion was distributed in the Midwest (18% vs. 26%). Additionally, more than 95% of the surgically treated back pain admissions were in the urban area.

To compare the overall health status among surgically treated back pain patients, a Charlson comorbidity index was constructed from the ICD-9 codes associated with each admission. The Charlson comorbidity index identifies a list of diagnoses representing various levels of disease severity and comorbid illness and assigns a comorbidity score for each identified diagnosis[25]. For example, admissions with a diagnosis of diabetes (ICD-9-CM 250–250.3, and 250.7) would be given a comorbidity score one, whereas admissions with a renal disease diagnosis would have a comorbidity score two. Table 10.3 shows that the proportion of back pain admissions with a comorbidity score of one or higher was actually lower among the workers' compensation group; 5.2% of the workers' compensation admissions (compared with 6.9% in admissions not paid by workers' compensation) had a comorbidity score one. In addition, 0.4% of the workers' compensation admissions, compared with 0.8% in the non-workers' compensation group, had a higher than one Charlson comorbidity score. This finding suggests that the overall health status of surgically treated workers' compensation patients was better than those not covered by workers' compensation.

Table 10.3 Patient and provider characteristics of surgical back pain admissions, age 18–65, NIS, 1995

	Workers' compensation	Not workers' compensation
Total charges	$ 11,540 (9,694)	$11,110 (11,520)
Length of stay	2.89 days (2.0)	3.0 days (3.15)
Age	41.1 year (9.50)	44.65 years (10.54)
Male	73.8%	54.0%
Race: White	73.4%	69.5%
Black	5.7%	3.8%
Other	20.9%	26.7%
Hospital size: Small	7.0%	7.7%
Medium	31.8%	31.4%
Large	61.2%	60.9%
Ownership status: Government	6.1%	6.0%
Not for profit	80.6%	84.9%
For profit	13.3%	9.1%
Teaching hospital	34.1%	41.4%
Regions: North East	19.7%	20.4%
Midwest	18.0%	26.0%
South	38.4%	35.2%
West	23.9%	18.4%
Urban	96.0%	95.5%
Comorbidity index: None	94.4%	92.3%
One	5.2%	6.9%
More than one	0.4%	0.8%

4.2 Regression Analysis

Descriptive statistics reported in Tables 10.2 and 10.3 suggested that workers' compensation patients appeared to have higher (though not the highest) charges than those covered by other payers. Regression models based on equation (10.1) are used to examine whether these observed differences could be attributed to differences in payment sources, after controlling for other factors affecting charges. The dependent variable in the first specification of the regression model in Table 10.4 is 'hospital

Table 10.4 Regression model without sample selection adjustment
         (surgical data only)

	Model (1): charges	Model (2): log (charge)
Age	−186.5 (109.95)	−0.01 (0.01)
Age * age	0.84 (1.24)*	0.0002 (0.0001)*
Male	−819.9 (317.9)*	−0.07 (0.02)*
Race (reference group: white)		
Black	651.7 (774.4)	0.07 (0.05)
Other race	−1451.5 (373.6)*	−0.10 (0.02)*
Payer (reference group: workers' compensation)		
Blue Cross	−1714.3 (580.0)*	−0.19 (0.03)*
HMO	−786.8 (475.3)	−0.09 (0.03)*
Other private	−222.0 (409.4)	−0.05 (0.02)
Self-pay	2662.6 (947.1)*	0.16 (0.06)*
Hospital size (reference group: large)		
Small	−966.4 (631.9)	−0.10 (0.04)*
Medium	−644.6 (355.0)	−0.05 (0.02)*
Ownership status (reference group: for profit)		
Government	1664.9 (801.2)*	−0.04 (0.05)
Not-for-profit	−3450.6 (562.0)*	−0.38 (0.03)*
Teaching hospital	1333.5 (364.6)*	0.09 (0.02)*
Region (reference group: North East)		
Midwest	1670.7 (493.7)*	0.16 (0.03)*
South	693.5 (471.3)	0.06 (0.03)*
West	5311.2 (537.1)*	0.44 (0.03)*
Urban	4288.4 (761.1)*	0.36 (0.05)*
Charlson's comorbidity index (reference group: non)		
One	201.8 (644.2)	0.05 (0.04)
More than one	4119.9(1828.6)*	0.31 (0.11)*
Constant	11 546.3(2587.3)*	9.14 (0.15)*
Adjusted R^2	0.0592	0.1172
N (total number of observations)	4689	4689

Notes
Numbers in parentheses are standard errors.
* indicates statistically significant at the 5 percent level.

charge of a surgically treated back pain admission', whereas the second specification used the 'logarithm transformation of the hospital surgical charge' as its dependent variable. It is common in empirical studies to take a logarithm transformation of a dependent variable composed of positive dollar amounts, such as wages, salaries, and charges. The purpose of such a transformation is to mitigate skewed distribution and to make estimates less sensitive to outliers[26]. Because of the skewed distribution of hospital charges, the second model specification is a better fit for this type of data structure.

Explanatory variables include patient demographics, primary source of payment, facility characteristics, regions, treatment characteristics, and comorbidity status. Age square is included to capture a possibly non-linear association between age and charges. Race is categorized into three groups: white (reference group), black, and others. Primary payers are described by four binary variables: Blue Cross, HMOs, other private insurance, and self-pay, using workers' compensation as the reference group. Facility characteristics include hospital size (small, medium, and large), ownership (government, not-for-profit, and for-profit), and teaching status. Geographic regions are described by four Census regions (North East, Midwest, South, and West) and urban versus rural status. Comorbidity status associated with a surgical admission is categorized as no comorbidity, one comorbidity, and more than one comorbidity.

Table 10.4 presents the estimates of the above two regression specifications based on equation (10.1). Model (1), using total charge as the dependent variable, found that compared with workers' compensation patients, charges for hospitalized back pain patients undergoing surgical treatment were significantly lower for Blue Cross patients, and significantly higher for the self-pay patients, after controlling factors other than payment source. However, no significant differences were observed between workers' compensation back pain surgical charges and charges paid by HMOs, PHPs, or other private insurance. Using natural logs of total charges as the dependent variables, Model (2) reached a somewhat different conclusion: the negative association between log(charges) and HMOs/PHPs became statistically significant. The negative association between log(charges) and Blue Cross and the positive association between log(charges) and self-pay remained significant. The higher R^2 (adjusted) value of Model (2) (0.117 vs. 0.059) indicates that this semilogarithmic model is a superior model specification for hospital charges.

The following relationships were also found in Model (2): (a) A negative (but not significant) association was found between back pain charges and patients' age, and this negative association significantly accelerates with age. (b) Hospital charges of surgically treated male back pain patients were significantly lower (approximately 6.7% lower) than those of their female counterparts. (c) Compared with 'white', black back pain patients had higher (but not significant) surgical charges, whereas 'other race' had significantly lower (9.5% lower) charges. (d) Compared with surgically treated back pain patients who were covered by workers' compensation, hospital charges of those covered by Blue Cross, HMOs/PHPs, and other private insurance were 17.3%, 8.6%, and 4.9% lower, respectively, though the charge differential between claims paid by workers' compensation and those by other private insurance was not statistically significant. On the other hand, charges of self-pay back pain patients treated surgically were significantly higher (17.4%) than those of workers' compensation patients. (e) Back pain patients treated in small or medium size hospitals had significantly lower charges than those treated in hospitals with large bed size. (f) Compared with for-profit hospitals, back pain surgical patients treated in government or not-for-profit facilities had lower charges. (g) Back pain patients treated in teaching hospitals had significantly higher charges. (h) Compared with back pain patients in the North East region, those in Midwest, South or West had significantly higher charges. (i) Urban patients had significantly higher charges. And (j) back pain admissions with more than one comorbidity had significantly higher charges (36.3% higher). Note that the regression coefficients associated with binary variables in Model (2) were transformed as $100*(\exp(\beta) - 1)$ to provide correct interpretation of these coefficients in terms of percentage changes (Halvorsen and Palmquist, 1980)[27].

However, the above relationships may be susceptible to sample selection bias since back pain admissions with certain characteristics may be more likely to be treated surgically. A logit regression analysis was conducted to examine the association between the choice of surgical treatment and a variety of patients and facility characteristics, including primary payer. Model (3) in Table 10.5 presents the logit regression results. For ease of interpretation, odds ratios were reported in Table 10.5. Compared with back pain hospitalizations covered primarily by workers' compensation, the odds of receiving surgical treatment were lower among patients covered by Blue Cross (odds ratio (OR): 0.84), HMOs/PHPs (OR: 0.89), other private insurance (OR: 0.61), or self-pay (OR: 0.17), though the difference observed in patients covered by Blue Cross and HMOs/PHPs was not statistically significant.

The odds of receiving surgical treatment were found to increase with age at a decreasing rate. Hospitalized male back pain patients were 1.28 times more likely to be treated surgically than their female counterparts.

Table 10.5 Regression models to verify exclusion restriction requirement

	Model (3): logit model	Model (4): weighted LS
Dependent variable:	= 1 if surgical treatment; = 0 otherwise	Log(charges)
Age	1.13 (0.025)*	−0.014 (0.007)*
Age * age	0.99 (0.0002)*	0.0002 (0.0001)*
Male	1.28 (0.09)*	−0.07 (0.19)*
Race (reference group: white)		
Black	0.59 (0.096)*	0.08 (0.05)
Other race	0.73 (0.59)*	−0.09 (0.02)*
Payer (reference group: workers' compensation)		
Blue Cross	0.84 (0.11)	−0.195 (0.035)*
HMO	0.89 (0.11)	−0.10 (0.03)*
Other private	0.61 (0.06)*	−0.05 (0.025)
Self-pay	0.17 (0.03)*	0.14 (0.06)*
Hospital size (reference group: large)		
Small	0.30 (0.035)*	−0.11 (0.04)*
Medium	0.75 (0.06)*	−0.05 (0.02)*
Ownership status (reference group: for profit)		
Government	0.51 (0.08)*	−0.04 (0.05)
Not-for-profit	1.14 (0.14)*	−0.39 (0.03)*
Teaching hospital	2.03 (0.18)*	0.08 (0.02)*
Region (reference group: North East)		
Midwest	1.60 (0.16)*	0.16 (0.03)*
South	2.00 (0.21)*	0.05 (0.03)*
West	2.66 (0.34)*	0.42 (0.03)*
Urban	3.81 (0.47)*	0.34 (0.05)*
Charlson's comorbidity index (reference group: non)		
One	0.82 (0.11)	0.05 (0.04)
More than one	0.85 (0.28)	0.31 (0.11)*
Income class	*0.94 (0.03)**	*0.01 (0.01)*
Constant	–	9.19 (0.16)*
Adjusted R^2	0.1219**	0.1137
N	6145	4689

Notes
Numbers in parentheses are standard errors.
* indicates statistically significant at the 5 percent level.
** number presented is pseudo R^2 generated by logistic regression model in STATA.

Compared with hospitalized white back pain patients, the odds of operation were significantly lower in blacks (OR: 0.59) and other races (OR: 0.73). Also, back pain patients admitted to small or medium sized facilities were less likely to be treated surgically. Compared with back pain patients admitted to for-profit hospitals, the odds of surgery was 0.51 and 1.14 for those admitted to government and not for profit hospitals, respectively. Patients treated in teaching hospitals were twice as likely to receive surgical treatment than those not in teaching hospitals. Large geographic variations of treatment pattern were found. In general, back pain hospitalizations in the West, South, and Midwest were 2.7, 2.0, and 1.6 times more likely to have surgery than those in the North East. The odds of operation were 3.8 times for back pain patients admitted to urban hospitals than those to rural hospitals. Interestingly, no association was found between treatment choice and patients' comorbidity status.

Patients' income class was found to be significantly associated with treatment choice. Back pain patients in higher income class were actually less likely to be treated surgically, after controlling for other factors. Note that this is the only explanatory variable in model (3) that does not overlap with the variables used in model (2), the log(charges) regression. Model (4) added the income class variable as an additional explanatory variable, but found that this variable did not have a partial effect on log(charges). An exclusion restriction can therefore be established due to the fact that the income variable affected selection, but not log(charges). In the Heckman model estimated below, the income class variable was included in the probit model (for example, selection equation) as the exclusion restriction imposed on Heckman's two-step estimation method.

Table 10.6 compares regression model (2) with estimates from Heckman's sample selection model, denoted as model (5). The previous speculation regarding the sample selection problem was confirmed by the statistical significance of the regression parameter associated with the Mill's ratio. After adjusting for payers' preference in back pain treatment, charge differentials between surgically treated back pain patients covered by workers' compensation and those covered by other private or non-public payers became even more evident across all payers. The significantly negative association found in patients covered by Blue Cross or HMOs/PHPs increased in magnitude after adjusting for sample selection. The significantly positive association found in self-pay patients and the negative (but not significant) association found in patients covered by 'other private insurance' both turned significantly negative after the sample selection adjustment. Using the transformation equation provided by Halvorsen and Palmquist (1980)[27], model (5) indicates

Table 10.6 Sample selection model

	Model (5): Sample Selection model		Model (2): weighted LS	
Age	0.01	(0.01)	−0.01	(0.01)
Age * age	−0.00005	(0.0001)	0.0002	(0.0001)*
Male	−0.02	(0.03)	−0.07	(0.02)*
Race (reference group: white)				
Black	−0.03	(0.06)	0.07	(0.05)
Other race	−0.15	(0.03)*	−0.10	(0.02)*
Payer (reference group: workers' compensation)				
Blue Cross	−0.22	(0.04)*	−0.19	(0.03)*
HMO	−0.12	(0.03)*	−0.09	(0.03)*
Other private	−0.15	(0.04)*	−0.05	(0.02)
Self-pay	−0.32	(0.16)*	0.16	(0.06)*
Hospital size (reference group: large)				
Small	−0.41	(0.10)*	−0.10	(0.04)*
Medium	−0.12	(0.03)*	−0.05	(0.02)*
Ownership status (reference group: for profit)				
Government	−0.17	(0.06)*	−0.04	(0.05)
Not-for-profit	−0.35	(0.04)*	−0.38	(0.03)*
Teaching hospital	0.22	(0.05)*	0.09	(0.02)*
Region (reference group: North East)				
Midwest	0.21	(0.03)*	0.16	(0.03)*
South	0.17	(0.05)*	0.06	(0.03)
West	0.58	(0.06)*	0.44	(0.03)*
Urban	0.73	(0.13)*	0.36	(0.05)*
Charlson's comorbidity index (reference group: none)				
One	−0.01	(0.04)	0.05	(0.04)
More than one	0.29	(0.11)*	0.31	(0.11)*
Mill's ratio	0.96	(0.32)*	–	
Constant	7.86	(0.47)*	9.14	(0.15)*
Adjusted R^2	0.1152		0.1172	
N	4689		4689	

Notes
Numbers in parentheses are standard errors.
* indicates statistically significant at the 5 percent level.

that hospital charges of surgical back pain patients covered by Blue Cross, HMOs/PHPs, other private insurance, and self-pay were 24.6%, 12.8%, 16.2%, and 37.7% lower, respectively, than those covered by workers' compensation.

No significant association was found between patient demographics and surgical charges, except for the charge differential between whites and other race, with charges of the latter group 16.2% lower than those of the former group. Charge differential among hospital in different sizes was enlarged after sample selection adjustment; surgical charges of back pain patients treated in small and medium size hospitals were 50.7% and 12.8% lower than those in large hospitals. Charges incurred in teaching hospitals were 24.6% higher than those in non-teaching hospitals. Charge difference across geographic regions also became more substantial after adjusting for sample selection; back pain admissions treated surgically in the West, Midwest, and South were 78.6%, 23.4%, and 18.5% more expensive than those treated in the North East. Additionally, charges of surgical back pain admissions in urban hospitals were 1.07 times higher than those in rural hospitals. Limited changes were found in the effects of patient comorbidity after the sample selection adjustment; surgical charges of back pain patients with at least one comorbidity (based on the Charlson comorbidity index) were 33.6% higher than those who had no comorbidity.

5   DISCUSSION

Empirical findings from this study provide supporting evidence of hospital cost shifting in the form of price differentiation among surgically treated working age back pain patients. This study also finds that different insurance payers appeared to have different treatment patterns for back pain patients. In general, workers' compensation back pain patients were more likely to be treated surgically than hospitalized back pain patients covered by either employment-based or non-public insurance. As a consequence of treatment pattern variation across payers, the pool of surgical patients not covered by workers' compensation was overall sicker than those covered by workers' compensation. Failure to adjust for sample selection would underestimate charge differences between surgically treated back pain patients covered by workers' compensation and those covered by other payers.

This study compares workers' compensation with either employment-based or other non-public payment source. Patients whose primary payer was Medicare, Medicaid or other public insurance were excluded from the study. This exclusion criterion was to select a more homogeneous group for charge comparisons. For working age men or women (that is, persons age between 18 and 65) to be eligible for these public programs, they are probably disabled, unemployed, or suffered from permanent kidney failure. Since back pain conditions for this group are likely to be much more debilitating in nature, comparing charges of workers' compensation patients with patients covered in public programs is not very meaningful.

Patients' income class – the variable that met the requirement of exclusion restriction in the Heckman model – deserves more discussion. Initially, the author expected to observe a positive association between patients' income class and the selection of surgery. However, a significantly negative association was concluded in the estimation. A possible explanation is that patients' income class closely resembles their education level. Though higher income makes a back pain patient more financially capable of paying his or her share of the treatment cost, a more educated patient is also likely to be more informed on the treatment options available. For back pain conditions, the lack of consensus regarding clinical management of back pain in the medical society certainly casts doubts on the effectiveness of surgical treatment and increases the uncertainty of this treatment option. Therefore, people with a higher education level may choose not to undergo back pain surgery unless it is absolutely necessary. This preference is then reflected in the slightly negative association between income class and the selection of surgical treatment.

Findings from this study are subject to the following limitations. NIS, the data set used in this study, was not collected specifically for back pain patients, therefore, did not provide detailed information regarding the severity of patients' back pain conditions. It is possible that some of the observed differences in treatment patterns and charge differentials may be attributed to variations in the severity-mix across payers. Additionally, only charge information, rather than costs, was provided in this claims database. Given that many third party payers are able to negotiate a rate lower than the official charges, the observed charge differences between surgically treated workers' compensation back pain patients and those covered by Blue Cross, HMOs/PHPs, or other private insurance may be increased if cost information is used. On the other hand, charge differentials between workers' compensation and self-pay patients may be decreased when cost information is used because the latter group is unlikely to be able to exercise any type of price negotiation.

This study focuses only on one part of the health care system – inpatient care. However, a back pain patient is likely to have several office visits prior to hospitalization, and different payers may have different preferences in the choice of inpatient versus outpatient treatment. If the preference of inpatient versus outpatient treatment indeed differs across payers, then the inpatient back pain population selected in this study would already be subject to selection bias. The possibility of this hierarchy of selections needs to be explored by future studies. In addition, some studies suggested that cost shifting may be done more subtly[28]. For example, rather than charging different prices for the same type of care, higher frequencies of care may be induced for workers' compensation patients. However, the episode-based data set used in this study does not contain sufficient information to examine the latter type of cost shifting, since the outpatient data file for back pain patients examined in this study was not collected.

A more integrated system should reduce the chance of cost shifting from private payers to workers' compensation. Proposals such as 24-hour coverage have been discussed in several states. The 24-hour coverage plan proposes to combine the medical component of workers' compensation with the traditional employer-provided health insurance[29]. Advocates of the 24-hour coverage plan claimed that it would reduce price discrimination by providers, alleviate the moral hazard effects, streamline the delivery of care, and decrease administrative and legal costs. However, due to high administrative costs associated with the system integration and also to political concerns, very limited number of regions have implemented this plan. Evaluations of areas with experience of 24-hour coverage will provide valuable information to consider in the reform of the workers' compensation program.

REFERENCES

1. Folland, S., A.C. Goodmand and M. Stano (1997), *The Economics of Health and Health Care*, Second edition, Prentice Hall, NJ, p. 598.
2. Morrisey, M.A. (1994), Chapter 1 in *Cost Shifting in Health Care: Separating Evidence from Rhetoric*, Washington, DC: The AEI Press.
3. Meyer, J.A. and W.R. Johnson (1983), 'Cost shifting in health care: an economic analysis', *Health Affairs*, Summer, **2**(2): 20–35.
4. Ginsburg, P.B. and F.A. Sloan (1984), 'Hospital cost shifting', *New England Journal of Medicine*, 5 April, **310**(14): 893–8.
5. Rosko, M.D. and R.W. Broyes (1984), 'Unintended consequences of prospective payment: erosion of hospital financial position and cost shifting', *Health Care Management Review*, Summer, **9**(3): 35–43.
6. Kramer, O. and R. Briffault (1991), *Workers' Compensation: Strengthening the Social Compact*, New York: I.I.I. Press.

7. Worrall, J.D. (1983), Chapter 1 in *Safety and the Work Force: Incentives and Disincentives in Workers' Compensation*, Ithaca, NY: ILR Press, pp. 2–6.

8. Burton, J.F. (1990), 'Benefit and costs continue to climb: led by health care payments', *Workers' Compensation Monitor*, 3(2): 2.

9. Boden, L.I. and C.A. Fleischman (1989), *Medical Costs in Workers' Compensation: Trends and Interstate Comparisons*, Workers' Compensation Research Institute, Cambridge, MA.

10. Boden, L.I. (1992), 'Workers' compensation medical costs: a special case', in J. Greenwood and A. Taricco (eds), *Workers' Compensation Health Care Cost Containment*, Horsham, PA: LRP Publications, pp 27–54.

11. Gots, R. (1987), 'Workers' compensation: the last bastion of the open checkbook', *International Association of Industrial Accident Boards and Commissions Journal*, Summer, pp 66–9.

12. *Hospital Utilization in Workers' Compensation* (1992), California Workers' Compensation Institute Research Update, April.

13. Zaidman, B. (1990), *Industrial Strength Medicine: A Comparison of Workers' Compensation and Blue Cross Health Care in Minnesota*, Minnesota Department of Labor and Industry.

14. Baker, L.C. and A.B. Krueger (1995), 'Medical costs in workers' compensation insurance', *Journal of Health Economics*, 14: 531–49.

15. Johnson, W.G., M.L. Baldwin and J.F. Burton Jr. (1996), 'Why is the treatment of work-related injuries so costly? New evidence from California', *Inquiry*, Spring, 33(1): 53–65.

16. Leigh, J.P. (1989), 'Specific illness, injuries, and job hazards associated with absenteeism', *Journal of Occupational Medicine*, 31: 792–7.

17. Feffer, H.L. and A.L. Nachemson (1992), 'Standards for assessment and management of low back pain', Chapter 8 in *Health Care Cost Containment*, Horsham, PA: LPR Publications, pp 155–86.

18. Deyo, R.A., J.D. Loeser and S.J. Bigos (1990), 'Herniated lumbar intervertebral discectomy', *Annual of Internal Medicine*, 112: 598–603.

19. Frymoyer, J.W. (1988), 'Back pain and sciatica', *New England Journal of Medicine*, 318(5): 291–300.

20. Mroz, T.A. (1987), 'The sensitivity of an empirical model of married women's hours of work to economic and statistical assumptions', *Econometrica*, 55: 765–99.

21. Maddala, G.S. (1983), *Limited-dependent and Qualitative Variables in Econometrics*, Cambridge, MA: Cambridge University Press.

22. Heckman, J. (1976), 'The common structure of statistical models of

truncation, sample selection and limited dependent variables and a simple estimator for such models', *Annals of Economic and Social Measurement*, **5**: 475–92.
23. Wooldridge, J.M. (2000), Chapter 17 in *Introductory Econometrics – A Modern Approach*, Cincinnati, OH: South-Western College Publishing. Thomson Learning_{TM}.
24. Leung, S.F. and S. Yu (1996), 'On the choice between sample selection and two-part models', *Journal of Econometrics*, **72**: 197–229.
25. Deyo R.A., D.C. Cherkin and M.A. Ciol (1992), 'Adapting a clinical comorbidity index for use with ICD-9-CM administrative databases', *Journal of Clinical Epidemiology*, **45**(6): 613–9.
26. Wooldridge, J.M. (2000), Chapter 6 in *Introductory Econometrics – A Modern Approach*, Cincinnati, OH: South-Western College Publishing. Thomson Learning_{TM}.
27. Halvorsen, R. and R. Palmquist (1980), 'The interpretation of dummy variables in semilogarithmic equations', *American Economics Review*, **70**(3): 474–5.
28. Butler, R.J., R.P. Hartwig and H. Gardner (1997), 'HMOs, moral hazard and cost shifting in workers' compensation', *Journal of Health Economics*, **16**: 191–206.
29. Baker, L.C. and A.B. Kruger (1993), 'Twenty-four-hour coverage and workers' compensation insurance', *Health Affairs*, **12** (Suppl): 271–81.

11. Hospital services under a national health insurance system: transition from a fee-for-service to a capitation system

Tetsuji Yamada, Tadashi Yamada, Seiritsu Ogura and Reiko Suzuki*

1 INTRODUCTION

There has been a substantial increase in health care expenditure under the National Health Insurance (NHI) scheme in Japan. Under NHI, the Japanese government maintains the fee-for-service (FFS) payment as a retrospective cost-based method of reimbursement for health care services. Recent studies have shown an annual increase in the national health care expenditures on an average of about 5 percent per annum. In 1997, the elderly aged 65 and over had more than seven times the hospital care expenditure of people under the age of 65.

In 1990, the Japanese government implemented a cost containment policy by introducing a partial capitation fee (CAP) on elderly care services in geriatric and general hospitals.[1] A government-approved geriatric hospital for CAP reimbursement is called a managed geriatric hospital. Those that are not approved by the government are called general geriatric hospitals with lower FFS reimbursement rates for elderly care.[2] Despite the urgency for the development of a new health care financing system in an aging society like Japan, there is still no consensus, from either theoretical or empirical perspectives, as to the effects of the Japanese partial prospective payment system regarding the performance of health care delivery since the implementation of the CAP.

In other industrialized countries, there has been a rapid increase in the cost of health care programs over the decades. Policy debates in these countries include controlling health care costs, quality of care, and cost-containment programs. For example, Medicare's prospective payment

213

system (PPS) in the United States has reduced hospital service utilization, which has then controlled the rapid increase in health care expenditures (Sloan et al. 1988; Feinglass and Holloway 1991).[3] It is the common view that this cost-containment policy has been effective. Yet an ambiguity still remains over the relationship between the level of health care expenditure and intensity of health care services. DesHarnais et al. (1987) and DesHarnais et al. (1988) state that the PPS has reduced hospital utilization without adverse effects on the quality of care. Newhouse and Byrne (1988) claim that the PPS decreases length of stay among Medicare patients. More recently Hodgkin and McGuire (1994), Dor and Farley (1996) and Kesteloot and Voet (1998) support the theory that the PPS decreases the resource intensity of hospital services.[4]

For the relationship between Medicare and managed care, Baker (1995), Baker and Shankarkumar (1997) and Cutler and Sheiner (1997) show that the structural change caused by an increase in managed care, known as capitation in the US, is negatively associated with a decrease in Medicare expenditure. Baker and Brown (1997) and Feldman and Scharfstein (1998) note that managed care patients tend to be treated with a smaller range of services than those with a cost-based fee-for-service health care plan.

In this study, our purpose is threefold. First, we will examine the choice of the capitation program by geriatric hospitals in Japan. Second, we will analyze the different effects of the capitation and the fee-for-service programs on intensity per day, units of service, length of hospitalization and intensity per treatment, as well as their interactions in terms of the quantity and the intensity of hospital services in geriatric and general hospitals. Third, we will fill the literature gap regarding the effects of the Japanese prospective payment system on hospital services.

2   BACKGROUND

The insurance system for the elderly in Japan consists of five insurers under government supervision. Government-managed Health Insurance covers employees at places of work (mainly small and medium sized enterprises). Social Health Insurance covers employees at places of work (mainly large enterprises, or enterprises with 700 or more employees). The Seamen's Insurance covers seamen and those working on ships and boats. Mutual Aid Associations' Insurance covers national public service employees, local public service employees, and private school teachers and employees. The National Health Insurance covers people who are not covered by employee insurance (farmers, the self-employed, such as carpenters, doctors, and so on.) and retirees formerly under employees' insurance and their dependants. About 70 percent of the 11 million elderly belong to the National Health Insurance, while 17 percent are general employees under the Government-managed Health Insurance. The Social Health Insurance, Seamen's Insurance and Mutual Aid Associations' Insurance cover the remaining 13 percent.

Medical service providers follow the reimbursement schedules with a point system as set by the Ministry of Health, Labour and Welfare. The reimbursement price, based on a system, is a unified system applicable to all medical service providers, regardless of the types of health insurance cover provided. The role of the point system is to generate enough revenue to cover the costs incurred. Each kind of medical service is assigned a certain number of points, and providers are reimbursed a sum of the total points multiplied by 10 yen (approximately 10 cents, assuming one dollar equals 100 yen).

The point system classifies 13 service categories: medication, injection, examination, hospital service, general treatment, radiology, mental treatment, anesthesia, basic consultation, home care, image diagnosis, operation and physiotherapy. Within these groups there are further classifications. For example an initial consultation is accorded 195 points and 450 points with referrals; nursing at hospitals is accorded 318 points; injection ranges from 15 to 150 points, depending on the skill required. As an exception, medication is awarded 1 point per 15 yen, and the material purchasing price plus the prescription are 74 points per unit. These changes in points are dependent on whether the patients are children, adults, or the elderly, the degree of skill required, the quantity of material needed, and the patient's length of treatment. The government reimbursement price consists of these complicated pricing classifications on a fee-for-service basis.

For the elderly, the criteria for government reimbursement differ slightly from the general case. Table 11.1 shows points given according to the types of services. Services such as medication, injection, operation, anesthesia, and radiology do not have specific point criteria for the elderly. These consist of so many kinds of services and treatments that the differences between maximum and minimum points are large, for example, 120–80 000 points for operations, 31–5100 points for anesthesia, and 80–10 000 points for radiology.

In the United States, a prospective reimbursement system based on diagnosis-related groups (DRGs) was instituted by the Health Care Financing Administration (HCFA) in 1984 for Medicare inpatient hospital services. Unlike the US Medicare system, the Japanese system is a partially prospective payment system for hospital services. The general health insurance program for those under the age of 70 has the FFS. The

Table 11.1 Point system for the elderly (health and medical care services)

Type of service	Points
1. Consultation	
First hospital visit	195
Hospital visit more than once	43
2. Home care (per month)	2200
3. *Medication	
Preparation (a)	1–4
Prescription	24
4. Injection (b)	15–250
5. Physiotherapy (per day)	
Equal to or less than 6 months since the first consultation	
Complicated physiotherapy	500
Simple physiotherapy	170
More than 6 months since the first consultation	
Complicated physiotherapy	460
Simple physiotherapy	150
6. Image diagnosis	
Simple computer tomogram	
Head	800
Body	1100
Limbs	800
Computer tomogram for cerebral functions	2300
7. Examination	
Basic examination when an admission to a hospital (per month)	60
8. Treatment (per day)	12
9. *Operation	120–80 000
10. *Anesthesia	31–5100
11. *Radiology	80–10 000
12. Hospital day (per day)	
Basic nursing care	
Less than 6 months since the first consultation	318
More than 6 months since the first consultation	308

Notes
* follows the same criteria as for all other ages.
(a) 1 point for a dose and 4 points a day internal medicine.
(b) for example, 15 for hypodermic injection, 120 for venous injection and 250 for spinal injection.

Source: Department of Insurance, and Department of Health Insurance and Welfare of the Elderly, *Tensu Hyo no Kaishaku* 1993 (Interpretation of points table 1993), Tokyo, the Ministry of Health, Labour and Welfare, 1993.

Elderly Health Insurance Program (EHIP) for those aged 70 years and over, including the bedridden elderly aged 65 to 70, has two types: the FFS which is a retrospective cost-based method of reimbursement with the point system; and the CAP, which is a prospective reimbursement with the same point system.[5]

Hospital services under the capitation program are classified into four categories: medication, injection, examinations, and inpatient care, including nursing care. These services are collectively called managed medical hospitalization treatment. As the capitation program is in its early trial stage, all hospital services are not subject to the program. The Japanese government has not fully implemented capitation, and hospital services other than the four mentioned service categories are still provided with points under the FFS.

3   ANALYTICAL FRAMEWORK

This section briefly addresses the empirical framework in which our estimations are attempted. Suppose that hospital j makes its revenue per period, Z_j:

$$Z_j = \Sigma_i \, p_i q_i d_i \qquad (11.1)$$

where i denotes patient i, and p is a reimbursement system ($p = \theta CAP + (1-\theta)FFS$), $0 \le \theta \le 1$. p is the weighted sum of capitation (CAP) based reimbursement and the FFS of cost based reimbursement.[6] q and d denote intensity of health care services (for example, amount of medical care per day or intensity per day) and length of hospitalization in number of days, respectively. Since the CAP reimbursement is made on the basis of a lump sum for health care per person per day, this will give a hospital an incentive not to provide health care beyond the maximum reimbursement per person per day.[7] In this framework we assume that physicians have no direct role in the model because physicians in Japan are basically *salary-based* employees. However, they do balance the hospital's interest in profit on funds and the patient's interest in services. Therefore, in our framework, intensity, units of service, and number of treatment days play important roles.[8] Average intensity per day and intensity per treatment are included to measure two types of health care intensity; this is done by controlling the length of hospitalization days, the technical sophistication involved (for example, intensive care unit and coronary care unit), and the patient's severity.

The intensity of services provided by hospital j to a patient i is expressed as a function of the reimbursement system and other factors:

$$g_{d,i,j} = f(p_{i,j}, d_{i,j}, g_{t,i,j}, X_{i,j}),\tag{11.2a}$$

where g_d, and g_t denote intensity per day and intensity per treatment, respectively. X denotes other influential factors that include patient characteristics, severity control measures, resource inputs, hospital characteristics, and so on.

The units of service provided ($q_{i,j}$) and length of hospitalization ($d_{i,j}$) are expressed to be a function of the reimbursement system and other factors:

$$q_{i,j} = h(p_{i,j}, g_{d,i,j}, g_{t,i,j}, X_{i,j}),\tag{11.2b}$$

and

$$d_{i,j} = k(p_{i,j}, g_{d,i,j}, g_{t,i,j}, X_{i,j}),\tag{11.2c}$$

Similarly, the intensity per treatment is expressed as:

$$g_{t,i,j} = m(p_{i,j}, q_{i,j}, g_{d,i,j}, X_{i,j}),\tag{11.2d}$$

The decisions the hospital makes include intensity (per day and per treatment), units of service and length of hospitalization with the behavior of other hospitals taken as given. In addition, the factors and production processes that are influenced by the decision-making staff may generate hospital service decisions. Therefore, intensity in some underlying production function is embodied in services that are expected to be correlated. Thus the production endogeneity requires an instrumental variable approach. Breyer (1987) builds a simultaneous equation model that considers cost per case, average length of stay and average occupancy rate as jointly dependent variables in his cost analysis. Newhouse (1994) intensively discusses the difficulties in measuring output and adjustment for quality (that is, intensity) in hospital services, and states there is a distortion of findings because of the omitted variable problem. Thus misspecification will lead to a cross-level bias, such as intensity of day and treatment, units of service and length of hospitalization.

We estimate a simultaneous equation model with intensity per day equation (11.2a), units of service (11.2b), length of hospitalization (11.2c) and intensity per treatment (11.2d) as jointly dependent variables by incorporating intensity-related factors. We employ two-stage least squares estimation by using instrument variables. These are estimated in the first stage by patient characteristics, types of insurance cover, hospital characteristics, and resource inputs. Our instruments are expected to remove biases that may stem from omitted variables and simultaneity. For identification purposes, we exclude units of service per day from equations (11.2a) and (11.2c), and length of hospitalization from equations (11.2b) and (11.2d).

To estimate the effect of capitation on hospital services, we consider the regression analogue to the equations (11.2a) to (11.2d) as:

$$\text{Hospital services}_{j,h} = \alpha_0 + \alpha_1 \text{Capitation}_j +$$
$$\Sigma_h \ \beta_h \text{Hospital service}_{j,h} + X_j\gamma + \varepsilon_{j,h} \qquad (11.3)$$

With the procedure subscripts (i) dropped, h denotes intensity per day, units of service, length of hospitalization, or intensity per treatment by hospital j. $X_j\gamma$ denotes a vector of patient and hospital related variables that may influence intensity, units of service and length of hospitalization. ε_j in equation (11.3) is a random disturbance stemming from components of intensity per day, units of service, length of hospitalization and intensity per treatment that are affected by immeasurable factors. For h, length of hospitalization is not part of the intensity of care in our analysis (Hodgkin and McGuire 1994); rather, we employ the number of procedures performed per day for intensity per day and the number of procedures performed per treatment for intensity per treatment.

The focus of the analysis is on the influence of the capitation program on hospital services by considering intensity. Given the available data, we group variables into patient characteristics, severity control measures, resource inputs, and hospital characteristics. Patient characteristics include age, sex, type of insurance cover, duration of hospitalization, and types of diseases. For adjusting the intensity of hospital services, we include in our estimation such factors as types of operation and frequency of equipment usage as severity control measures, physicians, nurses and technicians as labor inputs, number of equipment types, bed types and clinical space as capital inputs, and hospital ownership types, emergency medical hospital treatment, and additional special service as hospital characteristics. Table 11.2 contains the definitions of these variables.

4   DATA

In this study we used three different survey data. The first, Iryo Shisetsu Jittai Chosa ('Statistic Survey of Medical Facility'), is the 1993 Medical Facility Survey of 9896 hospitals, which include accredited geriatric

Table 11.2 Definitions of variables

Variable	Definition
Policy factors	
Capitation	geriatric hospitals with capitation (that is, managed geriatric hospitals) = 1, otherwise = 0; individuals in managed geriatric hospitals = 1, otherwise = 0.
Points	total points for a patient per month.
Length of hospitalization	total hospital days per month.
Units of service	total number of treatments per month.
Intensity per day	total points per patient/hospital days per month.
Intensity per treatment	total points of a treatment /treatments per month.
Patient characteristics	
Outpatient	the number of outpatient admissions per month.
Inpatient	the number of inpatient admissions per month.
Gender	sex of patient: male = 1, female = 0.
Age	age of patient.
Health insurance	general occupational health insurance (those are employee's health insurance, seamen's health insurance, and mutual aid associations' health insurance) = 1, otherwise = 0.
Compensation	employee's accident compensation insurance = 1, otherwise = 0.
Geriatric	geriatric medical care = 1, otherwise = 0.
In/out	inpatient = 1, otherwise = 0.
< 1 month	length of stay: days between a week and a month.
1–2.9 months	between more than month and less than three months.
3–5.9 months	between more than three months and less than six months.
6–12 months	between more than six months and less than one year.
1–1.5 years	between more than one year and less than one year and a half.
> 1.5 years	more than one year and a half.
CIRCUL	diseases of the circulatory system = 1, otherwise = 0.
MUSCUL	diseases of the muscular skeletal system and connective tissue = 1, otherwise =0.
DIGEST	diseases of the digestive system = 1, otherwise = 0.
NERVOU	diseases of the nervous system and sense organs = 1, otherwise = 0.
Severity control measure	
ICU	the average number of patients per bed in an intensive care unit (ICU) per month.
RADIOTHERAPY	the average number of patients per bed in radio-therapeutics unit per month.
ANESTHESIA	the number of general anesthetics per month.
FEMUR	the number of operations of femora per month.
CORONARY	the number of coronary operations per month.
FIBERSCOPE	the frequency of usage of fiberscope of (upper) digestive tract per week.
DIGITAL-RADIO	the frequency of usage of digital radiography per week.
X-RAY CT	the frequency of usage of general computed tomography (X-ray CT) per week.
MRI	the frequency of usage of nuclear magnetic resonator-tomography (NMR-CT or MRI) per week.
BONE	the frequency of usage of bone-salt measuring apparatus (or equipment) per week.
HIGH-ENERGY	the frequency of usage of medical high-energy radiograph (or radiographic equipment) per week.

Table 11.2 Definitions of variables (cont.)

Variable	Definition
Labor inputs	
Physician	the number of full-time physicians.
Pharmacist	the number of pharmacists.
Nurse	the number of nurses.
Asso-nurse	the number of associate nurses.
Assistant	the number of nursing assistants.
Radio-tech	the number of radiology technicians.
Labo-tech	the number of clinical laboratory technicians.
Nutritionist	the number of nutritionists.
Administration	the number of employees in an administrative department.
Capital inputs	
Fiberscope(K)	the number of fiberscopes of (upper) digestive tract.
High-energy(K)	the number of medical high-energy radiographs (or radiographic equipment).
Dialyzator	the number of renographic dialyzators.
Gene-bed	the number of general beds.
Geria-bed	the number of geriatric beds.
Ward	size of ward in square meters.
Clinical	size of clinical section in square meters.
Admini	size of administrative section in square meters.
Hospital characteristics	
Prefectural	hospitals run by prefectural government.
Municipal	hospitals run by municipal government.
Non-profit	hospitals run by non-profit organization (insurance, union, and so on).
Private	hospitals run by private individual.
Emergency	emergency hospital for medical care treatment system = 1, otherwise= 0.
Meal	meal preparation for patients (by outside providers) = 1, otherwise = 0.
Cleaning	cleaning hospitals (by outside providers) = 1, otherwise = 0.
Nursing care and other services	
Ergo-therapy	the number of patients treated in ergo-therapy unit per month.
Psychiatric	the number of patients treated in psychiatric ergo-therapy unit per month.
Geria-day-care	the number of patients treated in geriatric day-care unit per month.
Vaccination	hospitals practicing vaccination.
Prescription	the number of prescriptions issued per week.
Regional dummy	
D1	district dummy = 1 (Hokkaido and Touhoku), otherwise = 0.
D2	district dummy = 1 (North Kantou), otherwise = 0.
D3	omitted district (East Kantou where includes Tokyo).
D4	district dummy = 1 (Hokuriku), otherwise = 0.
D5	district dummy = 1 (Tokai), otherwise = 0.
D6	district dummy = 1 (Kinki), otherwise = 0.
D7	district dummy = 1 (Chugoku), otherwise = 0.
D8	district dummy = 1 (Shikoku), otherwise = 0.
D9	district dummy = 1 (Kyushu and Okinawa), otherwise = 0.

hospitals with the capitation program, accredited geriatric hospitals without the program, general hospitals and clinics. In this study, we excluded the data from clinics in order to focus on hospitals. The data include establishment, health insurance accredited types, patient types and all kind of information regarding medical facilities except costs. The second, Byoin Houkoku Chosa ('Survey of Hospital Report'), is the 1993 hospital employee of survey of 9844 hospitals. The data provide information of medical personnel, that is, physicians, nurses, pharmacists, dietitians, technicians, administrative staffs, and so on. The third, Shakai Iryo Shinryo Koibetsu Chosa ('Survey of Medical Treatments'), is the 1994 medical services survey of 311 292 patients. The data provide types of illness of patients, age, sex, health insurance, types of medical services, reimbursement points, hospital types, and so on. These survey data are useful for the purposes of our analysis, since they are the most recent since the implementation of the capitation program in 1990. We merged the first and second hospital survey data so as to obtain the data relevant for this study. We examined the three types of hospitals: managed geriatric, general geriatric, and general hospitals. We then selected the inpatients and outpatients in those hospitals whose ages were 65 and over.

5   EMPIRICAL RESULTS

5.1   Choice of Capitation (Results of Logit Procedure)

We present the results of the logit model of capitation in Table 11.3. The sample of 546 hospitals is composed of managed and general geriatric hospitals. Holding labor and capital inputs, patient severity, and hospital characteristics constant, hospitals with a higher number of outpatients are more likely to choose the CAP program. The negative sign of inpatients indicates that hospitals with a higher number of patients are less likely to choose the CAP program. From the policy implication position, geriatric hospitals have incentives to apply the capitation program to outpatients while applying the fee-for-service program to inpatients. Outpatients, who are less severe but in need of medical care, visit geriatric hospitals more often than general hospitals. An application of the CAP to outpatients is more profitable and is a feasible option for hospitals.

There is a theoretical possibility of the transfer of inpatient-based services to outpatient-based services (Newhouse 1996). The effect of capitation on admission is theoretically ambiguous in US studies, however. The experiences of the US prospective payment show that the average severity of cases treated on an inpatient basis may increase

Table 11.3 Logit model of capitation: managed geriatric and general geriatric hospitals (dependent variable: CAP (capitation))

Independent variable	Estimated coefficient	*t*-statistic	*P*-value	$\partial CAP/\partial X$
Constant	2.126	1.090	[0.276]	0.316
Patient characteristics				
Outpatient*	0.2209	1.833	[0.067]	0.032
Inpatient*	−1.243	−3.022	[0.003]	−0.185
Severity control				
ICU*	0.0677	0.3868	0.699]	0.010
ANESTHESIA*	0.9163	2.628	[0.009]	0.136
FEMUR*	−0.5007	−0.7486	[0.454]	−0.074
FIBERSCOPE*	−0.2218	−1.459	[0.144]	−0.033
DIGITAL-RADIO*	−0.2083	−0.7892	[0.430]	−0.031
X-RAY CT*	−0.1271	−1.260	[0.208]	−0.018
MRI*	−0.1096	−0.5475	[0.584]	−0.016
BONE*	−0.6491	−1.797	[0.072]	−0.096
HIGH-ENERGY*	−0.1841	−0.7774	[0.437]	−0.027
Labor inputs				
Physician*	−0.8743	−1.744	[0.081]	−0.130
Pharmacist*	−1.193	−3.765	[0.000]	−0.177
Nurse*	1.432	6.052	[0.000]	0.213
Asso-nurse*	1.439	3.389	[0.001]	0.214
Assistant*	1.834	6.647	[0.000]	0.272
Radio-tech*	−0.1144	−0.2922	[0.770]	−0.017
Labo-tech*	−0.4085	−0.9830	[0.326]	−0.060
Nutritionist*	0.0621	0.1616	[0.872]	0.009
Administration*	0.2235	0.6925	[0.489]	0.033
Capital inputs				
Fiborscope(K)*	−0.6410	−1.883	[0.060]	−0.095
High-energy(K)*	−1.272	−0.9829	[0.326]	−0.189
Dialyzator*	−0.5825	−2.757	[0.006]	−0.086
Gene-bed*	0.4171	1.297	[0.194]	0.062
Geria-bed*	−0.2715	−1.801	[0.072]	−0.040
Ward*	−0.9622	−2.947	[0.003]	−0.143
Clinical*	0.0783	0.4232	[0.672]	0.011
Admini*	−0.3273	−2.042	[0.041]	−0.048

Table 11.3 Logit model of capitation: managed geriatric and general geriatric hospitals (dependent variable: CAP (capitation)) (cont.)

Independent variable	Estimated coefficient	t-statistic	P-value	∂CAP/∂X
Hospital characteristics				
Private	−0.3052	−1.171	[0.241]	−0.045
Emergency	0.1854	0.6224	[0.534]	0.027
Nursing care and other services				
Ergo-therapy*	0.0998	1.462	[0.144]	0.014
Psychiatric*	0.2779	1.894	[0.058]	0.041
Geria-day-care*	0.3959	2.223	[0.026]	0.058
Prescription*	0.0444	0.6337	[0.526]	0.006
Regional dummy				
D1	0.4248	0.9742	[0.330]	0.063
D2	1.103	1.793	[0.073]	0.164
D4	1.017	1.810	[0.070]	0.151
D5	0.1434	0.2961	[0.767]	0.021
D6	0.8956	2.116	[0.034]	0.133
D7	0.7008	1.221	[0.222]	0.104
D8	1.715	3.144	[0.002]	0.255
D9	0.6679	1.720	[0.085]	0.099

Number of observation = 546
R-squared = 0.388326
Log likelihood = −249.069
Fraction of correct predictions = 0.798535

Notes
∂CAP/∂X is the marginal effect of independent variable on the dependent variable.
* indicates natural logarithm.

subsequent to the PPS. Less sick patients may be treated in non-capitation settings, that is, as outpatients and in other non-capitation settings of inpatient treatment. Thus outpatient treatment will increase because non-prospective payment settings may be more profitable.

5.2   Influence of Capitation on Hospitals

As mentioned above, we estimated the choice of the capitation program by geriatric hospitals with the logit procedure. Does the capitation program provide financial incentives to geriatric hospitals? It is of interest to examine whether the Japanese capitation program discourages hospitals from participating in the program or encourages them to reduce their financial risks by participation.

Our quasi output function of points per patient per month is examined by the 2SLS procedure in order to evaluate the effect of capitation on points; results are in Tables 11.4a and 11.4b. Table 11.4a presents the results of the combined sample of patients in managed geriatric and general geriatric hospitals with the capitation program. Similarly Table 11.4b presents the results for the combined sample in managed geriatric and general hospitals. For tests of exogeneity, the variable 'capitation' is not endogenous as shown by the Hausman test in the notes to Tables 11.4a and 11.4b.

The estimated coefficient of capitation in Table 11.4a is statistically significant and positive. This implies that the capitation program increases output by an additional 2150 points per patient per month in a managed geriatric hospital, as compared to the points per patient per month in a general geriatric hospital. For the combined sample in managed geriatric and general hospitals shown in Table 11.4b, the capitation rises 706 points per patient relative to points per patient in general hospitals. The results indicate that acute-care oriented general hospitals produce more points per patient per month than the long-term care oriented general geriatric hospitals. In other words, the government provides strong and increased incentives to general geriatric hospitals to change to managed geriatric hospital settings more than to general hospitals. Patients under the fee-for-service plan are treated in significantly higher volume in general hospitals than in general geriatric hospitals. The results imply that the Japanese government provides financial incentives and encourages geriatric hospitals to participate in the capitation program by specializing in the treatment of elderly patients in the capacity of a managed geriatric hospital.[9]

It is interesting to note that the estimated coefficient of intensity per day is 3.96 in the combined sample in managed geriatric and general geriatric hospitals in Table 11.4a. This is slightly higher than the 2.85 (Table 11.4b) of the combined sample in managed geriatric and general hospitals. Although the difference in the two estimates of intensity of care for the elderly is only 1.1 points (= 3.96 − 2.85), the government seems to be providing better incentives to geriatric hospitals to treat elderly patients than they are to general hospitals. This result reflects the current diminishing point system by the government, which gives strong disincentives to general hospitals to keep elderly inpatients for long-term

Table 11.4a Two-stage least squares of points for patient: combined sample of patients in managed geriatric and general geriatric hospitals with capitation program (dependent variable: points)

Independent variable	Estimated coefficient	*t*-statistic	*P*-value
Constant	80.2687E+2	−1.060	[0.289]
Policy factors			
Capitation	21.5013E+2	7.418	[0.000]
Units of service	19.6653E+1	3.718	[0.000]
Intensity per day	39.6828E−1	3.651	[0.000]
Patient characteristics			
Gender	96.0492E−1	0.0714	[0.943]
Age	−11.2959	−1.163	[0.245]
Health insurance	94.3591E+1	0.6731	[0.501]
Compensation	−20.1084E+1	−1.367	[0.162]
Geriatric	83.4726	0.4372	[0.662]
In/out	30.3092E+2	4.215	[0.000]
< 1 month	28.1437E+2	0.3871	[0.699]
1–2.9 months	−17.1824E+2	−15.60	[0.000]
3–5.9 months	19.1236E+2	2.361	[0.018]
6–12 months	28.0309E+2	3.475	[0.001]
1–1.5 years	23.9278E+2	3.008	[0.003]
> 1.5 years	30.9530E+2	3.842	[0.000]
CIRCUL	35.2937E+1	2.519	[0.012]
MUSCUL	88.1558E+1	3.310	[0.001]
DIGEST	14.5495E+1	0.5634	[0.573]
NERVOU	88.6275E+1	1.881	[0.060]
Severity control			
ICU	−13.3843	−1.233	[0.217]
ANESTHESIA	−18.0271	−1.439	[0.150]
FEMUR	−34.3375	−0.4270	[0.669]
CORONARY	14.7727E+2	2.146	[0.032]
FIBERSCOPE	−44.0454	−3.233	[0.001]
DIGITAL-RADIO	−19.6163E−1	−1.070	[0.284]
X-RAY CT	53.7186E−1	1.307	[0.191]
MRI	−48.5328E−1	−0.5920	[0.554]
BONE	22.1602	1.018	[0.308]
HIGH-ENERGY	17.2421	2.980	[0.003]
Labor inputs			
Physician	−60.2768	−1.674	[0.094]
Pharmacist	−37.6024E−1	−0.0665	[0.947]
Nurse	48.2786	7.183	[0.000]

Table 11.4a Two-stage least squares of points for patient: combined sample of patients in managed geriatric and general geriatric hospitals with capitation progran (dependent variable: points) (cont.)

Independent variable	Estimated coefficient	t-statistic	P-value
Labor inputs			
Asso-nurse	−15.2641	−1.863	[0.062]
Assistant	26.4927	4.965	[0.000]
Radio-tech	15.4306E+1	1.922	[0.055]
Labo-tech	−20.1873E+1	−4.365	[0.000]
Nutritionist	79.8457	2.142	[0.032]
Administration	−38.4582	−2.769	[0.006]
Capital inputs			
Fiborscope(K)	−17.1221E+1	−2.134	[0.033]
High-energy(K)	−31.6195E+1	−0.9179	[0.359]
Dialyzator	86.7803E−1	−0.6122	[0.540]
Gene-bed	42.0721E−1	2.060	[0.039]
Geria-bed	−26.6319E−1	−1.547	[0.122]
Ward	−26.4405E−2	−4.268	[0.000]
Clinical	−5.8870E−2	−0.4429	[0.658]
Admini	0.0840E−1	0.1159	[0.908]
Hospital Characteristics			
Prefectural	83.8545E+2	0.9431	[0.346]
Municipal	16.9096E+2	2.579	[0.010]
Non-profit	−54.2234E+1	−1.543	[0.146]
Emergency	23.4512E+1	1.768	[0.077]
Nursing care and other services			
Ergo-therapy	3.2587E−2	0.2183	[0.827]
Psychiatric	−94.0749E−2	−2.028	[0.042]
Geria-day-care	11.3512E−1	3.394	[0.001]
Prescription	10.0328E−1	2.789	[0.005]

Number of observations = 16 970
R-squared = 0.833646
Adjusted R-squared = 0.833115
Standard error of regression = 7107.33

Note: Unit of service and intensity per day are endogenous variables. The exogenous variables, which are excluded from the above equation but are included in the first stage equation, are meals, cleaning, vaccination, and radiotherapy, and eight regional dummies. The variable of capitation is not endogenous based on the Hausman specification test: Chi-square (d.f. = 55) = 3.958.

Table 11.4b Two-stage least squares of points for patient: combined sample of patients in managed geriatric and general hospitals with capitation program (dependent variable: points)

Independent variable	Estimated coefficient	*t*-statistic	*P*-value
Constant	30.9878E+2	0.884	[0.377]
Policy factors			
Capitation	70.6628E+1	3.143	[0.002]
Units of service	20.8959E+1	2.166	[0.030]
Intensity per day	28.5315E−1	2.518	[0.012]
Patient characteristics			
Gender	50.9174E−1	0.0351	[0.972]
Age	−15.9828	−1.746	[0.081]
Health insurance	12.5469E+2	1.555	[0.120]
Compensation	−26.8434E+1	−1.381	[0.167]
Geriatric	39.6638	0.2493	[0.803]
In/out	21.0853E+3	10.277	[0.000]
< 1 month	−64.9293E+2	−2.243	[0.025]
1–2.9 months	−12.0554E+3	−6.531	[0.000]
3–5.9 months	54.7165E+2	6.744	[0.000]
6–12 months	55.6762E+2	6.962	[0.000]
1–1.5 years	40.6561E+2	4.580	[0.000]
> 1.5 years	60.7255E+2	4.792	[0.000]
CIRCUL	19.3821E+1	1.112	[0.266]
MUSCUL	54.4687E+1	1.564	[0.118]
DIGEST	−55.6238E+1	−2.321	[0.020]
NERVOU	63.7735E+1	1.301	[0.193]
Severity control			
ICU	−22.7115E−1	−0.4165	[0.677]
ANESTHESIA	−44.2757E−1	−1.622	[0.105]
FEMUR	−16.4852	−0.6592	[0.510]
CORONARY	10.6867E−1	0.0333	[0.973]
FIBERSCOPE	−17.4141	−2.344	[0.019]
DIGITAL-RADIO	12.0743E−1	1.188	[0.235]
X-RAY CT	38.4148E−1	2.255	[0.024]
MRI	−97.7509E−2	−0.7760	[0.438]
BONE	36.2993E−1	0.2221	[0.824]
HIGH-ENERGY	−91.0354E−1	−5.138	[0.000]

Table 11.4b Two-stage least squares of points for patient: combined
sample of patients in managed geriatric and general hospitals
with capitation program (dependent variable: points)(cont.)

Independent variable	Estimated coefficient	*t*-statistic	*P*-value
Labor inputs			
Physician	−77.9683E−1	2.003	[0.045]
Pharmacist	−35.0205	−1.107	[0.268]
Nurse	64.2118E−1	2.643	[0.008]
Asso-nurse	−36.1372E−1	−0.9942	[0.320]
Assistant	−66.1582E−1	−1.288	[0.198]
Radio-tech	39.9880	1.061	[0.288]
Labo-tech	−26.6757	−1.267	[0.205]
Nutritionist	47.1315E−1	0.1798	[0.857]
Administration	−40.7374E−2	−0.0655	[0.948]
Capital inputs			
Fiborscope(K)	−55.5533	−2.867	[0.004]
High-energy(K)	34.6610E+1	1.507	[0.132]
Dialyzator	22.1655	3.533	[0.000]
Gene-bed	55.8713E−2	0.5475	[0.584]
Geria-bed	28.2309E−1	2.418	[0.016]
Ward	−0.2948E−2	−0.0735	[0.941]
Clinical	5.8706E−2	1.929	[0.054]
Admini	−5.8524E−2	−2.286	[0.022]
Hospital characteristics			
Prefectural	76.1635	0.2442	[0.807]
Municipal	−23.3696E+1	−1.363	[0.173]
Non-profit	36.3094E+1	1.843	[0.065]
Emergency	−17.4949E+1	−1.484	[0.138]
Nursing care and other services			
Ergo-therapy	9.6482E−2	0.7759	[0.438]
Psychiatric	−96.6834E−2	−2.948	[0.003]
Geria-day-care	10.8592E−1	2.365	[0.018]
Prescription	9.6293E−2	1.178	[0.239]

Number of observations = 45 643
R-squared = 0.702739
Adjusted R-squared = 0.702386
Standard error of regression = 9886.46

Note: Unit of service and intensity per day are endogenous variables. The exogenous variables, which are excluded from the above equation but are included in the first stage equation, are meals, cleaning, vaccination, radiotherapy, and eight regional dummies. The variable of capitation is not endogenous based on the Hausman specification test: Chi-square (d.f. = 55) = 3.039.

nursing care in the general beds wards even with the capitation program (Yamada et al. 1999).

On the other hand, the estimated coefficient of units of services, that is, quantity of treatment per month, is 208 in Table 11.4b and is larger than the 196 in Table 11.4a. Thus on a monthly basis, more treatment may be provided to elderly patients at general hospitals with the fee-for-service plan than at geriatric hospitals. Hence, the points are higher at general hospitals.[10]

5.3   Simultaneous Estimation of Hospital Services

For each of the four measures, we estimate a simultaneous equation model by a two-stage least squares estimation with 'intensity per day' (equation (11.2a)), 'units of service' (equation (11.2b)), 'length of hospitalization' (equation (11.2c)) and 'intensity per treatment' (equation (11.2d)) as jointly dependent variables. For evaluation purposes, we present the estimated coefficients of policy relevant variables in Table 11.5. The results of (II) and (IV) include the product terms of each of the four variables mentioned multiplied by the CAP variable. Those of (I) and (III) do not include the product terms of (x CAP).

For the impact of capitation (CAP) on intensity per day in column [1], the managed geriatric hospitals seem to provide more intensity per day by 117.79 in (I) and by 378.91 in (II) than the general geriatric hospitals do. These results show the robustness of the findings of logit estimation in the previous section. Managed geriatric hospitals seem to produce more points through to the government reimbursement scheme than the fee-for-service oriented general geriatric hospitals do. The government intends to develop the capitation program for elderly health care in preparation for the future aging society. The results imply that transferring elderly care from general hospitals, which specialize in acute care, to the managed geriatric hospitals, which emphasize less acute care for the elderly, is a cost containment policy option.

The influence of capitation (CAP) on intensity per treatment in column [4] of Table 11.5, another intensity measure in this analysis, does not show a clear-cut difference between 299.86 (I) and 207.41 (III) at a glance. However, applying the capitation program with an intensity measure, we find a clear-cut difference in intensity per day without the term (x CAP) in (II) to intensity per day with the capitation x CAP in (II) (see columns 2, 3, and 4) as well as similar comparisons between them in (IV). This clearly shows the negative effects of intensity per day with CAP on units of service (column 2), length of hospitalization (column 3) and intensity per treatment (column 4) with statistically significant

*Table 11.5 Regression results: capitation, intensity per day, units of
service, length of hospitalization and intensity per treatment**

Dependent variable	Intensity per day [1]	Units of service [2]	Length of hospitalization [3]	Intensity per treatment [4]
(I) Managed geriatric hospitals and general geriatric hospitals				
• Capitation (CAP)	117.79^a	−1.15^b	−0.07	299.86^a
• Intensity per day	−	0.01^a	−0.001^c	0.36^c
• Units of service	−	−	−	−46.82^a
• Length of hospitalization	−27.39^c	−	−	−
• Intensity per treatment	−0.11^c	−0.006^a	0.47E–04	−
(II) Managed geriatric hospitals and general geriatric hospitals				
• Capitation (CAP)	378.91	6.44^c	0.61	215.51
• Intensity per day	−	0.017^a	−0.002^c	1.41^a
• Units of service	−	−	−	−119.99^a
• Length of hospitalization	−146.37^a	−	−	−
• Intensity per treatment	4.01^a	−0.018	0.006	−
• Intensity per day x CAP	−	−0.012^b	0.001	−2.13^a
• Units of service x CAP	−	−	−	143.28^b
• Length of hospitalization x CAP	189.63^a	−	−	−
• Intensity per treatment x CAP	−4.53^a	0.01	−0.005	−
(III) Managed geriatric hospitals and general hospitals				
• Capitation (CAP)	50.12	1.07^c	0.11	207.41^a
• Intensity per day	−	0.004^a	−0.001^a	0.004
• Units of service	−	−	−	−19.79^b
• Length of hospitalization	−76.21^b	−	−	−
• Intensity per treatment	−0.43	−0.01^a	0.98E–03	−
(IV) Managed geriatric hospitals and general hospitals				
• Capitation (CAP)	−996.61^b	25.85^a	9.17^a	883.42
• Intensity per day	−	0.008^a	0.9E–04	0.33^c
• Units of service	−	−	−	−47.37
• Length of hospitalization	−311.67^a	−	−	−
• Intensity per treatment	5.22^a	0.002	0.006^b	−
• Intensity per day x CAP	−	−0.01^b	−0.005^a	−1.18^c
• Units of service x CAP	−	−	−	41.03
• Length of hospitalization x CAP	484.34^a	−	−	−
• Intensity per treatment x CAP	−6.25^a	−0.01^c	−0.007^a	−

Notes

[a], [b] and [c] represent statistically significant levels of coefficients as follows: 99 percent level
([a]), 95 percent level ([b]) and 90 percent level ([c]) for a two-tailed test.

* The entire results of the regressions are available on request.

coefficients. Clearly, one of the major effects of the capitation program is to shift the site of care from the acute-care oriented general hospitals to the less technologically but qualitatively oriented geriatric hospitals, particularly to managed geriatric hospitals.

Looking at the influences of intensity per treatment with capitation (x CAP) on Intensity per day in column [1], we find negative signs of –4.53 in (II) and –6.25 in (IV), while the intensity per treatment without the term (x CAP) has the estimated values of 4.01 in (II) and 5.22 in (IV). Thus these findings indicate intensity per day decreases when there is capitation on the intensity per treatment. The marginal impact of intensity per treatment with CAP on intensity per day in column [1] is –135.9 (–4.53 x 30 days) per month in (II) and is –187.5 (–6.25 x 30 days) in (IV). This impact is much larger than the influence of intensity per day (x CAP) on intensity per treatment in column [4], which is –63.9 (–2.13 x 30 days) in (II) and –35.4 (–1.18 x 30 days) in (IV). The results suggest that the hospitals are not easily able to raise intensity of care, that is, intensity per treatment, through a daily-base intensity because the point system restrains intensity efforts through the capitation program. In contrast, the hospitals generate higher intensity enhancement efforts through daily-based intensity. When the capitation program is not implemented, that is, under fee-for-service, hospitals tend to increase both intensity measures, which will result in higher medical costs to the government.

A similar inverse relationship exists between length of hospitalization in number of days and intensity per day without (x CAP) in (I), (II), (III) and (IV) in Table 11.5.The results show that length of hospitalization has a negative effect on intensity per day (–27.39) in group (I) of column [1], while intensity per day also has a negative effect on length of hospitalization (–0.001) in group (I) of column [3]. The reason is that the consistent results above show that an increase in resource intensity reduces the length of treatment days for a given level of patient severity. Conversely, an increase (decrease) in length of treatment days is usually assumed to be less (more) of a financial incentive in raising resource intensity per day under the cost-based fee-for-service program.

To shed further light on the issue of capitation, we computed the elasticities of intensity per day, units of service, length of hospitalization and intensity of treatment in Table 11.6. The results we present suggest that in general there is a substantial decrease of various hospital services covered by the capitation program on the introduction of the program in general hospitals. An introduction of capitation clearly depicts changes from positive (capitation = 0) to negative signs (capitation = 1) in the sample group of managed geriatric and general hospitals (IV).[11]

Table 11.6 Elasticities: effects of capitation on intensity per day, units of service, length of hospitalization and intensity per treatment*

Dependent variable	Intensity per day [1]	Units of service [2]	Length of hospitalization [3]	Intensity per treatment [4]
(II) Managed geriatric hospitals and general geriatric hospitals				
Elasticity with capitation = 0				
• Intensity per day	–	1.230ᵃ	–0.188ᶜ	1.579ᵃ
• Units of service	–	–	–	–1.907ᵃ
• Length of hospitalization	1.624ᵃ	–	–	–
• Intensity per treatment	3.589ᵃ	–1.137	0.493	–
Elasticity with capitation = 1				
• Intensity per day	–	0.380ᵇ	–0.039	–0.811ᵃ
• Units of service	–	–	–	0.370ᵇ
• Length of hospitalization	0.480ᵃ	–	–	–
• Intensity per treatment	–0.463ᵃ	–0.496	0.038	–
(IV) Managed geriatric hospitals and general hospitals				
Elasticity with capitation = 0				
• Intensity per day	–	0.765ᵃ	0.017	0.747ᶜ
• Units of service	–	–	–	–1.224
• Length of hospitalization	–1.744ᵃ	–	–	–
• Intensity per treatment	2.354ᵃ	0.088	0.503ᵇ	–
Elasticity with capitation = 1				
• Intensity per day	–	–0.524ᵇ	–0.915ᵃ	–1.873ᶜ
• Units of service	–	–	–	–0.163
• Length of hospitalization	0.966ᵃ	–	–	–
• Intensity per treatment	–0.466ᵃ	–0.647ᶜ	–0.110ᵃ	–

Notes

ᵃ, ᵇ and ᶜ represent statistically significant levels of coefficients as follows: 99 percent level (ᵃ), 95 percent level (ᵇ) and 90 percent level (ᶜ) for a two-tailed test.

* Elasticities are based on the regression results from groups II and IV in Table 11.5.

For example, a 1 percent increase in intensity per day (capitation = 1) will lower units of services by 0.524 percent in group IV of column [2], length of hospitalization by 0.915 percent in column [3], and intensity per treatment by 1.873 percent in column [4]. Similarly, a 1 percent increase in intensity per treatment will lower intensity per day by 0.466 percent in group IV of column [1], units of service by 0.647 percent in   column [2], and length of hospitalization by 0.11 percent in column [3]. If these results constitute the case for general hospitals, shifting hospital management from general hospital settings to managed geriatric hospital settings would lead to a straightforward reduction in resource-intensive hospital services. If the CAP is implemented in general hospitals, these estimates suggest a resulting decrease in medical care expenditure, and by extension, a decrease in government health care expenditure.

6   SUMMARY AND POLICY IMPLICATIONS

This chapter researches the role of the capitation program in a partial transition from the cost-based fee-for-service payment to the capitation program among general and geriatric hospitals under the point system of the national health insurance framework. A large number of the elderly in Japan are long-term care inpatients in acute-care hospitals, namely general hospitals. The reason is twofold: first, the national health insurance system allows the elderly to stay in hospitals at minimum cost; second, there has been a shortage of institutional long-term care facilities for the elderly. By providing higher reimbursement levels through the capitation program for less acute elderly care, the Japanese government provides financial incentives to general geriatric hospitals and less well equipped general hospitals with the fee-for-service program to acquire managed geriatric hospital settings. Increasing reimbursement through the capitation program for elderly care leads to an increase in the resource intensity of services provided in managed geriatric hospitals. Also, by changing hospital management settings from fee-for-service to the capitation settings, a higher amount of revenue will be left to hospitals.

Understanding hospital behavior is especially important at the current health care financing stage in order to implement the capitation program for elderly care in Japan. The partial implementation of the transition from the retrospective payment to the prospective payment system is anticipated to reduce hospital health care expenditure of the government by shifting elderly care from acute-care oriented general hospitals to less well equipped, staffed and resource-intensive geriatric hospitals. Our findings show evidence of a reduction in inpatient admissions and a rise in outpatient admissions in both the non-capitated geriatric hospitals and general hospitals. This comes about because the fee-for-service setting of inpatient elderly care treatment provides fewer financial incentives to general geriatric and acute-care oriented general hospitals. Thus the implementation of the capitation program encourages general geriatric hospitals and less well equipped general hospitals to shift to managed geriatric hospital settings.

Under the FFS, acute-care oriented general hospitals generally and theoretically favor admitting inpatients. The general hospitals in Japan are, however, used as a substitute for geriatric hospital services. This situation leads to higher health care expenditure. Our findings show that the current mixed reimbursement systems of cost-based fee-for-service and capitation payments in managed geriatric hospitals generate higher intensity enhancement efforts for elderly care in Japan.

Finally, our results also indicate that if the capitation program is introduced to general hospitals with the prospective payment, this will lead to a substantial decrease in health care services, namely expenditures, as shown by the points. It is possible that an expansion of the capitation program from the current partial prospective to full prospective payment may have effects of more quality improvement efforts by general hospitals. Efficient health care resource utilization while maintaining the current mixed payment system, the FFS and the CAP, can be achieved by transferring the current high volume of elderly patients from the acute-care oriented general hospitals to the less resource intensive managed geriatric hospitals. Thus an expansion of the capitation program in geriatric hospitals seems to be one of the viable options for the government as a cost-containment policy in order to restrain the rapid increase in the current hospital health care expenditures.

NOTES

*   We thank the participants of the Taipei International Conference on Health Economics by Academia Sinica and also those at the Japan Economic Seminar of the Columbia University. This study is a part of the report entitled 'Study on the Natural Increase in Medical Expenditure', which was made to the Institute for Health Economics Policy (IHEP) by the research members of the Japan Center for Economic Research (JCER). We acknowledge the research supports given by the Japan Ministry of Education, Culture, Sports, Science and Technology (Grant #11630034), IHEP, JCER, and the Research Council of Rutgers University. The views presented here are those of the authors and do not necessarily represent those of the affiliated institutions mentioned above.

[1]   Under a partial capitation system, the NHI under the Japan Ministry of Health, Labour and Welfare reimburses hospitals for the costs of four categories: medication, injection, examination, and inpatient care including nursing care. The CAP reimbursement does not fully cover all other hospital services for the elderly; those are radiology, mental treatment, anesthesia, image diagnosis, operation and physiotherapy.

[2]   A hospital is able to obtain CAP approval by the government if it meets the

government guidelines: three doctors, 17 nurses and 13 nursing assistants per 100 patients, where 60 percent of the patients are aged 65 and over. Suppose that the hospital has to decide whether to improve its personnel and facilities in order to meet the government requirements. By doing so, the hospital will be accredited, and thus will be able to use the CAP program to reimburse its medical costs. The choice of the CAP depends on the hospital decision-makers (Yamada et al. 1999).

[3]   The studies referred to are DesHarnais et al. 1987; DesHarnais et al. 1988; Newhouse and Byrne 1988; Sloan et al. 1988; Hodgkin and McGuire 1994; Dor and Farley 1996; and Kesteloot and Voet 1998.

[4]   According to Steinwald and Dummit (1989), the onset of the PPS tends to have an effect on an increase in case-mix indices. A higher value index leads to a greater degree of complexity, which in turn leads to higher medical expenditure per patient with greater input resources.

[5]   Abe (1983) intensively discusses a lack of strict internal controls by medical service providers, who create a failure to perform efficiently, under the Japanese point system.

[6]   When $\theta = 1$, all medical care provided to a patient is subject to the capitation based reimbursement; if $0 < \theta < 1$, this is called a partial capitation-based reimbursement; and if $\theta = 0$, then this is the FFS reimbursement. The Japanese system is a form of partial capitation program, since not all health care services are subject to the capitation fee even at managed geriatric hospitals.

[7]   While the capitation-based reimbursement is a lump sum payment, the Japanese government gives handsome reimbursement rates for the services of the capitation program. On the other hand, other geriatric hospitals have had to accept low rates of reimbursement because they do not meet the government requirements for the number of medical personnel as well as for facilities.

[8]   'Quality of care' is often defined as 'resource intensity of care'. As a consequence, additional tests, longer hospital stays, use of the intensive care unit, new technology adoption for services, volume of services and treatment per day or per month, and so on are always seen as quality improvements, which often results in cost augmentation. For hospital services, quality of medical intervention may be harder to measure than quality of certain types of surgical intervention to cure illness. From a different perspective 'quality' may also be measured by health outcomes, an improved scheduling of diagnostic testing, and patient satisfaction (for example, less waiting time, accessibility to hospital services) (DesHarnais et al. 1988; Dor and Farley 1996; Cutler and Sheiner 1997; Baker and Brown 1997; and Kesteloot and Voet 1998). For hospital services, quality of medical intervention may be harder to measure than the quality of certain types of surgical intervention to cure illness (McClellan and Staiger 1999). Thus, an implication of our quality measurement in this chapter is to use length of hospitalization, units of service per month, average intensity per day

and intensity per treatment.

9   Managed geriatric hospitals are required to meet the Medical Law Regulatory Standard by staffing three physicians per 100 inpatients, one nurse per six inpatients and one nursing assistant per eight inpatients. Requirements for a general hospital are six physicians per 100 inpatients, and a nurse per four inpatients.

10 The variable 'length of hospitalization' is not included as another policy factor in addition to 'unit of service' and 'intensity per day' in Tables 11.4a and 11.4b because of the identity problem.

11 There is one exception of the influence of length of hospitalization on intensity per day; the effects are -1.744 (capitation = 0) and 0.966 (capitation = 1).

REFERENCES

Abe, M.A. (1983), 'Hospital reimbursement schemes: Japan's point system and the United States' diagnosis-related groups', *Medical Care*, **23**: 1055–66.

Baker, Laurence C. (1995), 'HMOs and fee-for-service health care expenditures: evidence from Medicare', National Bureau of Economic Research, Working Paper 5360.

Baker, Laurence C. and Martin L. Brown (1997), 'The effect of managed care on health care providers', National Bureau of Economic Research, Working Paper 5987.

Baker, Laurence C. and Sharmila Shankarkumar (1997), 'Managed care and health care expenditures: evidence from Medicare, 1990–1994', National Bureau of Economic Research, Working Paper 6187.

Breyer, Friedrich (1987), 'The specification of a hospital cost function: a comment on the recent literature', *Journal of Health Economics*, **16**(2): 147–57.

Cutler, David M. and Louise Sheiner (1997), 'Managed care and the growth of medical expenditures', National Bureau of Economic Research, Working Paper 6140.

DesHarnais, Susan, James Chesney and Steven Fleming (1988), 'Trends and regional variations in hospital utilization and quality during the first two years of the prospective payment system', *Inquiry*, **25**: 374–82.

DesHarnais, Susan, Edward Kobrinski, James Chesney, Michael Long, Richard Ament and Steven Fleming (1987), 'The early effects of the prospective payment system on inpatient utilization and the quality of care', *Inquiry*, **24**: 7–16.

Dor, Avi and Dean E. Farley (1996), 'Payment source and the cost of hospital care: evidence from a multiproduct cost function with multiple payers', *Journal of Health Economics*, **15**(1): 1–21.

Feinglass, Joe and James J. Holloway (1991), 'The initial impact of the Medicare prospective payment system on US health care: a review of the literature', *Medical Care Review*, **48**: 91–115.

Feldman, Sarah and David Scharfstein (1998), 'Managed care and provider volume', National Bureau of Economic Research, Working Paper 6523.

Hodgkin, Dominic and Thomas G. McGuire (1994), 'Payment levels and hospital response to prospective payment', *Journal of Health Economics*, **13**: 1–29.

Kesteloot, K. and N. Voet (1998), 'Incentives for cooperation in quality improvement among hospitals – the impact of the reimbursement system', *Journal of Health Economics*, **17**(6): 701–28.

McClellan, Mark and Douglas Staiger (1999), 'The quality of health care providers', National Bureau of Economic Research, Working Paper 7327.

Newhouse, Joseph P. (1994), 'Frontier estimation: how useful a tool for health economics?', *Journal of Health Economics*, **13**(3): 317–22.

Newhouse, Joseph P. (1996), 'Reimbursing health plans and health providers: selection versus efficiency in production', *Journal of Economic Literature*, **34**(3): 1236–63.

Newhouse, Joseph P. and Daniel J. Byrne (1988), 'Did Medicare's prospective payment system cause length of stay to fall?', *Journal of Health Economics*, **7**: 413–6.

Sloan, Frank A., Michael A. Morrisey and Joseph Volvona (1988), 'Effects of the Medicare prospective payment system on hospital cost containment: an early appraisal', *Milbank Quarterly*, **66**(2): 191–220.

Steinwald, Bruce and Laura A. Dummit (1989), 'Hospital case-mix change: sicker patients or DRG creep?', *Health Affairs*, **8**: 35–47.

Yamada, Tadashi, Tetsuji Yamada, Seiritsu Ogura and Reiko Suzuki (1999), 'Technical efficiency of production in hospitals in Japan', Institute of Policy and Planning Sciences, Discussion Paper Series No. 826.

PART V

Health Care Financing

12. Financing health care for the elderly: will an aging population end 'health for all' in South Korea?

John W. Peabody, Paul J. Gertler, Bong-Min Yang and Duk Hyoung Lee

1   INTRODUCTION

In 1955, South Korea emerged from civil war desperately poor, technologically underdeveloped, and beset by starvation and disease. However, during the 1960s, South Korea began an impressive process of turning all this around. Between 1965 and 1994, its economy grew at an average rate of about 10 percent per annum[1]; as a result, it has achieved a per-capita income level of more than $8000 and is now a member of OECD[2].

Commensurate with its rapid economic development, South Korea's health status also improved dramatically. Starting from a virtually nonexistent health infrastructure, South Korea has improved its life expectancy at birth from 55 for males and 58 for females in 1965 to 74 and 68 years, just a generation later, in 1993[3]. Over the same period, infant mortality fell from 62 per 100 births to 12, and maternal mortality declined from 83 per 100 000 births to 30[3].

Just as impressively, Korea has gone from providing few social benefits in the 1950s and 1960s to establishing universal health insurance coverage for its population. Beginning in 1977, Korea's National Health Insurance (NHI) – a pay-as-you go system funded through a combination of earmarked payroll taxes and government subsidies – has been incrementally expanded; by 1989, Korea achieved universal coverage, and today the NHI is financially solvent and has been steadily accumulating asset reserves since 1990[4].

At the root of South Korea's impressive health care accomplishment is the fact that it has managed to complete a demographic transition – substantially reducing fertility and infant mortality – within one generation.

This means that Korea's population pyramid is now inverting rapidly. Specifically, while the population aged 65 and over was constant at about 3.3 percent until 1975, the proportion of the elderly rose to 5.3 percent in 1995 and is expected to rise to about 11.4 percent by the year 2020[5].

While this accelerated rate of aging has a number of health care implications, one of the more serious ones has to do with the effect it will have on the financial stability of the NHI program. Just six years after attaining universal coverage, the NHI is now faced with the burden of providing benefits for a rapidly increasing elderly population.

In this chapter, we examine the effects this rapid aging process will have on the NHI's financial solvency. Using data from government and public records we first analyze the trends in demography, utilization, revenues and expenditures[5,6]. These trends are then modeled to make projections regarding on the future financial viability of health care in the Republic of Korea (South Korea). Finally, we examine the implications of South Korea's health care financing problems for other countries in Asia, the Philippines and Singapore, and take a closer look at parallels with the impending insolvency of Medicare in the United States.

2   THE RAPID GROWTH IN SOUTH KOREA'S ELDERLY POPULATION WILL DRIVE THE NHI TOWARD INSOLVENCY

A pay-as-you-go system, such as Korea's NHI, means that current revenues are used to cover current expenditures. In countries experiencing a growing elderly population, such health insurance systems are vulnerable to both declining revenue and rising expenditure.

2.1   Revenues

Since the NHI program is primarily funded by earmarked payroll taxes on the work force, revenue going into the system will inevitably decline as the population ages, because the work force relative to the number of elderly dependants will shrink. In South Korea, the ratio of the numbers of workers available to pay premiums to support each older South Korean will decline by more than 50 percent through the year 2010 and by more than 100 percent through the year 2020. Specifically, while there were almost 16 workers per elderly person in 1980, the ratio at the time of writing has dropped to 13.4 workers. By the year 2010, there will be only 8.3 workers per elderly person and by 2020 this will decline to 6.3.

If this trend becomes manifest, it will have profound implications for the financial solvency of the national health insurance system. To maintain its current level of revenue per beneficiary, the NHI would have to increase the payroll tax rate on workers by one-third in 2010 and double it in 2020.

2.2 Expenditures

An aging population also increases the expenditure per beneficiary. Except for newborns and young children, the elderly use more health care services than any other demographic group. For example, while the elderly in South Korea accounted for only 5.4 percent of the population in 1993, they utilized the health care system at a disproportionately higher rate, accounting, for example, for 9.2 percent of all admissions and 17.4 percent of all admissions for chronic diseases. Not only do the elderly utilize the system more than the non-elderly, this utilization has increased over time. For individuals over age 65, outpatient utilization has increased by over one and a half visits per person per year in just five years. Inpatient visits have also increased, albeit not as rapidly.

And beyond using more health care services, the elderly, because they are more likely to suffer from chronic diseases or catastrophic illnesses, also use more expensive health care services, such as CT and MRI scanners. The epidemiological changes in the leading causes of death in South Korea support this notion. In 1965, the main causes of death were respiratory infections, gastrointestinal disease, and parasitic infections; today, the leading causes are cancer, cerebrovascular accidents, and heart disease, all of which have been increasing over time[7,8]. Clearly, chronic diseases are on the rise, and chronic diseases, by definition, require more sophisticated diagnostic strategies, longer therapy, and more extensive support services.

Thus, from a health delivery perspective, no other interval in life places such a combination of costly and frequent demands on the health care system. As the population ages, there are more elderly who have larger health care demands but who do not contribute premiums, and fewer workers available to pay the premiums. In pay-as-you-go systems, rapid population aging implies that expenditure will grow faster than revenue, leading to ever increasing NHI deficits.

3   IF DEFICITS ARE LEFT UNCHECKED, PROJECTIONS SHOW THAT THE NHI WILL BE INSOLVENT IN LESS THAN 15 YEARS

The real question, then, is not whether there will be NHI deficits, but how big will they be and, more important, how fast they will increase. By modeling both the revenue and expenditure sides of the problem, we show in this section that if nothing is done to stop the growth of the deficits, the NHI program will erode its large asset reserves and become insolvent in less than 10 years.

3.1   Forecasting Projected NHI Revenues

Since NHI revenues are primarily based on payroll taxes, we calculated the revenues contributed in any given year as the premium contribution per worker times the number of workers. We computed the contribution rate based on past contribution trends and expected wage growth, and computed the expected number of workers based on future population trends. Since it is difficult to forecast the exact size of the work force, we instead used the potential work force, defined as the number of individuals aged 15 to 59. While not all these individuals will work or be fully employed, many individuals aged 65 and over will continue to work and pay into the NHI fund. We expect the two factors to approximately offset one another. The potential work force data was used to compute support ratios.

The contribution per potential worker was computed by taking total NHI contributions divided by the potential work force and then converting these numbers into contributions per potential worker by dividing by the number of individuals between ages 15 and 59. After an initial adjustment, contributions per potential worker are shown to have grown approximately 10 percent per year between 1991 and 1993.

Finally, we extrapolated future contributions per potential worker based on expected real GDP growth and expected inflation. Government projections expect GDP to grow at 6.6 percent through 1999, at 4.9 percent through 2005, and at 4.3 percent after that. Inflation is expected to be around 8 percent – a level consistent with recent history[5].

3.2   Forecasting Projected Expenditures

Table 12.1 shows NHI expenditures from 1990 (the first full year of NHI operation) until 1993. Since 1990, nominal expenditures per capita have risen 41 percent, averaging 13.5 percent per year. In real terms, the

Table 12.1 NHI Inpatient and outpatient expenditures

Year	Inpatient admissions			Outpatient visits		
	Expend./ capita	Admission rate	Expend./ admission	Expend./ capita	Clinical utilization	Expend./ clinic visit
1990	19.34	0.06	1238	25.13	3.17	7.93
1991	21.46	0.07	1395	25.36	3.15	8.06
1992	25.22	0.07	1740	28.63	3.35	8.66
1993	28.74	0.07	2011	33.87	3.61	9.38

Source: Korea Medical Insurance Corporation (1990–94) *Medical Insurance Statistical Yearbook*, Seoul.

growth in NHI expenditures per capita fast outpaced inflation over the same four years. In fact, in the last two years of operation, real expenditures per capita grew on average about 7.5 percent per annum[9].

This increase in real expenditure can be attributed to growth in heath care utilization per capita and to growth in the expenditure per outpatient visit and per inpatient admission. As shown in Table 12.1, inpatient admissions per capita rose less than 3 percent per year on average over the four-year period, while outpatient visits per capita rose over 4 percent per year on average. Nominal expenditure per inpatient admission rose 10 percent per year, while nominal expenditure per outpatient visit rose about 6 percent per year. But after controlling for inflation using the consumer price index, real inpatient expenditure per inpatient admission grew only 2 percent per year on average, while the real expenditure per outpatient visit actually decreased by 1 percent per year.

Thus, of the 41 percent increase in total NHI expenditure between 1990 and 1993, general inflation accounted for about 60 percent of it, with the remaining 40 percent split equally between increases in inpatient and outpatient expenditures. The increase in total NHI expenditure from outpatient care was driven by a dramatic rise in the outpatient visit rate, since, as mentioned above, the expenditure per outpatient visit actually declined. Half the increase from inpatient care occurred because of a rise in the admission rate and the other half because of a rise in the expenditure per admission.

To forecast future expenditure, we assumed the expenditure per inpatient admission and outpatient visit would rise at the same rate as the average growth rate experienced in the last two years reported in Table 12.1, i.e. 11.5 percent for inpatient admissions and 8 percent for outpatient

Table 12.2 Outpatient and inpatient utilization rates per beneficiary by age group

	Individuals less than 65		Individuals 65 and over	
Year	Outpatient visits	Inpatient admissions	Outpatient visits	Inpatient admissions
1990	3.316	0.064	3.532	0.103
1991	3.300	0.062	3.729	0.110
1992	3.513	0.066	4.038	0.115
1993	3.811	0.066	4.605	0.121

Source: Korea Medical Insurance Corporation (1990–94) *Medical Insurance Statistical Yearbook*, Seoul.

visits. Overall, these rates are comparable with expected inflation rates over the next 10 years (8 percent).

To get at the impact of the aging population on expenditure, we broke down the outpatient visit and inpatient admission rates for those individuals less than 65 years of age and for those more than 65 years of age. Table 12.2 shows the growth rates from 1990 to 1993, from which the forecast for future growth was derived.

In Table 12.1, we saw that the cost of an inpatient admission is growing faster than that of an outpatient visit. This difference will have a significant impact on NHI expenditure growth, because, as shown in Table 12.2, older individuals have much higher inpatient admission rates than do younger individuals. As the population ages, this fact combined with the faster rising cost of inpatient admissions will lead to an exponential increase in NHI expenditures.

Not only do older South Koreans have greater outpatient and inpatient utilization rates, but, as shown in Table 12.2, the rates for the elderly have been growing at a faster pace than those for the young. Specifically, in 1994, older Koreans' outpatient visit rates were close to 40 percent higher and inpatient admissions rates were almost twice those of younger South Koreans. Moreover, while the outpatient visit rate for young individuals grew on average about 4 percent per year, the visit rate for older individuals grew at over 9 percent per year on average. Similarly, where the inpatient admission rate grew at about 1 percent on average per year for the young, the admission rate grew by over 5 percent per year on average for the elderly.

These results suggest that not only will utilization rates increase as the

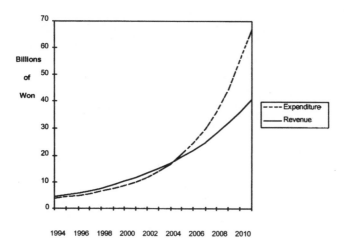

Figure 12.1 Projected NHI expenditure and revenue

population ages, but that they will grow at an increasing rate. However, utilization rates will not increase forever. There is a natural bound. We used the average growth rate in utilization from the last two observed years to forecast the utilization rates to 1995, and then fixed the rates at the 1995 rate thereafter. This assumption probability understates the future differences in utilization between young and old, which again implies that our estimates are lower bounds.

3.3 Forecasting NHI Financial Status

We then examined how aging is likely to affect NHI's financial position. Projected expenditures and revenues are pictured in Figure 12.1. Notice that expenditure rises exponentially while revenue rises linearly, with the exponential expenditure growth driven by the exponential increase in the elderly population. When expenditure exceeds revenue (sometime in 2004), the NHI will begin running deficits, which will increase significantly each subsequent year.

To finance annual budget deficits, NHI must use its asset reserves, which include both surplus (reserves) plus interest on past reserves (10 percent). Figure 12.2 shows that NHI's asset reserves are forecast to

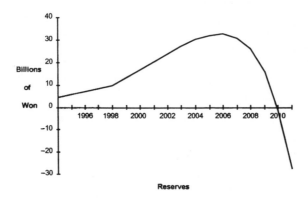

Figure 12.2 Projected NHI asset reserves

increase through 2005 and decline thereafter. This deficit financing will erode NHI reserves by 2010, when the asset reserves are exhausted.

4   THE PROBLEM OF FUTURE NHI INSOLVENCY IS UNDERSTATED BECAUSE OF 'UNMET NEED' AMONG THE ELDERLY

Even though the elderly utilize health care more than other population groups, they do not use it as much as they could because there is poor access to providers, because out-of-pocket costs for services are very high, and because there is no or limited coverage for some conditions that affect the elderly[10]. Filling this unmet need will require large increases in NHI expenditure, which would place further financial pressure on NHI. Below, we discuss each of the problems in turn.

4.1   Poor Access to Providers

In Korea, the urban population has grown significantly, but this shift has been primarily a shift of the skilled, younger, and more mobile work force. In 1960, the elderly comprised 4.2 percent of the population who lived in rural areas, whereas in 1990, they comprised 9 percent of the population. In 1974, for example, only 13 percent of the poor urban and 18 percent of rural households were over 65. But by 1989, 25 percent of all urban poor households and 31 percent of all rural households belonged to this group[5].

This presents an access problem for the elderly, because very few private providers and hospitals have been willing to locate in rural areas[11,12]. While 24 percent of Koreans live in rural areas, only 10 percent of physicians and 15 percent of inpatient beds are located there. The physician to patient ratio in urban areas is 1 to 600 compared to 1 to 2400 in rural areas.

4.2 The High Cost of Services

While the elderly have more serious health problems, they are less likely to be able to afford the required medical care. Out-of-pocket costs for outpatient health care in South Korea are extremely high, and even with NHI-covered services, the rate of cost sharing is still high compared to coinsurance rates in other countries' health insurance schemes[13,14]. Payments for health care services are, therefore, mostly the responsibility of individual patients. For example, household survey data reveals that the proportion of out-of-pocket patient payment for health services (hospital care, dental care, oriental medicine care, drugs) is over 70 percent of the total health care bill, leaving only about 30 percent as the responsibility of NHI[15].

When the coinsurance rate is applied irrespective of family income, as is the case in South Korea, it represents a greater burden to low-income families than to high-income families. This aspect is particularly important for the elderly, who are typically poor[16].

4.3 The Lack of Coverage for Certain Conditions

While NHI covers everybody, there are significant gaps for services critical to the diagnosis and treatment of diseases that greatly affect the elderly. Table 12.3 shows a list of services not covered by NHI in 1995 that are associated with conditions affecting the elderly. As the table shows, many of the services involve use of high-cost diagnostic and testing tools, such as MR and CT scanners[17].

One reason why NHI fails to cover expensive high-technology services is the way it pays providers. South Korea pays fee-for-service, but regulates prices by trying to keep them around 5 percent above costs. Providers receive the fee covered under NHI and cannot balance the bill, but they are free to charge what that market will bear for non-covered services, which generate high profit margins. For example, the actual

Table 12.3 Services not covered by NHI and associated elderly health conditions in 1995

Services not covered	Associated elderly health conditions
CT scan of the body	Cancer (solid tumor diagnosis)
CT scan of the head	Cerebrovascular accident
MR scan of the head	Cerebrovascular accident/CNS tumor
Abdominal ultrasound	Diseases of the gallbladder/other
Dentures	Edentula
Glasses	Presbyopia
Hearing aid	Presbycusis
Wheel chairs	Cerebrovascular accident/other

Source: Ministry of Health and Welfare *Medical Insurance Benefit Criteria and Fee Schedule*, Seoul, 1995.

costs of a CT, an MR, and an ultrasound study are $57, $163, and $10, respectively, but the market prices for the same services are $240, $475, and $63, respectively. In these cases, the markups range from three to over six times the actual costs. Hence, there is a strong provider lobby to exclude these technologies from coverage[18,19].

In 1995, the Ministry of Health and Welfare attempted to include some of these high-cost testing tools within the NHI fee schedule. If this goes into effect, it would clearly benefit the elderly and the treatment of chronic diseases, but it would also undoubtedly increase NHI expenditure through direct costs and higher utilization.

Besides not covering some services, the NHI also imposes limits for services that are covered. For example, NHI benefits, with few exceptions such as dialysis for chronic renal failure, cover only 180 days a year for each beneficiary. As for diagnostic studies, the Ministry of Health and Welfare has been working to increase the limit to 210 days a year, with the aim of abolishing any limitations before the end of the 1999. Again, such changes will affect NHI expenditure through direct costs and higher utilization[17].

4.4　Social/Demographic Changes will Increase Elderly Need for Health Care

Traditionally, long-term care for the elderly in South Korea has been dealt with within the extended family structure of Korean society. But as populations shift to the city and away from rural areas, more nuclear family structures are taking hold, which means there will be increasing demands for institutional care for the elderly.

Two types of institutional care are generally available – nursing health care facilities and elderly homes. Unfortunately, neither is sufficient to meet even current demands[20]. As at the end of 1993, Korea had 49 nursing home-like health care facilities for the elderly that could accommodate approximately 3200 patients. However, most of these institutes do not satisfy minimal government manpower and facility requirements. In addition, there are 86 elderly homes, but these only have the capacity to care for 9500 persons[21].

5 POLICY OPTIONS

South Korea's rapid population aging has created a looming financial crisis for NHI. Unless steps are taken, Korea's NHI will begin deficit financing around the year 2004 and exhaust its asset reserves around 2010. The real questions, then, are what kinds of steps can South Korea take and which of these steps will be effective without worsening the provision of health care services to the elderly?

The two most common (and logical) strategies for improving the financial position of insurance plans such as NHI are to reduce expenditure by improving the efficiency of the system through consumer incentives such as cost-sharing and provider incentives such as capitation, and/or to increase revenue by mobilizing resources through increased premiums and government subsidies. Unfortunately, neither option addresses the fundamental problem that the number of people financing the system relative to the number of dependant beneficiaries falls as the population ages.

Approaching the problem from the expenditure side by improving efficiency in medical services through the use of better incentives – that is, decreasing utilization by, for example, limiting hospital reimbursement; or decreasing hospital, physician, and pharmacy reimbursements and/or introducing uniform fees – can help, but they provide at best a one-time cost saving. Moreover, limiting the benefits package is not an option, since the elderly clearly need expanded benefits[22]. Finally, the impact of introducing global budgeting/capitation is limited, since demand is growing and the support ratio is dropping.

Approaching the problem from the revenue side by increasing workers' payroll contributions beyond the current tax maximum of 8 percent or by increasing the percentage paid by firms above 50 percent can help, but such actions affect labor demand and economic growth. Moreover, increasing contributions from income taxes or ad valorum taxes results in a choice between progressive/regressive tax effects. Finally, raising user co-payments risks decreasing utilization by the elderly poor, who already pay as much as 70 percent out of pocket.

An alternative to these approaches is medical saving accounts (MSAs). Under this system individuals save for the future when they are young and pay actuarially fair health insurance premiums from their savings after they retire. Since retirees would pay into this system, the support ratio would not change as the population aged, thus breaking the relationship between aging and the support ratio and thereby smoothing NHI financing over the demographic transition. The public would still have to subsidize the poor, but this is not a problem of aging. In essence, the proposal is to create a social security-like savings program or include in a social security program the feature that individuals should save for their health care needs just as they should save for other financial needs when they retire.

The hard part of this alternative is figuring out how many individuals have to save. Most individuals would have a work life of about 40 to 50 years to save enough to finance health insurance premiums over a 10–20-year retirement life. Given that premiums stay around 5 percent of annual income and that the savings earn interest over the work life, individuals would have to save a lot less than 5 percent per year to fund insurance premiums during their retirement life. However, health care costs are hard to predict far in the future, primarily because of technological change. This makes it difficult to determine the exact savings rate. More research is needed to determine the feasibility and savings rate required to fund this option.

Singapore exemplifies how MSAs can be utilized. Medisave, Singapore's medical savings account, is a compulsory national health care savings program where individuals contribute 6–8 percent of their wages to a savings account to be used for medical expenses. This system transfers the cost of health care to the individual over time. This provides a powerful incentive to curb health care cost and unnecessary utilization of the health care system. In addition, Singapore has a voluntary supplemental insurance, Medishield, to cover catastrophic illness and extraordinary hospital expenses. There is also a government-funded program, Medifund, to provide financial assistance to the lower-wage worker and those with few resources to pay for health care. The MSA of Singapore provides a good example of how this system can be effectively used.

Such a solution in South Korea would mean gradually shifting from a system that distributes risk from a pay-as-you-go system to one that distributes risks across a changing demographic base to smooth risk across an individual's life time. This approach has the added incentive of curbing demand because financial risk is transferred to the individual.

Policy Approaches from Two Asian Countries and the United States

The health of the elderly is at risk if poor policy choices are made because older populations have fewer income possibilities and because they are more dependent on publicly financed care. The elderly and other marginalized groups, for example, have assets that are often limited to fixed incomes and savings. Many countries, however, face demographic and macroeconomic pressures to decrease public spending. Currency devaluation, inflation, rising unemployment, and the fragile financing health care systems, all increase these pressures to curb spending and place the elderly at even greater risk[23].

South Korea's health care financing problem has clear implications for other East and South-East Asian countries that are aging at a similarly rapid rate and that have, or are moving toward, social health insurance plans (for example, Indonesia, Malaysia, the Philippines, Thailand, and Taiwan). The lesson from the Korean experience is that when a large population cohort becomes older, it will do so very fast and quickly put financial strains on the health care system. Therefore, developing country governments need to plan today for the implications of aging tomorrow.

The South Korea experience is illustrative of problems faced by two Asian countries at different stages of social insurance development. The Philippines is undergoing a demographic transition while Singapore, which has a stable, older population, is faced with the challenge of paying for the rising cost of care of a stable elderly population. In the Philippines the National Health Insurance, which covers retirees, is unable to pay for basic services for more than 7 percent of the population. And as demand for services continues to grow as the elderly population increases this demand for services outstrips PHIC revenue because payroll contribution are capped at 7000 PP (US$188/year) regardless of income (GDP per capita is $1190/year). Financing reform options now focus on increasing revenue by introducing co-payments and eliminating first-Peso coverage. Reform to control utilization will have to curb demand by introducing price incentives that favor less expensive outpatient care. Despite these policies, like South Korea, the Philippines is unlikely to be able to curb rising expenditures sufficiently. This will jeopardize expansion of PHIC coverage to the remainder of the population.

In Singapore, universal coverage was accomplished in 1984, five years before South Korea. However, unlike South Korea, financing national health insurance used compulsory medical savings accounts. This strategy spreads risk over time instead of across a demographically changing population. Saving accounts while providing powerful cost containment incentives, provide only limited insurance against catastrophic illness for the elderly[24]. To provide supplementary coverage and additional health insurance financing the government has made available a separate Medishield plan although coverage is voluntary.

In the United State the elderly population is projected to grow in the next decade as life expectancies for the over-65 population increase and baby boomers reach retirement[25]. Already one third of health care spending in the United States is for the elderly, and two-thirds of this is paid for by Medicare. Part A Medicare funding under this demographic burden will be depleted by the year 2002[26,27]. The demand for health care in South Korea and the demand for Medicare have both increased dramatically; health care spending has also increased in both countries (in South Korea, from 2.8 percent of the gross domestic product (GDP) in 1975 to 7.1 percent in 1991; in the United States, from 9 percent of GDP in 1980 to 14 percent today); and attempts to solve the financing problems through the traditional means of reducing expenditure and increasing revenue have also been problematic. The forecast insolvency of South Korea's NHI program is remarkably close to the projected insolvency of the Medicare system. And both systems are beset by similar problems.

One can argue that the very fact that South Korea's problems are accelerating in this way provides a unique window of opportunity for policymakers in Asia and elsewhere to study and improve health care financing for the elderly.

REFERENCES

1. United Nations Development Program (1995), *Human Development Report*, UNDP, New York.
2. Asian Development Bank (1995), *Key Indicators of Developing Asian and Pacific Countries*, Manila, the Philippines.
3. International Bank for Reconstruction and Development (1996), *From Market to Plan*, World Development Report.
4. Peabody, J.W., S.W. Lee and S.R. Bickel (1995), 'Health for all in the Republic of Korea: one country's experience with implementing universal health care', *Health Policy*, **31**: 29–42.
5. Office of Statistics, Economic Planning Board, *Annual Statistics*

Yearbooks 1990–1995.

6. National Federation of Medical Insurance, *1990–1994, Yearbook of Health Insurance Statistics*, Seoul, Korea.
7. Kim, J.S. (1989) 'Transitions on cause of death in Korea', *Korean Journal of Epidemiology*, **1**(2): 155–74.
8. Koo, J. and D.O. Cogwell (1986), 'Health care of the aged in Korea', *Social Science and Medicine*, **23**: 1347–55.
9. Korean Medical Insurance Corporation, *1990–1994, Medical Insurance Statistical Yearbook*, Seoul, Korea.
10. Song, K.Y. (1994), 'Policy issues for health and social services in aging', *Journal of the Korean Medical Association*, **37**(10): 1147–53.
11. Moon, O.R. (1987), *A Critical Review on the Expansion of Rural Health Insurance*, Public testimony on the implementation of NHI, Seoul, Korea.
12. Yang, B.M. and J. Huh (1989), 'Physician distribution and health manpower in Korea', *Asia-Pacific Journal of Public Health*, **3**(1): 68–85.
13. Yang, B.M. and T.J. Lee (1989), *Rising Health Care Expenditures*, Korean Medical Insurance Corporation, Seoul, Korea.
14. Yoo, H.J. (1994), 'Geriatric medicine and medical care of the elderly in Korea: present status and problems', *Journal of the Korean Medical Association*, **37**(10): 1141–6.
15. Myung, J.I. (1994), *Trends and Structure of National Expenditures*, Korean Institute of Health Services Management, Seoul, Korea.
16. Kim, I.S. (1995), *Impact of Aging on Insurance Payment in Korea*, MPH thesis, School of Public Health, Seoul National University.
17. Ministry of Health and Welfare (1995), *Medical Insurance Benefit Criteria and Fee Schedule*, Seoul, Korea.
18. Yang, B.M. (1995), *Health Financing in Korea*, Workshop on Financing Human Resource Development in Asia, Asian Development Bank, Manila, 11–14 July.
19. National Federation of Medical Insurance (1994), *Medical Insurance in Korea*, Seoul, Korea.
20. Choi, S.J. (1994), 'Present state of Korean institutional care for the elderly and policy recommendations for development', *Journal of the Korean Medical Association*, **37**(10): 1154–9.
21. Rhee, K.O. (1994), *Development of Comprehensive National Policies on Aging: Life-long Preparatory Measures including Social Security*, Korean Institute for Health and Social Affairs, Working Paper 94–01; 54.
22. Ministry of Health Social Welfare (1992), *Research on the Direction for Improvement of Medical Welfare for the Elderly*, Social Republic

of Korea.

23. Kjellstrom, T., J. Koplan and R.B. Rothenberg (1992), 'Current and future determinants of adult ill-health', in R.G.A. Feachem, M.A. Philipps and R.A. Bulatao (eds), *The Health of Adults in the Developing World*, New York: Oxford University Press.

24. Peabody, J.W., M.O. Rahman, P.J. Gertler, J. Mann, D.O. Farley, J. Luck, D. Robalino and G.M. Carter (1999), *Policy and Health: Implications for Development in Asia*, Cambridge, United Kingdom: Cambridge University Press.

25. Lubitz, J., J. Beebe and C. Baker (1995), 'Longevity and Medicare expenditures', *New England Journal of Medicine*, **32**: 999–1003.

26. Fein, R. (1995), 'Assessing the proposed Medicare reforms', *New England Journal of Medicine*, **26**: 1777–81.

27. Wilensky, G.R. (1995), 'The score on Medicare reform minus the hype and hyperbole', *New England Journal of Medicine*, **26**: 1774–7.

13. Monitoring and enforcement in federal alcohol and drug abuse block grants

Ching-to Albert Ma, Thomas G. McGuire and Yong Weng*

1 INTRODUCTION

Block grants to fund state mental health and substance abuse services started with President Reagan's omnibus Budget Reconciliation Act of 1981. In 1982, the Alcohol, Drug Abuse and Mental Health (ADAMH) block grants replaced ten mental health and substance abuse grant programs. Before that time, federal funds were directly allocated to specific programs for drug abuse and prevention, community mental health, alcohol treatment and rehabilitation, and other services. Being direct allocations, these funds were unrelated to the mediatory roles of the states. Then in 1982, the Budget Reconciliation Act effectively combined the fundings of various mental health and related programs, reduced them by about 20 percent, and then allocated them entirely at the state level.[1]

Block grants to the states give the states more autonomy in targeting and assessing program needs and priorities. This mechanism may allow states better use of the resources to target clients as well as to reallocate existing funding among different services. In return, the overall amount of federal funding for substance abuse and mental health services was reduced from $585 million in 1981 to $432 million in 1982 (GAO 1985). The reduction meant that states would have to be more efficient than before if the same levels of services were to be maintained. The level of funding increased gradually over time, but it did not attain the real funding level of 1981 until the late 1980s.

To ensure that ADAMH block grants are used for the intended services, block grants are subject to 'set-aside' restrictions. Set-asides require that a specified minimum percentage of a block grant must be spent on particular groups of persons (or organizations), such as services for

257

women. They also determine the split of the ADAMH block grant between mental health and substance abuse services. For example, after 1989, states were supposed to have 10 percent of the full ADAMH block grant earmarked for alcohol and drug abuse services for women; states could not use more than 10 percent of the grant for administration, and after 1989, this limit was further reduced to 5 percent. For fiscal years 1981 through 1988, the set-asides were based on a 'hold-harmless' criterion – the amount and distribution between mental health and substance abuse being based on the respective allocations before 1981. These set-asides restrict states' control over block grants. Nevertheless, the set-asides have been offset by various transfer provisions, allowing states some freedom to move funds across services. In summary, the proportion of the ADAMH block grants for which a state had complete control over the distribution between mental health and substance abuse services changed over the years, with a maximum of 25 percent in 1985.

Clearly, the various restrictions on states' ability to reallocate funds reflects the major concern with the use of ADAMH block grants: a state may choose not to use ADAMH block grants for substance abuse and mental health services. In fact, once a state receives the block grants, it may choose to regard the funds as general revenue. Median voter theory (Musgrave and Musgrave 1989), which posits that politicians will allocate funds to maximize the preferences of the median voter, implies that the effect of block grants on behavioral health services will be very small if the preferences of the median voter do not value such services. However, earlier researchers have discovered a so-called 'fly-paper' effect (Wyckoff 1988). That is, states have actually responded by spending funds according to their intended use. Given these contrary views, and because states' responses to block grants fundings directly affect their efficacy, it is important to assess empirically the effectiveness of this funding mechanism.

Congress began requiring enforcement of block grant spending in the late 1980s. The Anti-Drug Abuse Act of 1986 legislated that 1 percent of block grant funds be used for data collection and evaluation. Congress imposed more restrictions in 1988: 20 percent of substance abuse portion as set-asides for prevention, and at least 10 percent of the drug portion to intravenous drug treatments (Institute of Medicine 1990). By 1990, enforcement of block grants was stepped up. The Center for Substance Abuse Treatment (CSAT) was asked to enforce maintenance-of-effort provisions. By 1992 and 1993, a new block grant application or report form was phased in, and states' accountability was increased. CSAT also sent audit teams to states to monitor compliance.

This chapter considers the effect of such monitoring and enforcement efforts using data on state spending. Earlier research has indicated that after federal enforcement of block grants was supposedly tightened in 1989, state spending on substance abuse services responded more to block grant funding. A previous paper by Jacobsen and McGuire (1996) used a post-1989 year dummy to capture the enhanced enforcement effect statistically. For this research, we collected data on technical review and waiver applications from CSAT, in an attempt to measure enforcement effects more precisely. We have used a post-1989 year dummy as well as the technical review and waiver application dummies for all states and all years for which these are applicable.

Because our new data are directly related to enforcement, our statistical analysis may be used to assess the effectiveness of these enforcement mechanisms. In addition, we collected data for years before and after the previous study. Our results are broadly consistent with earlier findings. State ADAMH spendings did respond to block grants, and this magnitude increased after 1989. Our results, however, indicate that technical reviews and waiver applications do not appear to explain states' responses. In other words, these specific enforcement mechanisms, after the step-up in enforcement has been controlled for, do not appear to lead to an increase in spending. There are two possible interpretations of these results. First, the effectiveness of general enforcement does not seem to be enhanced by the particular mechanisms under investigation. Second, states' compliance may depend more on a continuing relationship with the federal government or reputation rather than ex post auditing or inspection.

The next section contains some background information and describes our data set. The third section presents the regression results and their interpretations. We use a fixed-effects regression with interacted terms for our main model, and provide a set of specification checks. Concluding remarks are in the final section.

2 BACKGROUND AND DATA

The general background of the funding of substance abuse services by block grants to the states has been made available by earlier papers: GAO (1992), Hudson and Dubey (1985), Jacobsen and McGuire (1996), and Gamhkar and Sim (1999). Our research interest lies with the aspect of monitoring and enforcement of block grants. Therefore, we will review this particular issue only. First, federal block grants are subject to maintenance-of-effort requirements. When a state applies for a substance abuse block grant, the state governor pledges that appropriate steps will be taken to ensure that funded block grants will be spent according to the application. As we have said in the previous section, substance abuse (SA) block grants may contain set-asides, which direct fractions of the funds to provide services for certain groups, and states comply with these set-aside requirements unless they apply for waivers.[2] We have collected data on which states have applied for a waiver during our sample period.

Second, beginning in 1985, states that received over $100 000 in federal assistance must conduct an audit. The state is responsible for having an audit done by an independent firm.[3] CSAT is notified when the audit discovers a problem but does not automatically receive a report. However, we were unable to obtain any data on such notifications. Third, technical assistance reviews may be carried out. A site visit by a CSAT contractor helps to review states' needs with respect to types of substance abuse services and programs. Maintenance of efforts are included in these reviews. We have been able to collect data on technical reviews for our data period.

Our data set extends that used in Jacobsen and McGuire (1996). The substance abuse spending data for years 1984–94 were obtained from the annual survey of state alcohol and drug agencies – the State Alcohol and Drug Abuse Profile (SADAP), collected by the National Association of State Alcohol and Drug Abuse Directors (NASADAD) under contract to the National Institute on Drug Abuse (NIDA). Data of the ADAMH block grant allocations for substance abuse were obtained from the Substance Abuse and Mental Health Services Administration (SAMHSA).

All spending data are expressed in real terms, in constant 1988 dollars, using the US consumer price index as the deflator, and on a per capita basis. State income and population data were collected from the Statistical Abstract of the US. Additional data on state waiver application and approval over the time period and the data on phase one technical review are collected from CSAT.[4]

We use five main independent variables. Income refers to state per capita income, also in constant 1988 dollars. SABG is the substance abuse block grants. The next three variables are different measures of monitoring and enforcement of block grant administrations. Each of these variables has been interacted with the SABG variable.[5] The Post89 variable, a dummy that takes the value of 1 for years after 1989, simply captures the fact that enforcement has been stepped up since 1989. The 0–1 dummy variable that is used to create the Waiver variable takes a value of 1 when a state applies for a waiver. Similarly, for the TechRev variable, the corresponding 0–1 dummy takes a value of 1 when a technical review is carried out. Table 13.1 contains the definitions of the independent variables.[6] The regression analysis will also employ state and year fixed effects.

Table 13.1 Definitions and summary statistics of variables

Variables	Description
Dependent variable	Real state per capita SA expenditure
Income	Real state per capita income
SABG	Real state per capita SA revenue from ADAMH block grant
Waiver	Equals 1 if waiver in state i year j, interacted with SABG
TechRev	Equals 1 if technical review in state i year j, interacted with SABG
Post89	Equals 1 for years after 1989, interacted with SABG

	Observations	Mean	Std. dev.	Minimum	Maximum
Dependent variable	550	9.363	8.887	0.593	62.410
Income	550	1.578	1.076	0.153	8.381
SABG	561	2.017	1.136	0.371	9.899

Note: Means and standard deviations are statistics over all states and years. Dependent variable and income data are missing for the following states: Wyoming, 7 years; New Mexico, 1 year; District of Columbia, 1 year; Oregon, 2 years.

For six states, we graph the state total per capita substance abuse expenditures, and their shares of SA block grant in total SA expenditures; see Figure 13.1. Clearly, over time both per capita total substance abuse spendings as well as the percentages of block grants in total spendings change. These also vary according to the states, although they are seldom more than 40 percent. Some summary statistics of the enforcement variables are presented in Tables 13.2 and 13.3. Since 1989, only a minority of states have applied for waivers, although the majority of these waiver applications were accepted. On the other hand, the number of technical reviews on states since 1992 tends to be higher. For example in 1993, 40 percent of the states underwent technical reviews. There seems to be a downward trend in the number of states' waiver applications, but this does not appear to apply to the number of technical reviews during the four years (within our data set) for which they were applicable. Overall, we do observe some variations in the enforcement data that we analyze.

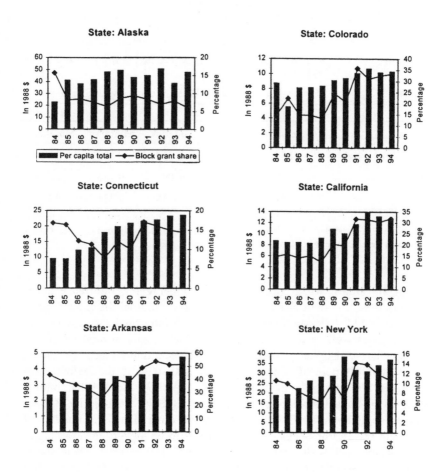

Figure 13.1 State substance abuse expenditure and the share of block grants for selected states

Table 13.2 Summary of state waiver applications

Fiscal year	Number of states applied	Approved	Rejected
1989	6	4	2
1990	8	7	1
1991	6	6	0
1992	5	5	0
1993	0	0	0
1994	2	2	0

Table 13.3 Summary of technical reviews

Fiscal Year	Number of states implemented
1992	11
1993	20
1994	5
1995	10

3   HYPOTHESES AND STATISTICAL RESULTS

Previously, researchers have confronted significant methodological problems when assessing the effect of block grants and state substance abuse spendings. The usual method of using cross-sectional data to estimate the effect of interest suffers from potential bias due to omitted variables. Very often only a few of the many factors influencing state spending can be included in a cross-sectional regression. It is by now well recognized that the omitted variable bias is empirically serious.[7] For our model, the variable measuring block grant funds may be correlated with omitted variables that also influence expenditure patterns (such as 'need').

Following Jacobsen and McGuire (1996), we use a 'fixed-effects model' to identify the regulatory effects of block grants on state SA expenditures. The fixed-effects approach enables us to control for many of these influences on state substance abuse spending without explicitly modelling them. Our data set spans a period of 11 years. This allows us to control for unspecified factors which influence substance abuse spending

Table 13.4 Regression results for state total spending on substance abuse, 1984–94

Variables	Eqn. 1	Eqn. 2	Eqn. 3	Eqn. 4	Eqn. 5
Income	−0.00004 (0.00029)	−0.00010 (0.00029)	−0.00004 (0.00029)	−0.00004 (0.00029)	−0.00010 (0.00029)
SABG	0.6598 (0.2426)	−0.0444 (0.2801)	0.6518 (0.2425)	0.6641 (0.2435)	−0.0429 (0.2804)
Post89		1.5554 (0.3294)			1.5829 (0.3335)
Waiver			−0.3181 (0.3500)		−0.2243 (0.3440)
TechRev				−0.0360 (0.1837)	−0.1637 (0.1818)
N	550	550	550	550	550
Overall-R^2	0.102	0.075	0.104	0.102	0.076

Note: Standard errors are in parentheses under each estimate.

and which are similar across observations of the same state. Each regression in this chapter includes a dummy variable for each state; the estimated coefficients on these variables represent the state fixed effects. Similarly, because we have many states in the data, we can include a fixed effect for each year. Given the fixed-effects variables, regression estimates of the effects of independent variables are identified by the changes in those variables. So the estimates measure how an increase or decrease in block grant funds affects changes in state substance abuse spending.

We estimate a number of regressions with the state agency substance abuse spending per capita in constant 1988 dollars as the dependent variable. The full model includes a number of independent variables. Common in all five regressions are states' real per capita incomes and real per capita SA block grants. Our full model makes use of all the independent variables (Table 13.4, equation 5). Each of the other four regression equations contains the per capita state income and block grant variables; these are the only variables for the benchmark model (Table 13.4, equation 1). Then the enforcement interaction variables are alternatively added to the benchmark model (equations 2–4). Table 13.4 presents the regression results.

Earlier research by Jacobsen and McGuire (1996) using a subset of the data here (for the years between 1987 and 1992) found that states did respond to increased SA block grants by increasing SA spending, and that this response was stronger after 1989, when federal enforcement was stepped up. Recall that the enforcement variables (Post89, Waiver and TechRev) are all interacted with the SABG variable. To obtain the full effect of a change in SA block grant on SA spending (the dependent variable), then the coefficient of the SABG variable should be added to those of the enforcement variables where relevant. For example, in equation 5 (Table 13.4) a $1 increase in SA block grant is estimated to lead to $ $(-0.0429 + 1.5829 - 0.2243 - 0.1637) = \$1.152$ increase in SA spending. We have performed a partial F test on the null hypothesis that the sum of the coefficients of SABG, Post89, Waiver and TechRev is equal to one. The F-statistic (with 1 and 484 degrees of freedom) turns out to be 0.09 and the p value is 0.7589. Therefore, we cannot reject the null hypothesis. In fact, we have also computed the asymptotic confidence interval, and it is [0.16, 2.14].

Equation 1 in Table 13.4 can be interpreted as a test of the median voter theory. Median voter theory asserts that block grants are just like general revenue, and predicts the regression coefficients of the income and block grant variables to be identical. If an SA block grant is regarded as general revenue, then an increase in SABG should not produce an increase in SA spending different from an increase in Income, and this is clearly rejected by the result in equation 1. In equation 1 (Table 13.4), the estimate of 0.6598 on the SABG variable should be interpreted as the 'average' response of SA expenditure to SA block grants, where the averaging is meant to apply over all states and all years in the sample period. We see that in both equations 2 and 5 in Table 13.4, the Post89 variable has a strongly positive estimate; this is consistent with earlier findings in Jacobsen and McGuire. From equation 2, we conclude that the block grants do have a significant effect on states' SA spendings, and this effect is stronger after 1989, when enforcement was supposed to have strengthened. Equation 5 reinforces this result: with all enforcement variables included, the estimated coefficient of the Post89 variable remains highly positive and significant. Equations 3 and 4 in the table omit the Post89 variable; instead each of these includes a more specific enforcement variable. In equation 3, the Waiver variable is used. The SABG estimates in both equations are similar to that in equation 1. Neither of the two enforcement variables is statistically significant. Our interpretation is that the specific enforcement information that we are able to gather does not appear to strengthen the compliance of SA block grants. Equation 5 again reinforces this point: there both the estimates of the

Table 13.5 Estimated within-state correlation matrix

Years	1984	1985	1986	1987	1988	1989	1990	1991	1992	1993
1984	1.0000									
1985	0.3544	1.0000								
1986	0.3782	0.6365	1.0000							
1987	0.4020	0.6917	0.7657	1.0000						
1988	0.4308	0.7992	0.8882	1.0000	1.0000					
1989	0.4377	0.7957	0.8870	1.0000	1.0000	1.0000				
1990	0.4523	0.8079	0.9378	1.0000	1.0000	1.0000	1.0000			
1991	0.4232	0.7673	0.8704	0.9652	1.0000	1.0000	1.0000	1.0000		
1992	0.4042	0.7663	0.8365	0.9245	1.0000	1.0000	1.0000	1.0000	1.0000	
1993	0.2517	0.4442	0.4724	0.5722	0.6594	0.7125	0.6296	0.6312	0.6813	1.0000
1994	0.3915	0.7387	0.8123	0.9344	1.0000	1.0000	1.0000	1.0000	1.0000	0.7609

Waiver and TechRev variables are negative and insignifcant, as in equations 3 and 4, and the Post89 variable captures most of the effect of block grants.

We perform a number of robustness tests on our regression analysis. We first address the issue of serial correlation and heteroskedasticity. We now discuss the methods and explain their results. It has been argued by Gamkhar and Sim (1999) that serial correlation could be a potential problem with the analysis of block grant spendings. To investigate, we begin with the decomposition of the error term of the basic regression: $\epsilon_{it} = \upsilon_i + \eta_t + \varepsilon_{it}$, where i is an index for the states, and t is an index for the years. In other words, the error term ϵ_{it} consists of the state-specific component, υ_i, time-specific component, η_t, as well as the residual ε_{it}. We first omit the time component, and use maxmium likelihood to estimate the correlation matrix of the state-specific component together with the residuals. This correlation matrix is reported in Table 13.5.

The result in Table 13.5 suggests that the correlation does not tend to decline over time. We further check the ratio of the variances of the state-specific components and the residuals. The value of this ratio is high, about 2.46. This indicates that variance of the state-specific component dominates that of the residual. We therefore conclude that serial correlation is unimportant. In other words, the contribution by the state-specific component, υ_i, to the error term, ϵ_{it}, is much stronger than the residual ε_{it}.

Table 13.6 Specification checks for serial correlation and heteroskedasticity

Variables	Reg 1	Reg 2	Reg 3	Reg 4	Reg 5	Reg 6
Income	0.0006	0.0008	0.0010	0.0007	0.0008	−0.0001
	(0.0002)	(0.0002)	(0.0002)	(0.0002)	(0.0003)	(0.0006)
SABG	0.5388	0.1240	0.3338	0.0440	0.1240	−0.0444
	(0.3627)	(0.2451)	(0.2531)	(0.1947)	(0.2717)	(0.3649)
Post89	0.5643	0.7861	0.5978	0.7885	0.7861	1.5554
	(0.2476)	(0.1648)	(0.1671)	(0.1455)	(0.2152)	(0.5504)
	unstructured error term	state-fixed effects	random effects	Reg 2 + AR(1)	Reg 2 + heteroskedasticity	Reg 5 + year dum
N	550	550	550	550	550	550

We further perform a number of specification checks. Estimation with an unstructured error term is reported in regression 1 in Table 13.6. Regression 2 in Table 13.6 presents the basic equation with only state fixed effects, whereas regression 3 presents the random effects model; the estimates differ somewhat. In the next regression, we report the results when an AR(1) process is assumed for the residual. Consistent with our previous analysis that serial correlation is unimportant, estimates in regression 4 are very similar to those in regression 2. Correcting for heteroskedasticity does not change the results. Regression 5 adds the heteroskedasticity correction but its estimates are the same as those in regression 2. Finally, regression 6 also adds the year fixed effects, and the estimates are similar to those in equation 2 of Table 13.4. Although the estimates in Table 13.6 change somewhat according to the statistical assumptions used, the result that in the post-1989 period, block grants are associated with about a dollar-for-dollar increase in spending emerges for all specifications.

4   CONCLUSION

Our results suggest that the precise way that enforcement affects ADAMH block grant spendings may not be directly related to the waiver and review monitoring that CSAT carried out. Rather, we hypothesize that the *threat* of rigorous enforcement may have been at work. Given that ADAMH block grants typically make up only a small percentage of a state's budget, perhaps it is not worthwhile for a state to acquire a bad reputation by using block grant funds inappropriately. A bad reputation in ADAMH block grant spendings may affect a state's ability to apply successfully for other funds. In other words, the benefit of 'cheating' may be too small and any potential penalties a state may experience in its ability to secure future funding may outweigh the gain.

Policy implications of our results are several. First, the use of waiver and review monitoring in substance abuse block grants may be regarded more as information gathering or assistance to states rather than explicit methods of reinforcement. While our results do not show that these particular enforcements have significant effects on substance abuse spendings originating from block grants, we do not want to imply that they are not worthwhile. These activities may well be useful to help states plan the ways they intend to use the block grant fundings. When states apply for waivers and are subject to reviews, it is expected that the effort that is being devoted to planning is increased. Second, we do not want to imply that results in our chapter can be extrapolated to other block grants. This is because the shares of substance abuse block grants in state budgets are typically very small. Again, our hypothesis of a reputation effect – that explicit enforcement may not be as powerful as a general 'announcement' effect – may work well for block grants that are relatively small. Third, our results do tend to support the efficacy of block grants as a means to fund substance abuse services provided by the states. The positive effect of block grants fundings on actual substance abuse spendings is actually quite robust: the earlier results in Jacobsen and McGuire (1996) are confirmed again in this analysis, which uses a larger data set and more stringent robustness checks.

NOTES

* National Institute of Alcohol Abuse and Alcoholism grant R03 AA10846 provided research support; McGuire also received support from the National Institute of Mental Health (KO5 MH01263). We thank Judith Uriyu, Public Health Advisor, Division of State and Community Program, Center for Substance Abuse Treatment, and James Sayers, Director of Block Grant Administration, Center for Substance Abuse Treatment for providing us with the waiver and technical review data. Margaret Stephens provided research and administrative support. Conclusions in the paper are the responsibility of the authors alone.

1   More background about the ADAMH block grants can be found in Jacobsen and McGuire (1996).

2   In unusual economic circumstances, states may be automatically granted a

waiver; for example, in a 'financial crisis' in which the total tax revenue declines at least 1.5 percent, and either unemployment increases by at least 1 percentage point or employment declines by at least 1.5 percentage points. See Federal Register Section 45 CFR Subtitle A, Part 96 – Block Grants; subpart L on 'Substance Abuse Prevent and Treatment Block Grant'.

[3] Neither the state nor the federal government actually conducts the audit.

[4] We thank James Sayers and Judith Uriyu from CSAT for kindly providing the waiver and technical review data.

[5] Interaction is obtained by multiplying variables together.

[6] Jacobsen and McGuire (1996) also used a block grant share variable in similar regressions. This variable was the ratio between the SA block grants and the state budget in 1988 and interacted with SABG; it measures the importance of SA block grants as a source of revenue. We have used some similar 'share' variables but discovered that regression results were very sensitive depending on the definitions. We suspect that an endogeneity problem led to this lack of robustness and have decided not to use it.

[7] Blank et al. (1994) in a different context, found that model identification using changes over time within states gives different estimates from those obtained using only cross-sectional variations.

REFERENCES

Blank, R.M., C.C. George and R.A. London (1994), 'State abortion rates: the impact of policy, provider availability, political climate, demography, and economics', Northwestern University.

Gamkhar, Shama and Shao-Chee Sim (1999), 'The impact of federal alcohol and drug abuse block grants on state and local government substance abuse program expenditure: the role of federal oversight', Lyndon B. Johnson School of Public Affairs, The University of Texas at Austin.

Hudson, C. and S. Dubey (1985), 'State mental health spending under the ADAMHA block grant', *Journal of Social Science Research*, **8**(2): 1–23.

Institute of Medicine (1990), *Treating Drug Problems*, Washington, DC: National Academy Press.

Jacobsen, Karen and Thomas G. McGuire (1996), 'Federal block grants and state spending: the alcohol, drug abuse, and mental health block grant and state agency behavior', *Journal of Health Politics, Policy and Law*, **21**(4): 753–70.

Musgrave, R.A. and P.B. Musgrave (1989), *Public Finance in Theory and Practice, Fifth Edition*, New York: McGraw-Hill.

United States General Accounting Office (GAO) (1985), *Report to the Congress: Block Grants Brought Funding Changes and Adjustments to Program Priorities*, GAO/HRD-85-33, Washington, DC: US Government Printing Office.

United States General Accounting Office (GAO) (1992), *Report to the Congress: Block Grants, Increases in Set-Asides and Cost Ceilings since 1982*, GAO/HRD-92-58FS, Washinton, DC: US Government Printing Office.

Wyckoff, P.G. (1988), 'A bureaucratic theory of flypaper effects', *Journal of Urban Economics*, **23**: 115–29.

Index

activities of daily living (ADL) 116
adult health 7, 111–3, 115–8, 120,
123, 125–6, 128–30, 132–3,
140
Akaike's criterion 102
back pain 10, 193–201, 203–4, 206,
208–9, 211
block grants 11, 257–69
capitation 2, 5, 10, 19, 21, 23–4, 26–
8, 30–1, 38–42, 46, 49, 52, 61–
2, 108, 194, 213–4, 217, 219–
20, 222–37, 251
caregiver 101
catastrophic illness 8–9, 160, 162–67,
169–70, 173–5, 243, 252, 254
child health 111–2, 114, 125, 135
China 3, 4, 7, 12, 19, 139, 143, 145–
6, 155, 157–8, 190
chronic energy defficiency (CED) 7,
113, 116–8, 126, 132, 134,
137–8
cognitive status 88–9, 92, 98
consolidation 6, 33, 36–7, 63, 71–2,
74–5, 79–80
cost shifting 10, 76, 193–4, 196, 208,
210, 212
cost 2, 5, 6, 8–10, 15–28, 30–2, 41–6,
48, 52, 58, 65, 67, 69–70, 75–7,
79–80, 85–6, 88, 90–5, 100,
103, 105, 107–9, 117, 124,
143–6, 148–9, 151, 154–7,
161–2, 174–7, 179, 187–8,
193–6, 208–10, 212–4, 217–8,
230, 232, 234–8, 246, 249–54,
dementia 93, 98
diagnosis related group 87
drug expenditures 2
efficiency 6, 19, 24, 28, 30, 63, 74,

76–7, 79, 135, 138, 143, 157,
238, 251
endogeneity 90, 92, 94, 96, 101–2,
105, 218, 269
equity 6, 8–9, 63, 74–6, 79, 145,
155–6, 159–62, 166, 174–6
formal care 88
functional status 94, 102, 105
health care expenditures 1–2, 4–5, 8,
18, 22, 32, 115, 147, 161, 163,
213–4, 235, 237
health care reform 4–6, 12, 15–7, 21,
23, 25, 29, 32, 71, 145, 158,
176, 189
health care utilization 5, 7–9, 32,
140, 161, 177–8, 180–2, 185,
187–9
health economics 1–2, 4–5, 12, 238
health insurance 4–6, 8–9, 11, 16–8,
20, 25, 26, 29, 32, 39, 44, 58,
61–4, 66–9, 71–2, 75–9, 81,
111, 115, 137, 144–5, 149,
154–5, 161, 176–82, 184–5,
187–90, 194, 210, 213, 215,
220, 222, 234, 241–2, 249,
252–4
health policy 1, 5–6, 16, 111, 135
health production function 7, 119,
122–5
heterogeneity 88, 90, 94, 102–4, 106,
139
hip fracture 7, 86–7, 90, 92, 97–8,
100, 104–9
hospital services 10, 86, 214–5,
217–9, 232, 234–6
hospital 2, 5, 9–10, 16–8, 20–1, 23,
26, 31, 37, 39, 47, 51–2, 56, 58,
60, 64–5, 67–70, 73, 76, 80,